Health Economics

Health Economics
A Critical and Global Analysis

George R. Palmer BSc, MEc, PhD
Emeritus Professor, Faculty of Medicine
The University of New South Wales

Maria Theresa Ho MBBS MHP MD
Associate Professor and Associate Dean (Curriculum),
Faculty of Medicine
University of Sydney

First published in 2008 by
PALGRAVE MACMILLAN
Houndmills, Basingstoke, Hampshire RG21 6XS and
175 Fifth Avenue, New York, N.Y. 10010
Companies and representatives throughout the world.

PALGRAVE MACMILLAN is the global academic imprint of the Palgrave Macmillan division of St. Martin's Press, LLC and of Palgrave Macmillan Ltd. Macmillan® is a registered trademark in the United States, United Kingdom and other countries. Palgrave is a registered trademark in the European Union and other countries.

ISBN-13: 978–1–4039–4082–7 hardback
ISBN-10: 1–4039–4082–7 hardback
ISBN-13: 978–1–4039–4083–4 paperback
ISBN-10: 1–4039–4083–5 paperback

This book is printed on paper suitable for recycling and made from fully managed and sustained forest sources. Logging, pulping and manufacturing processes are expected to conform to the environmental regulations of the country of origin.

A catalogue record for this book is available from the British Library.

10 9 8 7 6 5 4 3 2 1
17 16 15 14 13 12 11 10 09 08

Contents

List of Tables

List of Figures

Abbreviations

AHWAC	Australian Health Workforce Advisory Committee
AMWAC	Australian Medical Workforce Advisory Committee
CABG	Coronary artery bypass grafting
CAT	Computerised axial tomography
CBA	Cost-benefit analysis
CEA	Cost-effectiveness analysis
CUA	Cost utility analysis
DALY	Disability adjusted life years
DRG	Diagnosis-related group
EPOC	Effective Practice and Organisation of Care [Cochrane]
EU	European Union
FFS	Fee-for-service
GDP	Gross domestic product
HET	History of economic thought
HMO	Health Maintenance Organisation
HRG	Health resource group
IMF	International Monetary Fund
LMIC	Lower and middle income countries
MRI	Magnetic resonance imaging
MDCP	Multi-disciplinary clinical pathways
NICE	National Institute for Clinical Excellence
NHS	National Health Service (UK)
ODA	Overseas development and aid
OECD	Organisation for Economic Cooperation and Development
PAHO	Pan American Health Organisation
PBMA	Program budgeting and marginal analysis
PBS	Pharmaceutical Benefits Scheme
PPP	Purchasing Power Parity
QALY	Quality adjusted life year
RAWP	Resource Allocation Working Party
RBRVS	Resource-based relative value scale
RN	Registered nurse
SG	Standard gamble
SID	Supplier-induced demand

TTO	Time trade off
UK	United Kingdom
UN	United Nations
UNDP	United Nations Development Program
US	United States
USAID	United States Agency for International development
WHO	World Health Organisation
WTO	World Trade Organisation
WTP	Willingness to pay

Acknowledgements

We wish to acknowledge the role of Steven Kennedy of Palgrave Macmillan in initiating this project, and his continuing encouragement and support. Lynda Thompson of Palgrave Macmillan has been a patient and painstaking commissioning editor for which we are most grateful.

We wish to thank Helen Owens for providing generous and perceptive comments on earlier versions of most chapters. We are also grateful for the comprehensive critiques of an earlier draft by three anonymous reviewers, and their useful suggestions for amendments and improvements.

Gaeta Lafortune, OECD Health Division, was most helpful in our discussion of the OECD health data, and in alerting us to additional sources of information. We wish to thank him also for his permission to reproduce the large volume of OECD data we have included.

Sheryl Delacour has been of considerable help in compiling the bibliography, in carefully proof-reading the entire document, and for suggestions for improving the style.

The very skilled assistance of Lyn Broadway-Hill with the word processing tasks, including the preparation of the tables and graphs, has been greatly appreciated.

Finally, GP acknowledges his indebtedness to members of the Australian Health Economics Society over many years for stimulating discussions and presentations on numerous aspects of the material presented here. In particular he wishes to thank Jim Butler, John Deeble, Darrel Doessel, Stephen Duckett, Jane Hall, Jeff Richardson and Dick Scotton. They have all played notable roles, along with many others, in the development of health economics in Australia.

Preface

Health economics is concerned with applying the tools of economic analysis to the specific problems of health care finance and delivery. However, the application of economic principles and methods to the health services is fraught with difficulties of both a conceptual and practical nature. This is partly because of a number of special characteristics of health services, including the ability of providers to influence the utilisation of their services and the problematic relationship between these services and health status.

The book is designed to explain the nature of the available economic tools, their limitations and their strengths in examining crucial health policy and management issues. The emphasis is on the use of clear, non-technical language to explain these matters to students and others including those with a limited or no background in economics. It is a major objective that the book will be useful to those who have some knowledge of economics and wish to learn more about its application to health services issues, together with those whose background is largely in health and aim to learn more about the work of economists who may often be seen as the enemy of clinicians and other health professionals. For this reason collaboration between an economist and statistician and a medically qualified person with training in economics has been undertaken.

We emphasise that the book is not intended to enable students and other readers to become health economists. However, we have provided an extensive though not exhaustive list of key references to allow readers to follow up topics about which they may have a special interest. A further important aim has been to produce a text which differs from others in that it does not argue a case for the use of economics in the health field, but which is designed to produce an objective assessment of the various positions and methods espoused by health economists. From this should flow a body of knowledge for students, clinicians, managers and policy-makers that allows them to make better judgements about the appropriate role of health economics in health policy formation and implementation.

Health economics students undertaking courses in many institutions are drawn from a wide range of countries and professional backgrounds. Accordingly, it is also an important objective to draw on the experience of countries that differ in the way in which the health services are organised and funded. The Organisation for Economic Cooperation and Development (OECD) has made available a wide range of data and reports which assist greatly with this process. In addition there has been an increased interest in applying health economics to the problems of developing and transitional countries with their very limited resources for meeting the health needs of their populations.

Neoclassical economics, including welfare economics, has become the dominant paradigm in the applications and teachings of economics at present. This is also true of health economics, especially in the United States where much of the writing and research about the subject is produced. However, the extensive criticisms of neoclassical economics that exist in regard to its underpinnings in the theory of consumer demand and the theory of the firm must also be recognised, even though these have usually been ignored by most mainstream economists. As our title indicates we believe it has now become essential in a book dealing with health economics to adopt a critical approach to many of the theoretical bases of the study, applications and teaching of the subject.

Our perspective on the current state of many aspects of economics leads us to conclude that important insights about the discipline, and its application to the health services and health policy, are gained by reviewing briefly the history of economic thought. This history serves to highlight the great diversity of the approaches taken to economics by members of the various schools within the discipline, and the influences that economic and social interests, along with systems of values, have had on what becomes the dominant paradigm.

We wish to acknowledge that our own values embody a heavy emphasis on equity in all social arrangements, and the need for the more affluent and fortunate members of communities to support the more vulnerable citizens in their societies. We also cite the international and historical evidence that societies which share these values appear to achieve better health outcomes for their populations than those where more narrowly focused economic objectives prevail.

We are convinced that many of the uses of economic analysis to support specific policy initiatives in health care can be questioned by adopting a global perspective. For example, the attempts of some American health economists to advocate the greater use of competitive mechanisms, including higher user charges, to solve the financial problems of their system, ignore the patently obvious fact that all other comparable countries achieve outcomes for their populations which are substantially superior, cost far less, and are based on zero or modest payments by patients. This problem has wide implications since conservative political interests in many countries, including some developing countries, have looked to US 'experts' for guidance in achieving lower budgetary outlays and improved performance for their own systems.

We believe it is very important to consider the priorities established to date in the study of the economics of health and the health services. With some very important exceptions, these have been the product of the work of American and British health economists naturally concerned predominantly with the institutional arrangements of their own countries. Their relevance to other developed and developing countries is not self-evident.

Finally, we stress the importance of multi-disciplinary studies including the compelling need for health economists, in collaboration with others, to study the efficiency of individual institutions and services in this sector, which they are well equipped to undertake.

Introduction

What is economics and what is health economics?

There are numerous definitions of Economics as a discipline, most of which focus on the need to make choices between alternative uses of resources in the light of their scarcity. It is fundamental for many economists to recognise that the aspirations or wants of individuals and communities are insatiable but the resources required to satisfy these wants are finite. Hence, individually and collectively, decisions must be made about which wants are met and to what extent. The various definitions, their limitations and alternative approaches for exploring the phenomena comprising economic relationships, are discussed in Chapter 2.

Economic relationships conventionally refer to the production of goods and services, and the distribution of these goods and services for consumption or investment purposes. In general, consumption is taken to refer to the use of products or services by final consumers for the satisfaction yielded by the activity, whilst investment is distinguished by the notion that the goods and services involved are deployed in order to generate income, satisfactions or other returns in the future. In most systems flows of funds (money) are associated with each economic relationship.

Economists have developed a set of principles and concepts that they regard as being essential to gain an understanding of economic phenomena, and to throw light on how the performance of these systems of relationships might be improved. Much of the theory of economics is concerned with the operation of markets in which purchasers of goods and services interact with suppliers to establish the prices and quantities of the products.

Health economics

In the health arena the emphasis on scarcity and choices at first sight appears compelling. Diseases and trauma are all too common characteristics of the human (and other) species. The skilled personnel, drugs, materials and facilities that would be required to prevent, treat or cure all the conditions that afflict the human body and mind are clearly enormous, and often unavailable at our current level of medical and health care technology. It is also evident that even within affluent, developed countries the resources available to meet all these potential needs are limited. For example, where governments are providing most of the financial resources, allocations to the health services have to be assessed in the light of the competing requirements of education, defence, law and order, and the other responsibilities of these governments.

Hence it is hardly surprising that those economists who have specialised in health and health services issues have emphasised the choice and scarcity approach to the definition and applications of economics. As we discuss in more detail in later chapters, however, a concentration on this perspective in health economics may lead to a tendency to ignore or downplay those aspects of economic relationships that do not fit very comfortably within the framework of the conventional theory. These include the impact of health financing changes on the distribution of income and welfare, and the effects of cultural, sociological, psychological and other non-economic factors on health-related behaviour and outcomes.

It is important to understand in coming to grips with the subject matter of health economics that economists who specialise in this area use the special tools of their discipline to focus on both the services, commodities and financial relationships that characterise health systems, and on the implications of these for the well-being or *health status* of the relevant populations. Some health economists are primarily concerned with the health sector as an industry consisting of discrete entities, notably hospitals, other institutions for caring for the sick, health service providers and most importantly the funding arrangements, including health insurance, that are present in the industry. Those health economists who adopt this perspective wish to contribute to resolving such policy issues as improving the ability of the financing methods to achieve certain objectives, notably the effectiveness and efficiency with which the health care system operates.

Other health economists devote their efforts mainly to the health status issue. They argue that what is distinctive about health economics as compared with other branches of economics is the effect of the health services, including the institutions and providers, on the mortality and morbidity experience of the populations for which they are responsible. This perspective has led to virtually a whole industry of health economists who have endeavoured to quantify the measurement of health status as a method of evaluating health-related activities. Again, this group of economists wish to influence health policies about which programs and projects should be retained or expanded, and which might be improved on the basis of the results of their evaluations.

United States and British perspectives

We noted in the preface that the health economics literature has been dominated by contributions from the United States. United States-based health economists, with important exceptions, have emphasised the greater use of competitive market mechanisms to solve the perceived problems of the health services. They have been sceptical about the role of governments in health service funding, provision and regulation, including their subsidies of health insurance and the direct provision of services by governments.

British health economists have also made substantial contributions to health economics. With some important exceptions, they have been primarily concerned with the development and use of economic methods, including the measurement of health status, for evaluating projects and programs within the National Health Service(NHS). They have also taken a greater interest than their US counterparts in distributional and equity issues. Most other developed countries have very different health care systems from those of either the United States or the United Kingdom.

It is an important objective of the book to provide material that recognises the need for a more balanced approach to a range of health service issues, including those arising in developing and transitional countries. We believe that for students and practitioners of public health a change in their per-spectives about economics and health as derived from the existing text books and other sources would be highly beneficial.

Finally, it must be emphasised again that the book is not designed to be a means of enabling its readers to become practitioners of health economics. It is the intention, however, to provide a useful introduction for those students and others who aspire to undertake more advanced studies in health eco-nomics. We also hope that the book may serve to make some practising health economists indulge in a rethink of their own priorities in research and development in this important and contentious area.

Structuring of the content

In establishing the structure of the book we have provided an overview of economics from an historical perspective before proceeding to provide an account of some of the key concepts, notably demand and supply, used by economists. Our purpose here is to afford a basis for introducing our reservations about some of these tools of economic analysis before considering the details of the methods. We believe that it is very important in meeting our objectives to emphasise the diversity of schools of economic thought, and the quite fundamental disagreements amongst many of its most distinguished practitioners, than to commence with a non-critical summary of the apparatus of economic theory.

Similarly, we have decided to introduce material of a general kind on key controversies amongst health economists prior to our later discussion of the applications of health economics to health project evaluation, workforce planning and the characteristics of health systems. Again it is our intention to alert the reader to the fact that health economics, along with its parent discipline, cannot be regarded as an uncontested body of knowledge, and as presenting a single perspective on how the economic problems of health systems may be addressed.

Outline of chapter content

Chapter 2 is designed to present an overview of economics, including a review of the various definitions of the discipline, and the widely differing perspectives that economists have adopted in dealing with a number of key issues. The latter include the determinants of the price or value of commodities and services, the importance of economic incentives in influencing consumer and producer behaviour, and how to deal with income distribution issues.

The overview of economics thus includes a brief history of economic thought, covering the various 'schools' of economics that have emerged over the last two centuries. This overview emphasises that economics should not be regarded as a discipline with a unique set of theories, methods and policy relevant conclusions. In this regard it does not differ radically from most disciplines including other social and physical sciences. However, there may have been more of a tendency in economics, especially in the teaching of the subject, to gloss over the divisions between the various schools and their policy implications. We note also that economics has become divided into a number of sub-disciplines of greatly varying relevance to the study and application of health economics.

In Chapter 3 we describe the current state of health economics, especially the great expansion of interest in the subject as measured by the number of health services research projects that feature economic analysis, and the considerable increase in the literature dealing with health economics. To provide further perspectives on what health economists do, we present summary accounts of the main contributions of a number of prominent health economists, and of the very different positions taken by the members of this group from many of their colleagues on key issues.

In its pursuit of answers to questions about the determination of values as reflected in prices, economics has traditionally characterised influences into those operating on the demand side and those which affect the supply side. Despite the reservations we have about the assumed independence of these factors from each other, especially but not exclusively when dealing with health services and health, we regard it as useful for expository purposes to retain the notion of the health services as commodities of a special kind, notably as inputs to the production of health status.

Chapter 4 therefore deals with the factors that influence the supply of health services. This chapter includes a brief account of conventional supply and demand analysis, the concept of equilibrium and the notion of the margin. Costs are assumed to be the principal factor underlying the supply curve, leading on to a discussion of the definitions of average, marginal and total costs, and of opportunity costs. Other factors relevant to supply issues include production functions, cost functions and technical efficiency issues.

The chapter concludes with material on the measurement of the performance of health institutions and services, and a discussion of economic models of non-profit health organisations with particular reference to hospitals. The relationships between health service outputs and health outcomes are also reviewed.

In Chapter 5 we examine further health status and utility maximisation from the standpoint of the conventional theory of consumption. The existence and role of supplier-induced demand is emphasised as a key feature of health service 'markets'. We then discuss the major issue of the applicability of the notion of a demand curve to the health services. Finally, we note that the area of welfare economics and its application to health policy issues remains the source of many of the disagreements between health economists about policy conclusions based on economic analysis. These disagreements usually centre on the treatment or lack of it of income distribution problems in conventional welfare economics.

Chapter 6 covers a number of topics in what can be called the macroeconomics of health service provision. Included here is the flow of funds between financing sources, notably governments and the private sector, and the disposition of these funds between the major health services. A brief introduction is provided to the comparative data from a number of countries drawn from an Organisation for Economic Co-operation and Development (OECD) health database.

Together with data on the proportion of the total value of each country's production (gross domestic product) devoted to the health services, these data provide a useful basis for comparing individual countries, and arriving at broad conclusions about the effectiveness of health service expenditure in achieving policy goals. (These issues are pursued further in Chapter 10 which includes several case studies of the financing and related methods adopted across a range of developed countries.)

Chapter 6 also includes a discussion of the economics of health insurance, including the role of co-payments and deductibles, and risk sharing principles. The question is poised as to whether there is a 'welfare burden' of health insurance including a review of the shaky theoretical basis of this 'burden'. It concludes with a discussion of the methods of funding components of the health services, especially hospitals, including the use of casemix methods such as diagnosis-related groups.

Chapter 7 is designed to introduce key perspectives associated with the health workforce. Many students and health services personnel, especially those from a nursing background, will have become aware of the sudden shifts from a surplus to a shortage of staff, which have characterised many countries in the last few decades. The definitions of shortage and surplus will also be explored. Descriptive measures of key components of the health workforce are discussed including the numbers per thousand of population of doctors and nurses, the two most important groups. Forecasting health workforce requirements, the methods of workforce planning and their limitations, where the policy instruments available to governments are heavily constrained, are also reviewed. The potential for substituting less costly occupational groups for more expensive groups is illustrated by reference to doctors and nurses. In view of the key roles of medical personnel in the provision of health services, special attention is focused on how medical services are paid for including fee-for-service, capitation and salaries. The likely implications of each method are analysed for work incentives, the levels of service provision and the size of the workforce required in meeting the health needs of populations. The derivation of fee schedules for medical services where fee-for-service is the predominant method of payment is discussed, including the resource-based relative value scale method of fee setting being adopted in the United States.

Concern about the effectiveness and efficiency of health services provision in the face of rising costs and increasing pressures on government budgets has led in most countries to a greater emphasis on the use of economic methods for evaluating the components of health care systems. Chapter 8 is therefore devoted to the use and limitations of methods for evaluating proposed and existing health service projects. Much of the work of health economists in some countries, such as Britain, has concentrated on project and program evaluation.

Cost-benefit, cost-effectiveness and cost utility analysis are the principal methods used by health economists in evaluating health programs, projects and therapeutic procedures. A brief description of each technique is set out together with their relationships to one another. A review of their strengths and limitations and of their relationship with welfare economics is followed by concrete examples of how the evaluation procedures have been applied. Finally, we stress once more that the objective of this chapter is not to produce instant experts in economic evaluation but to enable students and policy makers to appraise critically the contributions health economists have made in this area.

The principal aim of Chapter 9 is to provide a better understanding of the relationship between the frameworks developed by health economists and the practical requirements of those who commission, deliver and manage clinical care. There is an increasing emphasis on providing efficient and equitable services from health care providers particularly in primary care and the public health care sector, against a background of increasing demands on limited sources and increased accountability. Health economics seeks to guide the directions of policies affecting this arena and the decisions made within it.

However, the impact of health economics, especially at the micro-economic level, has been limited because of the lack of recognition of the importance of context by those providing information on health economics. While evidence-based medicine and health economics have shifted the emphasis to frameworks supporting resource allocation, decisions based on the criteria of effectiveness and efficiency, the movement away from the health professional's consulting room has led to concerns about: conflicts between the traditional clinical focus on the individual patient versus the collective community, the limited evidence base for the effectiveness and efficiency of many programs/interventions, and the difficulties of extrapolating efficacy studies into practice. Thus literature on health economics is not accessible or readily accepted by clinical decision-makers. The chapter concludes with a number of proposals about how both health economists and clinicians may gain a better understanding of the positions adopted by each group. The role of the technique of program budgeting and marginal analysis is emphasised in these endeavours.

Chapter 10 is designed to provide a perspective on the diversity of methods of funding, organizing and delivering health services internationally. We set out a number of models of health care systems which endeavour to capture the salient features and variables of each type. It was noted in Chapter 3 that these include the British nationalised health service model with the direct provision of many health services by governments, a heavy reliance on direct taxation revenue for financing, a small private sector, only a limited reliance on fee-for-service doctor payments, and small or no user charges.

Other countries with national health service characteristics, notably Sweden and other Scandinavian countries, share important similarities to and differences from the UK model.

At the other extreme is the United States which may be regarded as having some of the characteristics of a market orientated, free enterprise model, with heavy reliance on private health insurance with large consumer payments and, alone amongst developed countries, the absence of coverage for a substantial proportion of the population.

Most developed countries have mixed models with a greater degree of reliance on private sector organizations than the NHS, notably for hospital care, as in Australia and France: use of health insurance, normally subsidised by governments, as in the Netherlands (including private health insurance) and Belgium; and a diversity of methods of doctor remuneration. It will be noted that economic variables, broadly defined, loom large in the construction of these models.

The chapter also canvasses the issue of the consequences for efficiency and equity, and other aspects of economic evaluation of the adoption of each model. The OECD data on both health expenditure and mortality experience presented in this chapter, together with a good deal of empirical work that has been undertaken recently, enables us to draw some important, though tentative, conclusions about these matters.

Chapter 11 addresses the important challenges that confront international health in the context of globalisation and sustainable growth, and the linkages of these global developments across health and other sectors with the issues of inequity, poverty and socioeconomic disadvantage faced by developing and transitional countries.

This chapter relates trends in international health policy to increased emphasis on effectiveness and with a diminished role of the state, and increasing provision of health care services by the private sector, together with the enhancement of various forms of evidentiary basis for decision-making.

In particular, with respect to developing countries, there are multilateral organisations (such as the World Bank) and bilateral organisations, transnational corporations and public/private partnerships which play important roles as decision-makers in international health. Until very recently, these organisations have been dominated by economists, working within the framework of conventional economic theory, who advocate greater use of market mechanisms including user charges. Emerging trends include the rise in concern with inequalities and inequities, often increased by previous policies, and a recognition of the power of consumer perspectives and advocacy.

Health care reforms include decentralisation of resource allocation in Asian and African countries, the advocacy of pro-poor health policy and the use of measures such as the Global Burden of Disease to guide economic evaluation of health programs.

Chapter 12 is designed to draw conclusions from the material presented in the previous chapters about the appropriate and inappropriate applications of health economics in health policy and health services management. We suggest that there are good reasons for a greater focus on the major institutions of the health services, especially where these are based on a multidisciplinary approach, with inputs from clinicians, epidemiologists, and financial experts as well as health economists.

Summary and conclusions

We believe that health economics, especially where coupled with sound empirical work, which often health economists are well equipped to undertake, has much to contribute to an improved understanding of health-related phenomena. We argue that health economists might be encouraged to give more emphasis than has been the case in the past to evaluating the efficiency of hospitals and other institutions and services. The preoccupation in Britain with the evaluation of health status *per se* via the attempt to measure the impact on life expectancy, adjusted for quality, may have diverted the intellectual energy of many health economists from what may turn out to be more important areas. Similarly, US health economists have focused on problems of how to make health insurance in its several forms in that country more efficient. Until very recently they have tended to ignore both the issues considered important in other countries, and the lessons to be learned from the experience of these countries.

An important outcome of studying and assimilating the contents of the book should be the ability to adopt a more critical approach to the nostrums for health care reform put forward by generalist economists and management consultants, often US-based, and international agencies, notably the World Bank. They typically have a very limited understanding of the complexities of health care systems (sometimes including their own) and the inappropriateness of applying simple economic models as the centrepiece of their proposals.

There is some evidence to suggest that in developing and transitional countries the free market approach in the United States, as we indicated above, may be taken as a model of how health services should be organised and funded. This may be part of the reason for the recent claim, from a former World Bank economist, that aid to these countries from the developed world has done more harm than good.

Overview of the Discipline of Economics

This chapter deals with a review of the several definitions of economics, the subject matter of economics and of what economists do. There are numerous definitions of economics as a discipline the most popular of which, as we noted previously, include the broad goal of making choices between alternative uses of resources in the light of their scarcity. These are discussed in more detail below. Economists have developed a set of tools and concepts that comprise economic analysis. It is noted that economic theory relies heavily on deductive reasoning from a limited set of assumptions, and that the validity of these assumptions requires careful appraisal in every instance, especially when applied in the complex area of health and health services.

Amongst economists there have been widely differing views about a number of key matters such as the determinants of price and 'value', the importance of economic incentives in affecting consumer and producer behaviour, the appropriate roles of governments in economic affairs and how to deal with income distributional issues. In these circumstances it is misleading to present economics as a discipline with a unique set of methods, theories and policy relevant conclusions. This conclusion is emphasised by outlining key elements of the history of economic thought and the variety of 'schools' that has arisen. Accordingly, we stress that as consumers of economic theories, principles, analyses and applications we should be very cautious about accepting uncritically the policy and management recommendations that flow from any economist's conclusions.

Definitions of 'economics'

Three methods of defining economics are in most common usage. The first and probably the most popular is to refer to economics as the discipline that studies the allocation of resources in the context of a scarcity of resources of all kinds to meet all needs and wants of consumers and providers in the various markets (Robbins, 1932). From the perspective of this definition the overall objective of economics is to guide the allocation of resources in such a way that all participants in economic transactions achieve their goals. For consumers this is assumed to be the maximisation of the satisfaction ('utilities') they derive from a set of goods and services; for producers the notion of profit maximisation is introduced as the principal goal. This definition of economics, and its implications, dominates neoclassical economics where the prime concerns are both to explain the nature of markets and the behaviour of the participants, and to point to methods of reforming the functioning of markets to achieve improved outcomes.

From the standpoint of this definition the focus of economics is upon the individuals who participate in these markets. Its origins are based on the philosophy of Jeremy Bentham who in the last decade of the eighteenth century enunciated the principle that the goal of all human beings was to maximise their pleasure and to minimise their pain. This philosophy is described by the term *Utilitarianism*.

Of course neither Bentham nor his followers would deny the role of other determinants of human behaviour, such as religious beliefs or of charitable impulses. However, these were seen as being of lesser importance than the pleasure and pain principle. Indeed, this principle is an early version of 'model building' in which the attempt is made to simplify a complex reality by a concentration on what are assumed to be the most important factors or influences. Alfred Marshall in his *Principles of Economics* (1961) stated that economics is a study of mankind in the ordinary business of life. It examines that part of individual and social action which is most closely connected with the attainment and with the use of the material requisites of well-being. Marshall went on to assert that economics is in part a study of wealth and in part a study of man. His classical predecessors would no doubt have accepted this definition. By including a notion of 'social action', his definition was of wider scope than the now generally accepted neoclassical one. It should be made clear that the term wealth was designed to cover what today we would refer to as income.

A third definition focuses on what economists actually do. Despite its obvious circularity, this definition has the advantage of bringing a much wider set of topics, where the application of the Robbins-based definition does not seem particularly relevant, into consideration as aspects of economics. For example, studies of industrial innovation, growth and development do not fit very comfortably into the neoclassical framework and its underlying definition of economics except in a very broad sense. Macroeconomics, including the building of econometric models of economic phenomena, largely based on

Keynesian economics and the Walrasian approach (see below), constitutes a further example, especially in view of the large number of people who would identify themselves as economists working in these areas.

One of the difficulties with this last definition is the fact that it is not clear who should be called an economist. Unlike most other professional and academic positions there is no requirement of a legal or formal kind to prevent any one calling him or her self 'an economist'. This may be a special problem for health economics, especially when other professional groups may base their perception of economics on the writings and pronouncements of those who are not well qualified in the discipline.

A perspective on the issues and controversies in the literature of economics is best gained by presenting a very brief history of economic thought (HET), including the various 'schools' of economics, for example, the classical, neo-classical, Keynesian and monetarist. It is also important to be aware of the many sub-divisions of the discipline – macro- and microeconomics, international trade, consumer and production economics, labour economics, welfare economics, development economics and econometrics. To this formidable list might be added the economics of regulation and public sector finance. The relevance of these sub-disciplines in the applications to the health arena varies considerably as does the ease with which they can be adapted to the special circumstances of health services and health.

Some acquaintance with elements of the history of the development of economic theory is necessary to counter the widespread assumption of those without any knowledge of economics, that there is and has been only one form of economics generally now labelled as 'economic rationalism' or 'market fundamentalism', especially by its opponents. We shall use the terms neoclassical economics and orthodox economics, to describe this approach to economics that dominates to date much of the contemporary study and outcomes of health economics. See Stigler (1965) and Bannock et al. (2003) for more details of HET.

We need to be aware of the trenchant criticisms that have emerged of the foundations of economic theory, especially of microeconomics. These have been explored in considerable depth in a number of books and journal articles, but with occasional exceptions they have been ignored in mainstream health economics. It is well beyond the scope of this book to reproduce the details of most of these criticisms.

However, where these impinge directly on important aspects of health economics, such as the theory of consumer demand, and the policy implications of the theory of welfare economics, a general outline of the criticisms cannot be avoided. The stress in economics on the motivations of individuals, as opposed to the position that a community is more than just a collection of individuals, has also been subjected to a great deal of critical analysis. In general, the question marks about the validity and relevance of aspects of economic theory are reinforced, as we shall see in later chapters, when attempts are made to apply the theory to health and to the health services.

A brief history of economic thought and theory

The earliest systematic attempt to develop an explanation of economic phenomena was provided by Adam Smith (1723–90) in *An Inquiry into the Nature and Causes of the Wealth of Nations* (1776). He sought to answer the question: how is it that without apparent outside intervention, the numerous transactions in a commercial economy come together so that the self-interested activities of buyers and sellers produce coordinated outcomes. The invisible hand of markets and the prices that emerge from these markets were viewed by Smith as the key to understanding these phenomena.

He also wished to explain why certain items such as diamonds, which were of limited use, were so much more valuable; that is, had very high exchange values, whilst essential items notably water were relatively inexpensive. He also explored the notion that a key to understanding the wealth of nations and its development was the division of labour. The skills and capability of the labour force were expanded greatly by their concentration on individual tasks (specialisation) rather than having to spread their productive capacity across a large number of activities.

The other towering figure in the early development of what has come to be called classical economics was David Ricardo (1772–1823). His agenda was to provide further understanding of economic phenomena by seeking to establish what determined the prices in markets, notably for agricultural products, and relied on a cost of production theory of value, building on the work of Smith for this purpose. This cost of production theory emphasised the cost of labour as the main determinant but did not exclude other costs (Ricardo, 1920; Stigler, 1965).

Ricardo, who was superb at logical analysis, relied heavily for his work in economic theory on deductive reasoning. From a limited set of assumptions about human behaviour he sought to derive conclusions about key issues regarding economic phenomena. This emphasis on deductive reasoning had both positive and negative effects on the later development of economics as a discipline; these have persisted up to the present day.

On the one hand it contributed, in the hands of the most intellectually able economists, to the creation of a very imposing set of structures and tools of analysis without recourse to much observational data. The latter data, especially that bearing on the actual behaviour of producers and consumers, were much slower in being generated. Even now there remain important gaps in the available data and hard evidence relevant to economic relationships.

On the other hand, the emphasis on the deductive method appears to have led to the according of a higher status in the discipline to economic theorists than to their more empirically minded colleagues. More importantly it has led, possibly, to a situation in which clear cut evidence of the divergence of the behaviour of key agents from that predicted by the theory is ignored, or as indicating that the agents ought to change their behaviour to conform to the conclusions of the theory. We return to this theme in later chapters with examples drawn from health economics.

Karl Marx (1818–83) was an important follower of Ricardo and endeavoured to use a labour theory of value that emphasised the exploitation of workers by capitalists in the creation of surplus value. His most lasting influence in economic phenomena, as distinct from his role in the study of history and politics, was to focus on an evolutionary view of the subject and the exploration of the determinants of future changes in the 'capitalist mode of production' leading to the formation of monopolies. His reliance on the notion of class conflict has continued to be felt in both politics and sociology. Some economists have been influenced by his theories and methods up to the present time and would identify themselves as Marxist economists.

Later economists, notably William Jevons (1835–82), in the *Theory of Political Economy* (1871), undertook detailed criticisms of the labour theory of value, especially the absence of an account of the role of demand. Jevons and others introduced the notion of marginal utility as the principal factor underlying the demand for commodities and services, and hence the prices paid for them.

Building on the utilitarian and individualistic philosophy of Bentham he argued that the goal of consumers was to derive satisfaction or utility from commodities. However he believed, largely on the basis of introspection, that the utility derived by individual consumers depended on the quantity of the commodity already consumed. Moreover, extra units of consumption yielded less utility according to this approach. Thus the principle of diminishing marginal utility emerged in his work as the key to understanding how market prices were determined.

Amongst a number of other important nineteenth century economists who contributed significantly to classical economic theory was the Swiss-based French scholar, Leon Walras (1834–1910). With a background in mathematics, Walras returned to the Smithian theme of how the markets for different commodities were related to one another. He conceptualised the totality of markets in an economy as a set of simultaneous equations in which the prices and quantities established were determined by the solution to these equations. His influence has continued well into the twentieth century with the building and quantification of econometric models of the whole or segments of the economy for policy and predictive purposes being based on the same underlying principle.

The other important figure in the early development of economics was Alfred Marshall (1842–1924). In his *Principles of Economics* (1961) first published in 1890, he introduced the notion of the equilibrium price of each commodity in a market being determined by the intersection of demand and supply schedules. These independent curves could be derived from the utility maximizing of each individual consumer and the profit maximizing aspiration of each producer. In his famous analogy he claimed that it was no more relevant to ask the question of whether it was demand or supply which determined prices than to ask which blade of a scissors was responsible for the cutting process. He also introduced the notion of distinguishing short-term and long-term economic phenomena. Nevertheless he recognized that his method was based on static principles and the absence of a theory incorporating changes over time.

Marshall had been educated as a mathematician at Cambridge and he realised the potential of the calculus for exploring economic concepts with greater rigor. He developed what have come to be regarded as the staple elements of micro-economic analysis such as the elasticity of demand and consumer surplus. In these enterprises he acknowledged his debt to the French economist Antoine Cournot (1801–77) as set out in his book *The Mathematical Principles of the Theory of Wealth* (1929). Moreover, Marshall, unlike many of his contemporaries and successors, recognised the need to integrate deductive and inductive methods if economics were to obtain the status of a scientific discipline, his longer term aspiration.

Increasingly economics in the latter part of the nineteenth and in the twentieth century was dominated by professional and academic economists largely based in Britain and the United States, as Stigler (1965) has documented in some detail. Nevertheless, important contributions were also forthcoming from several European economists including members of the so-called Austrian school, notably Carl Menger (1840–1921), Eugen Boem-Bawerk (1851–1914), and later Joseph Schumpeter (1883–1950). Menger contributed to the early development of marginal utility theory but he was also one of the founders of an evolutionary concept of economics. Boem-Bawerk was critical of labour theories of value especially those emanating from Marx and his followers. Schumpeter, however, was more interested in such phenomena as the business cycle, economic growth and development, and the role of entrepreneurs in the creation of innovations of both a technical and organisational kind.

Much of the impact of the Austrian school has been continued by their heirs to this tradition who migrated to the United States, often to the

University of Chicago. Of these the most notable was Friedrich von Hayek (1899–1992). He was a strong advocate of the use of free markets rather than government intervention to achieve economic and other social goals. Hayek was an advocate also of 'methodological individualism', based on the belief that human behaviour is only understandable in individual terms. He denied the existence of collective entities such as the 'community' and saw microeconomics, with its emphasis on the motivations of individuals, as the appropriate focus of economic theory (Drucker, 1981).

One of the most influential continental economists of this period was the Italian Vilfredo Pareto (1848–1923) whose name is perhaps the sole exception to the disregard in conventional health economics of the history of the subject. Pareto was largely responsible for what has come to be known as welfare economics which plays a major and controversial role in health economics. He set out the principle that any economic policy change is desirable if the change leads to at least one person's satisfactions being augmented and no one losing as a consequence. Recognising that economic policies of this kind would be unusual, two well-known theoretical economists J.R. Hicks (1904–89) and N. Kaldor (1908–86) set out the weaker version of Pareto's principle that a policy change was still desirable if, *in principle*, the winners could compensate the losers.

Later developments in demand theory in neoclassical economics included responses to the recognition that the utilities of individuals could not be compared and added together. Thus an ordinal concept of utility rather than a cardinal one emerged; for each commodity it was only necessary for an individual to rank the utilities derived from each commodity for the link to be established between marginal utility and the aggregate market demand for that commodity. Francis Edgeworth (1845–1925) in criticising Jevons's theory of value, especially his implicit assumption that interpersonal comparisons of utility could be made, invented along with Pareto, the notion of the indifference curve which continues to be one of central importance in microeconomics, including those aspects relevant to health economics.

The theory of the firm was developed by Marshall and others based on applying the same principles of marginal analysis to the decisions facing producers as had been applied to consumers. In determining their levels of output they were assumed to endeavour to maximise their profits by equating marginal costs with their marginal revenues.

The neoclassical theories of supply and demand are discussed further in Chapters 4 and 5, respectively, with a strong emphasis on their assumptions and limitations.

Further developments in economics in the early part of the twentieth century were concerned with monetary economics, international economic issues and the determinants of the trade cycle. However, these aspects of what is now called macroeconomics did not directly affect the assumptions or relevance of neoclassical economics. But this situation changed radically with the great depression of the 1930s and the work of Maynard Keynes (1883–1946) published in his *General Theory of Employment, Interest and Money* (1936). It is again of interest to note that Keynes had also been educated originally as a mathematician.

According to Keynes the 'classical' economists had denied the possibility of long lasting departures from a state of equilibrium in all markets, including the market for labour, by a reliance on Say's law. The essential feature of this law was that in the aggregate supply created its own demand. Producers of goods and services generated flows of income which were translated into demand for these products. For the neoclassicists, unemployment and trade cycle phenomena were either ignored or explained as being short run phenomena produced by departures from perfect competition, especially in the labour market, for example, caused by the actions of trade unions and of governments.

The details of Keynes's theory and of his attack on the conventional economics of the time do not concern us for our present purposes. In brief, he concentrated on the inter-relationships of aggregate consumption, investment and savings. In particular he emphasised an important source of disequilibrium as arising out of the failure of aggregate investment and savings to achieve equality. In general he ignored or downplayed the role in the economy of traditional microeconomics. His remedy for the problem of severe recessions was based on the need for governments to engage in investment and income generating activities even if this meant that overall deficits in their budgets arose.

Keynes has had a lasting influence on the creation of national accounting data including the aggregates generated in the systems of income and expenditure accounting that loom large in the health economics data of individual countries (see Chapter 6).

From the 1940s onwards economists have been divided in their reactions to Keynesian economics. Some, notably the American economist Paul Samuelson (1915–), have looked to a synthesis of neoclassical and Keynesian economics. Others such as members of the Cambridge (England) school, influenced by the Italian economist Piero Sraffa (1898–1983), have questioned the logical consistency of neoclassical economics especially in regard to the theory of the firm. The most prominent member of the Cambridge school has been Joan Robinson (1903–83) who was professor of economics at Cambridge University.

In the 1930s she queried the relevance of the perfect competition model of the neoclassicists based on the assumption that no single firm was responsible for a large enough proportion of output in the industry to influence the market price. Her theory of imperfect competition was derived from the observation that consumers may differentiate between very similar products so that individual firms may possess a degree of monopoly power (Robinson, 1969). This may lead to a situation in which the market price exceeded that which would be generated if the perfect competition assumptions held.

Joan Robinson's book *Economic Philosophy* (1962) set out a comprehensive debunking of some of the scientific pretensions of neoclassical economists, and their claims to have produced value-free theories untainted by ideology. That neoclassical economics remains the dominant paradigm of the discipline, despite these and other criticisms to which we refer below and in later chapters, may tell us more about the incentives and priorities in the profession than about the validity of these analyses (Evans, 1998).

In addition, in respect of economic policy in many countries there has been a resurgence of interest in monetary economics, in large part stimulated by the work of Milton Friedman (1902–2006). Monetarism, with its lesser role for government intervention in economies, was welcomed, especially in conservative political circles, as a desirable alternative to the approach of Keynes.

The division of economic thought into a number of different schools and policy perspectives has generated a reaction amongst some prominent economists that there is a crisis in the discipline (Bell and Kristol, 1981). It has also created an undercurrent of dissatisfaction with the notion of economics as a scientific discipline, since the prominence or decline of certain schools seems to have had more to do with shifting political attitudes and power rather than being based on new evidence or improved analytical techniques. A flurry of books and other writings, supporting this conclusion, has emerged with titles such as *Economic Theory and Ideology* (Fine, 1980), *Dangerous Currents: the State of Economics* (Thurow, 1983) and *Debunking Economics: The Naked Emperor of the Social Sciences*, (Keen, 2001).

The criticisms of neoclassical economics

Marginal utility theory

Almost from the time of its development marginal utility theory has been subjected to numerous criticisms. Many of these were articulated in cogent form by Gustav Cassel (1866–1945) in 1899. His most substantive criticism was that demand functions could be derived directly from empirical observations without recourse to a utility substructure (Stigler, 1965). His other criticisms asserted that the theory required a unit of utility that no one could define, that the underlying mathematics was intractable unless the commodities in question were divisible into small units and the utility functions were continuous.

The examples provided by marginal utility theorists almost invariably were based on food, with ice cream being a frequently quoted example. This tradition has continued at least in the elementary treatment of the subject up to the present (Samuelson and Nordhaus, 2005). In the nineteenth century a very high proportion of income was associated with expenditure on food. However, increasingly in developed countries, the proportion spent on non-food items has increased dramatically across all income groups. Marginal utility theory seems to verge on the fanciful when the attempt is made to apply it to consumer durables, for example.

Rather than being a successful attempt to incorporate a psychologically based theory into economics as some of the economists of the time claimed, professional psychologists, notably William James in the United States at the end of the nineteenth century, regarded the assumptions about human psychology of utility theory as being highly questionable. In particular he queried the Benthamite assertion that the main motivation of human behaviour was to maximise satisfaction (utility) and to minimize pain.

Do consumers and firms undertake maximising behaviour?

This theme has been taken up by behavioural economists, notably Herbert Simon, who have emphasised the notion of satisficing behaviour rather than maximizing behaviour (Simon, 1947). The extra effort, along with the data required in achieving the situation of a maximum of utility or profit may not be deemed worthwhile by many participants in markets. Entrepreneurs, for example, lacking information about their marginal costs, may be content with the use of rules of thumb in establishing the prices of their products.

Recent developments in evolutionary economics have also emphasised the limitations of the notion of optimising behaviour especially when applied to complex organisations subsumed in the conventional approach to the firm (Foster and Metcalfe, 2001; Foster, 2004). It is possible that the economic models developed for hospitals and other health service providers, which are discussed in Chapter 4, in the future might fruitfully be approached from an evolutionary economics standpoint based on the very complex networks of relationships which exist in these organisations.

Ideology and the role of government

Despite the assertions of economists that theirs is an objective discipline, political divisions within the discipline seem to form the basis of some of the controversy, especially between the various schools and their reactions to government intervention. The more conservative members of the profession, especially in the United States, in general regard the activities of government as often being counterproductive and that they should be replaced by greater reliance on market mechanisms. Their more liberal or radical counterparts look to governments as having more far reaching roles, especially in areas such as health, welfare and education.

Summary and conclusions

In summary, this review of aspects of the history of economic theory and thought has revealed the existence of a good deal of controversy about some of the fundamental tools of economic analysis. It has also revealed that the foundations of microeconomics, and hence of conventional neoclassical theory, have been criticised frequently, and in our view very effectively, in the literature of the subject. Marginal utility theory, the notion of the maximising behaviour of consumers and firms, and the individualistic basis of much of the theory, are points of contention that bedevil the discipline. As Keen (2001) pointed out, these controversies are rarely mentioned in the introductory treatment of the subject.

FURTHER READING

The book by Stigler (1965) quoted above, *Essays in the History of Economics*, provides an excellent and very readable account of the historical development of economic theory. Stigler's perspective is based within a neoclassical framework.

Schumpeter's (1954) *History of Economic Analysis*, is primarily concerned with issues about economic development, the role of innovation, and the 'waves of creative destruction' that he believed characterised capitalist economies. It provides a somewhat different approach to the history of the subject as compared with Stigler and others.

For those who wish to learn more about conventional economics, a large number of text books are on the market. Paul Samuelson's text, now in its eighteenth edition, (Samuelson and Nordhaus, 2005) is an excellent starting point.

Discussion questions

- In your view what are the main reasons why reputable economists have differed markedly in their views about key elements of economic theory and economic policy?
- Is there justification for the claim by some economists that theirs is a scientific discipline? If not, why not?
- Mrs Margaret Thatcher, when Prime Minister of the United Kingdom, asserted that there was no such thing as 'society'. The distinguished economist and Nobel Prize

winner, Milton Friedman, along with Friedrich von Hayek, another Nobel Prize winner, may have been the intellectual sources of her claim. What are the implications of this view for economics, and do you agree with the statement?

- Two famous quotations about the study of history are: 'We learn from history that we learn nothing from history' and 'Those who do not learn from history are doomed to repeat it.' Discuss in relation to the history of economic thought.

An Introduction to the Literature of Health Economics

Overview

In this chapter we describe the current state of health economics, especially the great expansion of interest in the subject as measured by the number of health services research projects that feature economic analysis, and the considerable increase in the literature dealing with health economics. To provide further perspectives on what health economists do, we present summary accounts of the main contributions of a number of prominent health economists whose views on key issues differ from many other health economists. We have also noted that the literature of health economics has been dominated by contributions from the United States and to a lesser extent from Britain. The interests of the majority of US-based health economists and those working in Britain differ considerably, as we have indicated previously, especially in regard to their preferred policy options and their approaches to the contentious area of welfare economics.

In its pursuit of answers to questions about the determination of values as reflected in prices, economics has traditionally characterised influences into those operating on the demand side and those which affect the supply side. Despite the reservations we have about the assumed independence of these factors from each other, especially but not exclusively when dealing with health services and health, we regard it as useful for expository purposes to retain the notion of health as a commodity, with one of the inputs to the production of this commodity being the outputs of health services.

This conceptualisation is not intended to deny the role of other factors in the determination of the health of individuals and communities. The issue of why some people are healthy and others unhealthy has been explored in considerable detail by Evans, Barer and Marmor (1994). Their conclusions stress the importance of the social environment and the status of individuals within occupational and other hierarchies in influencing health outcomes. The socio-economic determinants of health status have also been analysed recently by Fuchs (2004b) in a paper described later.

There has been an escalation of activity in health economics over the last 20 years, with a substantial increase in the number of economists who specialise in the area, a rapid expansion in the studies of the health services that are based on economic analysis, and of the literature on the subject. A recent detailed review of health economics articles in the *Econlit* database has shown an increase in the number of papers included under this heading from 273 in 1991 to 890 in 1999 (Rubin and Chang, 2003).

These developments have reflected, in part, the concerns of governments about the increases in the costs of providing health services and they have looked to economists to address this and related issues. Politicians have faced the task of limiting access to resources with budget constraints and they have increasingly sought the help of health economists in this endeavour. We explore the specific use of health economics for the purpose of evaluating health services programs, projects and clinical interventions in Chapter 8.

The sources of the health economics literature

Three specialised health economics journals are the *Journal of Health Economics, Health Economics* and *the European Journal of Health Economics*. A brief perusal of our bibliography will indicate that a large number of substantial contributions to the literature are contained in these journals. Many papers with a health economics focus are also featured in the journal *Health Affairs*, especially when they have important health policy implications.

There are also a large number of general textbooks on the subject. Examples include Feldstein, P. (1997), Folland et al. (1993), Jacobs (1997), and Santerre and Neun (2000). Most of these books are of US origin with an emphasis on the specific institutions, programs and policy issues of that country. An important exception is that of the English-based economists McPake, Kumaranayake and Normand (2002) who take an international perspective.

A further important addition to the health economics literature is that provided by the *Handbook of Health Economics* (Culyer and Newhouse eds, 2000). This mammoth work in two parts consists of nearly 2000 pages and covers a wide range of topics. Some of the individual chapters are quoted below and in later chapters of this book.

We have noted previously that US-based health economists, with important exceptions, have emphasised the greater use of competitive market mechanisms, including increased user charges, to solve the perceived problems. They have been sceptical about the roles of governments in health service funding, provision and regulation, including their subsidies of health insurance and the direct provision of services. Issues of equity in the funding and provision of services have not been prominent in their interests.

Whilst American health economists primarily write for a local readership, especially in regard to the recurring theme of health insurance reform in that country, it is often the case that their policy conclusions are taken up by economists and policy-makers in other countries, including developing and transitional countries. These recommendations have often reflected a simplistic belief in the benefits of the operation of free markets, with a noticeable lack of appreciation of the problems inherent in conventional neoclassical economics. This issue in regard to developing and transitional countries is explored in detail in Chapter 11.

We have also noted that British health economists, again with some very important exceptions, have been primarily concerned with the development and use of economic methods for evaluating projects and programs. National Health Service (NHS) reforms of the early nineties (in part wound back after the change in government in 1997) emphasised competition between providers of services, but the greater operation of market forces in influencing consumer behaviour has not been perceived as a realistic option politically in the context of the NHS, where most services are provided free at the point of service.

It is also the case that considerable caution must be exercised in applying the interests, conclusions and recommendations of British health economists to other countries that usually rely to a greater extent than the NHS on health insurance, user payments and the private sector. Moreover, the published literature indicates that British health economists, with a few exceptions, have not emphasised the measurement of the overall performance and efficiency of hospitals and other health services.

A literature search of the PubMed database has revealed numerous studies of the technical efficiency of hospitals from the United States, Canada, Germany, Italy, Norway, Ireland, the Netherlands, and a number of developing countries, but only one about UK hospitals. The comment of Alan Maynard about the lack of use of the Hospital Episode Statistics in the NHS is also highly relevant to this point (Maynard, 2005a).

The meaning of efficiency

One of the most important aims of economists is to improve the efficiency of the operation of economies. However, confusion is created in the literature of the discipline by the varying definitions of efficiency used or emphasised by different economists. To gain an understanding of the economics of the health services it is essential to be aware of how the term is used.

For many economists, the term efficiency is equated with the achievement of the situation in which no one can be made better off without someone being made worse off. This is the overall definition of what is usually referred to as 'economic' efficiency and is based on the application of the theory of welfare economics and the Paretian approach discussed previously. According to this theory, for efficiency to be achieved by the whole economy or a specific sector, a number of conditions must be present. These include the requirement that perfect competition is present in all markets which, in turn implies that there are no barriers to entry of new firms and that no firm is sufficiently large to influence the prices of its outputs and inputs, and that each firm is operating without any waste of resources.

Allocative efficiency is often treated as being identical with economic efficiency but it is also used to convey the notion that the distribution of resources is deployed in a manner that ensures that no redistribution of resources would generate higher satisfactions or other returns to the population. In the health services context, departures from maximum allocative efficiency would be present if it could be demonstrated that the health status of the population would be improved if resources were reallocated from hospitals to other activities such as health promotion and disease prevention.

In comparing the relative performance of the health systems of different countries (see Chapter 10) we have also used allocative efficiency to refer, somewhat loosely, to the relationship between measures of health status and the cost of providing these services.

Technical efficiency refers to the situation where a firm or other institution operates at the maximum level of production that can be generated by its available resources. For a profit maximising firm microeconomics establishes a number of formal conditions for this condition to be achieved. The notion of technical efficiency is closest to the way the term efficiency is used in engineering and physics: the maximum output of an engine for a given input of energy.

Note also that if some organisations were operating at less than the maximum achievable technical efficiency, allocative efficiency for the system would not be achieved; a reallocation of resources from the entities of lower technical efficiency to those of higher efficiency would improve the satisfactions or welfare of the population. In a competitive market the redistribution of resources would be an automatic process according to the economic theory concerning these markets.

It should be evident that each concept of efficiency, if interpreted in an absolute sense, is unlikely to be achieved in practice. Nevertheless, the pursuit of increased relative allocative or technical efficiency can be seen as a desirable objective, provided it does not conflict with other (social) objectives, notably the achievement of a more equitable society from the overall functioning of the economy, including the health care sector.

Economists in the neoclassical tradition emphasise the trade-off between efficiency and equity. Greater equity may only be achieved in their view at the expense of reduced efficiency. However, in the health area, there is a good deal of evidence that more equitable societies are able to achieve greater efficiency as reflected in enhanced levels of health status for their populations, often at lower cost. We return to this topic in Chapter 10.

The contributions of influential health economists

Background

Since the English language literature and research of health economics has been dominated to date by the United States and British contributions, an overview of the current status of the subject is best introduced by providing a brief account of the work of influential and prolific health economists from both sides of the Atlantic. It will be noted that most are of British or US origin with the exception being Robert Evans from Canada. Gavin Mooney, originally from Scotland, is now based in Australia.

Those we have chosen to include have all contributed substantially in terms of the number of publications dealing with health economics and the impact of their most significant work in this field, especially in respect of policy development and management. There are, of course, many health economists from other countries who have made significant contributions especially to issues such as health insurance development in their own country and in regard to equity and distributional problems. The Belgian economist van Doorslaer whose work with the English economist Wagstaff on international comparisons of the equity of health funding and utilisation is reviewed in Chapter 8, and the Swiss economist Peter Zweifel's work with its heavy emphasis on the econometrics of the health services (Zweifel and Breyer, 1997) merit special mention.

An account of the work of the health economists upon whom we have focused also serves to highlight most of the current controversies in this field. These cover the role of free markets in health, health insurance and co-payments, supplier-induced demand, managed competition, methods for funding health services, the optimum balance of public and private sector health activities, equity and efficiency objectives as applied to health, and income distributional issues. Many of these topics are examined in greater detail in subsequent chapters. Reference should also be made to the extensive *Glossary of Terms* appearing at the end of the book.

Whilst we believe that our comments about the positions and conclusions reached are as free of bias as we can make them, our objective has not been to assess the quality, originality and relevance of each person's contribution. It should be noted, however, that the health economists singled out in these summaries tend to lie outside the group of more conventional US-based economists who advocate the greater use of free market mechanisms in their own country and elsewhere. Finally, we should note that their values, as revealed in their scholarly and research studies and priorities, are largely consistent with our own as we have expressed them previously.

Professor Tony Culyer

As we have noted previously welfare economics based on the Paretian principle has been used extensively by economists to produce normative conclusions as an input into the creation of social policy programs. Tony Culyer has argued that the Paretian criterion of a desirable outcome for a policy change that at least one person is made better off and no one is made worse off, on the face of it seems to be an innocuous way of judging the social benefits of such a change (Culyer, 1998). If presented in these terms, it is likely to command widespread community support. Its application to policy issues had the commendable objective of minimising the intrusion of the values of the professional analyst, including the economist, into the policy-making process. Culyer emphasised that in his own early work on applying economic theory to social policy it seemed to be a potentially useful way of moving away from the politicisation of social policy issues (Culyer, 1973).

Culyer notes that the application of the Paretian criterion to health policy matters is of very limited utility in the light of the scope for policy changes to produce uncompensated losses, transfers and 'intrinsically involving distributive equity in resource allocation'. It is difficult to envisage any relevant policy initiative affecting how health services are funded or provided which does not produce winners and losers. Indeed funding policies designed to transfer resources from previously over funded areas to under funded areas, based, for example, on the Resource Allocation Working Party (RAWP) approach in Britain and elsewhere, are quite explicitly designed to achieve winners and losers as compared with the previous status quo. As Culyer also points out those who apply welfare economics to health policy issues do not address these problems, they simply ignore them.

In the United States, the underlying theme of many prominent health economists has been to draw normative conclusions about health policy from the application of welfare economics. These conclusions have encompassed such matters as the alleged deadweight loss of health insurance, and hence the need to adopt policies in which consumers take more responsibility for meeting their own health care costs. They have also denied the relevance of supplier-induced demand to health policy issues.

In an interchange between Culyer and Evans and Mark Pauly, the former entitled their response to an editorial of Pauly in the *Journal of Health Economics* as 'Normative Rabbits from Positive Hats' (Culyer and Evans, 1996). Pauly's main claim had been that, given its assumptions, normative policy conclusions could be drawn. Culyer and Evans pointed out that these assumptions are themselves based on the values of the people who make them. Where these are made by economists they should be accorded no more weight than if they were proposed by any one else. To assert that they are derived from welfare economics is simply misleading.

The problems in the application of welfare economics to the complex issue of health care provision and funding has led Culyer and others to advocate an extra-welfarist approach (Culyer, 1989). The essential feature of this approach is to move away from the utility maximisation basis of welfare economics to one in which the ultimate objective of health services is to maximise the health of the population. From this perspective, health policies and projects which can be demonstrated to produce health gains are those which should be implemented, subject to cost and resource constraints.

Culyer's extra-welfarism is linked with the role of the health economist being to provide policy advice to decision-makers based on their values. The values of the decision-makers may be obtained directly or inferred from other evidence. The role of the health economist is to spell out the consequences of each of the options and to ensure that all possible options are included. From this perspective health economists should act as consultants to the decision-makers and policy advisors. Culyer sees as an important additional advantage of the extra-welfarist approach that it would facilitate communication with other disciplines such as epidemiologists and doctors who may find welfare economics confusing or incomprehensible.

Tony Culyer has also written extensively on equity, equality and ethical issues in the health services (Culyer, 2001a,b). Most recently he has produced a comprehensive and valuable dictionary of health economics (Culyer, 2005b).

Professor Robert Evans

Robert Evans has written extensively about health economics, including two influential books *Strained Mercy: the Economics of the Canadian Health Care System* (Evans, 1984) and *Why are Some People Healthy and Others Not* (Evans, Barer and Marmor eds, 1994). *Strained Mercy* in our view is one of the most important books available about health economics. As the sub-title indicates the institutional material is primarily about the Canadian system.

In addition, Evans devoted a good deal of attention to the United States, especially in regard to debunking systematically many of the free market-based analyses of health economists. In later chapters of our book we have drawn freely on the salient ideas of Evans. The elegance and clarity with which Evans is able to express his ideas is also worthy of special note.

A paper by Evans and Stoddart which created considerable interest in public health and policy circles was entitled 'Producing health and consuming health care' (Evans and Stoddart, 1990). The paper dealt primarily with a large range of data dealing with systematic variations in mortality. A causal framework was established which was designed to integrate the determinants of health status as established or canvassed in a diverse set of disciplinary sources.

For our present purposes we concentrate on his contribution to an international conference on distribution issues in health economics (Evans, 1998). This paper summarises his writings and thoughts about many of the problems that have surfaced on the theoretical foundations of health economics. His perceptions of these problems, not surprisingly, have been influenced considerably by the proximity of the many health economists in the United States who subscribe to very different views about the role of free markets and prices in health care policies. He has also been concerned to counter the attempts by some economists and others in Canada to reform their health insurance program by introducing American style changes (Evans and Vujicic, 2005).

Evans in his paper, 'Towards a healthier economics, Ken Bassett's problem' starts off with an example drawn from medicine by a Canadian physician, Dr Ken Bassett, of why some clinicians continue to use a routine procedure, electronic foetal monitoring, when they know it confers no benefit to patients in normal deliveries. He poses the same question regarding health economists who, he claims, continue to apply conceptions of welfare economics to health matters without acknowledging the value judgements that are implicit in their policy conclusions.

As economists have long acknowledged it is fundamental to the application of welfare economics to policy recommendations that a rule is required to rank social outcomes. The ranking rule, a social welfare function, must incorporate a set of values that are derived from outside economics (Bator, 1957). Thus, for economic (Pareto) efficiency to be achieved the distribution of income implications of the policy must be assessed simultaneously with other outcomes of the policy. It is in respect of these assessments that the necessity for the introduction of value judgements must be recognised. Yet many health economists continue to make policy recommendations which ignore the distributional effects, or impose their own values that the distribution of incomes is ideal before and after the policy change.

Evans also included the claim of many health economists and others that technological developments in medicine were mainly responsible for increasing health care expenditure as a further example of Ken Bassett's problem. He made the point that health economists should be well aware that the international evidence points to the fact that the extent to which a technology is used is a product of other characteristics of health services, notably the amount of control that governments or other payers choose to deploy over its usage. He demonstrated that there are substantial differences in the use of many costly medical technologies between countries which cannot be accounted for by national income differences or access to the technologies.

In the jargon of economics Evans regards technology as an *endogenous* factor rather than an *exogenous* one in the context of the health services. That is its use is a product of other characteristics of the system, such as the roles of governments in evaluating, financing and restricting its applications. The exogenous nature of technology in creating cost escalation problems as assumed by many health economists is based on the belief that the use of technologies lies outside the control of health care policy-makers. A competitive, free market approach to health care policy issues is consistent with the exogenous role of technology.

Evans cited several reasons for the existence of Ken Bassett's problem in health economics. These include the fact that economists find it much easier to make up their underlying assumptions about consumer behaviour such as the exogenous nature of tastes, and of technology deployment, rather than finding out how relevant are these assumptions.

A further reason, Evans claimed, is that the assumptions made have 'powerful ideological and political content'. Those groups in the health care industry who stand to benefit from increased health care expenditure, including the manufacturers of health care equipment and other technology, and the pharmaceutical industry, do not wish to see measures such as cost controls introduced by governments which would threaten their sales and revenues. They strongly favour the exogenous role of technology and are likely to support, financially and otherwise, health economists who incorporate this assumption in their work and policy recommendations (Evans, 1998).

Professor Victor Fuchs

A major contribution of Victor Fuchs to health economics was made in his book: *Who Shall Live? Health, Economics and Social Choice* (Fuchs, 1974b). The book was amongst the first to set out in cogent form many of the principles underlying the application of economics to health issues based on notions of individual and social choice. Its overall theme was a critique of American medicine as it was organised, financed and practised in the early 70s. As reviewers at the time indicated, the book combined an excellent deployment of economic theory with a deep understanding of health services institutions.

In the United States, and elsewhere, the book provided a good deal of momentum to the recognition of health economics as a respectable sub-discipline of economics. An expanded edition was published in 1998 which included other papers by Fuchs. The respect of fellow economists for Fuchs was demonstrated by his elevation in 1995 to the presidency of the American Economics Association.

Fuchs has researched and written on a wide range of health economics topics, including the cost of medical care, the role of physician behaviour in influencing health care costs and the economics of ageing. He has taken a much wider perspective on health services and social issues, including an interest in the health systems of other countries, than most of his US health economist colleagues. Of considerable importance is Fuchs's recent contribution to the important issue of the socio-economic determinants of health (Fuchs, 2004b).

In the paper, Fuchs queried the possibility of rigorously establishing causal relationships in this complex area. Of the main socioeconomic variables usually considered in such studies, notably income, level of educational achievement, occupation and ethnicity, there is a high degree of correlation between each of these possible explanatory variables. This complicates the task of determining the separate effects of these factors despite the formal ability to control statistically for the effect of each variable in a statistical multiple regression estimation.

He noted that the correlation between income and health is well established empirically but he points to the fact that there are several possible interpretations of these data. In the US context it is usually assumed that people in the lower income groups, often uninsured, experience poorer health status because of financial obstacles to accessing health services. Fuchs points out that in principle poor health may lead to lower incomes or that both variables may be influenced by other factors. He notes that even in countries where universal health insurance exists studies have also revealed the high correlation between income and health. He also raises the issue of whether it is absolute income or relative income which is relevant to the postulated relationship.

Fuchs applied a similar approach to the high correlation found between health status and education level as measured by years of schooling. In this case, however, he recognised that the causal effect of health on years of education is unlikely to be present. However, he regarded it as unsatisfactory that the direct effect of level of education on health has not been explained and verified. He found it puzzling that the effect seems to be present at all levels of education so that an additional two years of college (tertiary) education has the same effect in improving health status as an additional two years of secondary education.

Fuchs suggested that other factors may influence both years of schooling and level of health. Those individuals who have a greater capacity to defer gratification, that is who have lower rates of time discount, may undertake more years of education and may be more likely to avoid unhealthy behaviour in spite of the short-term utility it might generate for them. Fuchs also emphasised the need in studies of income and health relationship to adjust or control for other factors that influence health status, notably age, sex and marital status.

Finally in this paper Fuchs claimed that health economists and others who have investigated this and similar relationships involving health status usually do not make clear the mechanism(s) at work when they infer a causal effect. He suggested a number of means of doing this, for example, by dis-aggregation of the data to individual age groups or by causes of death. His final suggestion was that interactions between genes and socio-economic variables should be further investigated. There is increasing evidence from genetic studies that health reactions to stress, such as the susceptibility to clinical depression, are influenced considerably according to the presence or absence of different (short and long) versions of the same gene.

Another major contribution of Fuchs was contained in his paper 'the future of health economics' (Fuchs, 2000). He provided convincing evidence of the enormous increase in the interest in health economics over the last 30 years as indicated by the 12-fold expansion in the number of PhD graduates in the field, the appointment of health economists in leading US economics departments and departments of public health and management, and the appointment of health economists to key government agencies in health-related areas. He also emphasised the expansion of health economics as an input to health policy and health services research. Along with other health economists he ascribed these developments to the ever increasing health care expenditure together with 'intellectual advances' and the greater availability of data.

Fuchs noted that some health economists' research interests and publications are close to the mainstream of economics as a behavioural science, whilst others work predominantly in health policy and health services research. However, he regarded each approach as of equal merit. For those who focus on economics as a behavioural science several research areas are worthy of further exploration. These are the endogenous nature of health technology and consumer preferences, the impact of social and professional roles and norms on economic behaviour, the principal-agency problem, and the measurement and analysis of the quality of life.

In the health policy and health services research areas Fuchs set out what he believes to be both the strengths and weaknesses of economics. He stressed that economists can approach new problems with the ability to bring to bear on them a well established framework of thinking and systematic theory. According to Fuchs, economists have also acquired considerable skill in drawing conclusions from imperfect data.

The chief criticism that Fuchs made of economists is that they give insufficient attention to institutions, history and language which he regards as especially important in the health services area. He claimed that it is not possible to understand why health funding arrangements differ so much between countries without investigating these matters. We shall return to further discussion of the issues raised by Fuchs when we consider in Chapter 12 the priorities for health economics activities and the possibilities of future changes in direction.

Professor Gavin Mooney

Gavin Mooney's two most important contributions to the literature of health economics are the notion that health policies should be concerned with communitarianism, and that the very different perspectives of clinicians and economists about key issues need to be recognised. Also he has clarified considerably our understanding of the various concepts of equity.

Communitarianism was defined by Mooney as incorporating the value of participating within a community. Thus to understand the behaviour of individuals one should first look at their communities and their communal relationships. In his view both the welfare and extra-welfarist frameworks, being based on individualist starting points and outcomes, ignore the element of process utility to which the communitarian approach contributes. Thus he claimed that it is not only the outcome in terms of health status that generates utility but the processes in place, including that of caring for the less fortunate members, which also yield satisfaction for communities.

The existence of universal health insurance in all advanced countries except the United States, including the direct provision by the state of health services in some of these countries, may reflect the fact that high values are placed by these communities on the access of all their citizens to affordable health care. In the United States, as judged by the absence of universal coverage for health care costs, the communitarian ethos may be much less well developed.

Mooney has argued at length (Mooney, 1992) that doctors regard their primary responsibility as being to their patients. Medical ethics supports this position where the emphasis is on doing one's best in the meeting of the medical needs of each patient. Economists look at health care issues from the perspective of allocating total scarce health resources between competing ends to maximise the utilities of individuals or the health status of their populations. Whilst the ethics of health economists have not been subjected to the same scrutiny and development of guidelines as in other professional groups, the tasks that health economists attempt to accomplish and their writings are consistent with this interpretation of their ethical background.

According to Mooney, these two perspectives lead to a very different set of concerns between the two groups especially about broad resource allocation issues. Economists stress the scarcity of resources and the need to ensure that these are deployed with maximum efficiency. Some doctors continue to subscribe to the myth that there are or should be unlimited resources for health services. Thus there is inevitably tension between these two very different perspectives.

The tension between doctors and economists, as we discuss further in Chapter 9, sometimes carries over into unhelpful debates in which economists may take the view that doctors need an elementary introduction to economic principles to enlighten them about opportunity costs and marginal analysis. On the other hand, doctors claim that economists do not understand the many pressures on their time and their legal and ethical responsibilities for their patients.

A further important contribution of Mooney to the health economics literature is represented in a book he has edited with Richard Scotton (Mooney and Scotton, 1998). The book contains an excellent set of chapters covering a wide range of topics written by a group of leading Australian health economists.

Professor Uwe Reinhardt

Uwe Reinhardt has also been concerned over a number of years with exposing the limitations of applying conventional welfare theory to health issues without giving due regard to distributional and equity issues (Reinhardt, 1998). Some of the principal points he makes overlap with those of Evans and will not be repeated for our present purposes. We also noted in the previous chapter that a major limitation in much of the use of economic welfare for prescriptive purposes, that is, in normative economics, lies in the failure to consider distributional and equity issues. Reinhardt explored these matters in considerable detail and he illustrates his arguments by examples of a compelling kind.

Thus he spelled out the consequences of a greater resort to market mechanisms, as favoured by most American health economists, of the implications of a market-based solution to resource allocation leading to a re-distribution of welfare from a poor family with a sick child to a rich family with a well child (Reinhardt, 1998).

Reinhardt also documented the remarkable growth in the number of health economists in recent times reflecting the fact that politicians have increasingly turned to them for advice in the belief that they are able to allocate limited budgetary resources more competently than others.

Reinhardt observed that in positive economic analysis, economists potentially have much to offer decision-makers in both the public and private sectors of health care delivery. They understand issues in costing such as the crucial distinction between fixed and variable costs much better than other professions. According to Reinhardt, the relevance of marginal costs to decision-making is also part of the important intellectual equipment that economists can bring to bear on policy issues.

The analytical framework of economists can also be a potent force in debunking many of the misconceptions that often underlie public health discussion and policy-making in health care. One notable example is the notion that human life is priceless. Economists, in Reinhardt's view, are also well placed to undertake empirical research into the behaviour of the providers and funders of health services. The extent, however, to which this potential has been realised, is one of the issues we address further in our concluding chapter.

Reinhardt has argued that the language used by economists may often be confusing, sometimes he claims, deliberately so. This is especially the case when terms such as efficiency which are in common usage, are applied by economists, with a very specific meaning, in the context of welfare economics. Greater efficiency may be construed by non-economists, including health policy-makers, as an unequivocal improvement in community welfare or social desirability. But when economists use this term, as we have observed above, they are often restricting it to the Pareto sense where the gainers from an efficiency enhancing change are better off and no one is worse off. Similar considerations apply to the use of the term 'optimal' as also being identifiable by non-economists as unequivocally the best.

In reviewing Reinhardt's contribution to the health economics literature it must be borne in mind that often his analysis is directed at countering the failure of his fellow health economists in the United States to recognise the limitations and pitfalls of many of their free market solutions to health policy-making. At the same time his criticisms of the free market approach are often directed at the material contained in microeconomics text books which do not directly address health economics issues, but where their conclusions about the 'welfare burden' of providing free services or of 'moral hazard' in these circumstances may be applied uncritically to the health services.

Some economists who lack knowledge of the specific issues addressed by health economists may also be guilty of promoting these misconceptions. In addition, as Reinhardt pointed out, there has been a tendency in other countries, including developing and transitional countries, for example, those of the former Soviet bloc, to base their health policies on the American free market policy principles and prescriptions.

A closely related problem is the redefinition of the patient as a consumer which has become popular even in the currently non-market-based British NHS. This is a further example of what Reinhardt has referred to as the use of language to convey an ideological point. It paves the way for the health services to be viewed as being akin to any other commodity, implying that the choices made by consumers in this area are subject to the same incentives, influences and responsibilities.

Professor Alan Williams

Alan Williams, another British health economist of note, has made at least two important contributions to the literature of health economics. The first of these was set out in a *British Medical Journal* article and was presumably designed to influence clinicians in their choices about medical interventions based on a framework which emphasised the costs of the treatment options (Williams, 1985). In this article Williams presented a set of results about the relative cost-effectiveness of a number of cardiac disease interventions. This paper has been very influential amongst British health economists and others in focusing attention on the relative cost-effectiveness of therapeutic and health projects and the use of quality adjusted life years (QALYs) as a measure of health outcomes in this process. The interpretations and limitations of OALYs are discussed at length in Chapter 8.

The other contribution of Williams has been to introduce the notion of a fair innings into the debate about the establishment of health service priorities (Williams, 1997, 1998a). According to this view there is a case for basing the allocation of the health resources provided to members of communities on their life expectancies as modified by QALY measures. It was Williams's primary intention in this endeavour to highlight the life expectancies of social classes 4 and 5 (lower income etc groups) in Britain as being substantially lower than for social classes 1 and 2. Since the former classes generally experience more ill health, the discrepancies become greater after QALY adjustment. According to his calculations for Britain, the discrepancy amounts to about nine QALYs.

Thus Williams argued that in the pursuit of greater fairness in resource allocation QALYs should be weighted by a set of equity weights applying to different groups in the community. These equity weights would be age specific and applied within groups as defined by social class and sex. He believed that such an approach would integrate equity and efficiency concerns in health service policy. He has also argued, more controversially, for according lower priority to the aged who have already exceeded their fair innings.

Williams has also published recently an excellent account of the role of ideology in the reforms touching on the privatisation movement in health care (Williams, 2005). Amongst his many perceptive observations is that instead of trying to make economic analysis as value-free as possible, the aim of much of neoclassical economics, we should be seeking to make it 'as value-compatible as possible'. In other words recommendations about economic policy should be compatible with whatever set of values we as individuals hold, or the community reveals. In the relation between ideology and analytical methods he stresses the danger of the *'belief that mainstream economics is value-free'*.

Summary and conclusions

In providing an introduction to the extensive literature on health economics, we have noted that it is dominated by contributions from North America and the United Kingdom. We have emphasised that the interests and priorities of health economists on each side of the Atlantic differ considerably.

We use a discussion of major contributions of six prominent health economists, three from North America and three from the United Kingdom, to foreshadow a number of important issues concerning health economics as a discipline which we examine in more detail in later chapters. These include the concept of supplier-induced demand, the role of welfare economics in health policy, income distributional matters and the very different perspectives of doctors and economists about health resource issues. All of the economists we discuss are characterised by a wider view of economics in relation to health than many of their colleagues.

In each case they have focused on the role of the medical profession and their relations with health economists as part of the need they perceive for economists to have a deep knowledge of health-related institutions, especially when having an input into health policy-making. To a lesser or greater extent they have been critical of aspects of conventional economic theory especially when it is applied uncritically to the health services, with insufficient allowance being made for their special characteristics.

──────────────── **FURTHER READING** ────────────────

In the light of the wealth of material generated by the health economists we have featured, it is not easy to arrive at a modest list of key references. However, for readers, including students undertaking courses in public health, the book edited by Evans, Barer and Marmor (1994) should be essential reading. The work takes a very wide multi-disciplinary perspective on the determinants of population health. Since the first two editors are health economists (Marmor is a political scientist) the book should help to undermine the commonly held view in clinical and public health circles that economists are only interested in money, especially cost-cutting.

The chapter in the book by Evans and Stoddart, 'Producing Health, Consuming Health Care' is a reprint of the article by the same authors (Evans and Stoddart, 1990). As we noted above, it presents a very useful framework for integrating the causal determinants of health status into a systematic model, combining social and individual characteristics.

For those who find health economics terminology confusing (most people?) Tony Culyer's *Dictionary of Health Economics* (2005) is to be commended. It provides clear definitions of a comprehensive range of concepts, including many drawn from statistics and epidemiology. The book also provides a number of useful mini-essays on topics such as his extra-welfarist concept, and the notion of market failure.

Discussion questions

- In your opinion what are the main reasons that the interests of American and British health economists differ substantially? What are the possible implications of these differences for people working or studying in the health field in other countries?
- Based on our necessarily brief accounts of the six prominent health economists discussed in this chapter, what do you regard as the main characteristics they have in common? Are you able to highlight any important differences they may have from one another?
- Some of the health economists we have discussed are very critical of their fellow economists and other health economists. What is the principal thrust of these criticisms? Do you agree or disagree with them?
- In our introductory discussion of the topics in which health economists are interested we have chosen only to present the views of those people whose approaches we have stated are often very different from the majority of their colleagues, especially of mainstream economists. Is this method justified and why have we adopted it?

The Tools of Economists as Applied to Health: The Supply Side

4

Background

Despite the reservations we have expressed about the application of neoclassical economics to health service issues, especially in regard to consumer/patient behaviour, we nevertheless regard it as useful to retain the notion of the health services as a commodity and one of several inputs into the process of improving the health status of populations. Without some discussion of the specific tools used by economists, moreover, it would not be feasible to commence the task of explaining and assessing the contributions of the discipline in this complex field.

A critical review of neoclassical economics, commencing with the supply or production aspects, serves the purpose of highlighting why differences have arisen between most health economists and those we have discussed in the previous chapter. The latter group are rather less inclined to take neoclassical economics as seriously in their analyses of the health services as those who focus on the role of market forces.

A review of the elements of microeconomics provides also a starting point for our later discussion about the priorities for future research and data gathering in health economics. The new directions, which we spell out in Chapter 12, we believe have more to contribute to the overall objectives of health economics than those which appear to be reflected in much of the existing literature and reports of research and development activities.

The representation of economic relationships

It must be emphasised that in this book, with its focus on students, clinicians and managers, we have kept to a minimum the use of the traditional smooth curves purporting to depict key economic relationships and much beloved by economists. Our reasons for this are twofold. First, we have observed that it is a source of considerable confusion for clinicians and other groups with a scientific background that the conceptual basis of these relationships and the resultant diagrams is very different from that of other disciplines. In physics, for example, smooth curves in two dimensions are normally used to portray functional relationships between two variables. These have been derived as exact relationships based on theoretical considerations, but verified experimentally where one variable is the exclusive cause of the other.

The curves in economics, for example the demand and supply curves of price theory, play a very different role. They are a graphical representation of a conceptual and hypothetical system which is designed to pose questions of the kind 'if the price took the value of y what would be the quantity supplied/demanded, x'. These relationships are always subject to the substantial qualification that other factors, notably income and tastes, remain unchanged. Economists refer to this condition as the *ceteris paribus* assumption – other things remaining equal.

Expressed in this way it is evident that the points on the curve are not based on any empirical evidence It should also be evident that the curves do not indeed purport to represent actual price and quantity values as measured in a market. Using a good deal of mathematical and statistical ingenuity empirical economists have been able to use market data to estimate the characteristics of the hypothetical curves such as the elasticity of supply/demand, but this process is a quite separate activity from the expository purpose of the original graphical portrayal.

Our second reason for not emphasising the graphs of conventional economics texts is a response to our view that the underlying theory on which they are based is often fatally flawed. Whilst it may be appropriate for those who aspire to become practising health economists to be drilled in the tools of the trade, we feel that other groups should be spared the trouble of this enterprise to concentrate on what we regard as the more important issues in the discipline.

The use of mathematics

Similar considerations apply to our reluctance to use mathematical symbols and expositions in our discussion of health economics. For many students and others mathematics affords a further barrier to the understanding of the subject. Moreover, we are conscious of the belief held by some health economists that in the literature of economics mathematical representations and manipulations may often conceal more than they reveal, especially in regard to the underlying assumptions of the analysis (Evans, 1998).

The role of models in economic theory

It is important to understand at the outset that the application of conventional economics is based on the construction of models of economic behaviour. These models are to be regarded, in part, as simplified versions of, or abstractions from, actual relationships which concentrate on the most important variables believed to be operating. Thus the construction of a model is normally derived from a set of assumptions about the relationships, including the objectives of the economic agents in undertaking their activities.

All disciplines rely on the creation of models to enable the complexities existing in the real world to be simplified and made manageable. However, the more scientific disciplines are normally able to test the relevance of their models by reference to experimental data. In economics, the scope for experimentation is usually very limited. Furthermore, as we have already noted, the ethos and rewards of economics for many practitioners have led them to concentrate on theoretical developments rather than on empirical verification.

In economics, the models developed are often *idealisations* of economic relationships. Runde (1997) has argued that idealisation may take the form in economic theory of 'limit types', entities or situations that are perfect or complete in some sense. Perfect competition, perfectly divisible commodities and perfect foresight are typical examples. Runde goes on to state that 'The limit types so characteristic of economic theory might more generally be labelled as *fictions* in the sense that they are the product of a transformation or deformation of something real into something that is a mere idea.' The problem that may arise in some economic theorising is that the analyst may lose sight of the fact that the concepts used are indeed fictions and treat them as if they existed in reality.

The assessment of their relevance and validity

In assessing the relevance and validity of economic models in particular applications, reliance has to be placed on appraising the validity of the assumptions. Frequently, this process may entail a careful review of what the assumptions are since the developers of the theory and its applications often may not make these assumptions explicit. Where the model is designed to facilitate predictions about economic behaviour it may be possible to use the accuracy of the predictions as a further test of the validity of the assumptions. As Keen (2001) has pointed out, the record of predictive accuracy of economists can only be described as woeful.

An additional use of idealised models of markets, such as the perfectly competitive market of neoclassical economics, that has been suggested is that it can be used as a method of comparing imperfect markets, the ones that actually exist, with the 'ideal' (McPake et al., 2002). This approach, however, avoids the issue of whether the ideal model is so divorced from reality in terms of the assumptions required to justify it, that it does not make a good starting point for further work It is also as well to point out that those who support the application of the principles of the free market to economic policy issues are in effect using the models as a reality that could be achieved.

Modelling the behaviour of the firm

Supply curves, costs and equilibrium

The supply side of economics in the conventional neoclassical accounts depends heavily on several key assumptions about the determinants of the behaviour of firms and the context in which they operate. In the first place the firm is a private organisation which desires to maximise its profits. Second, in the perfectly competitive market which is assumed to operate, no one firm is of sufficient size to influence the prices it receives for its product. Third, the individual firm bases its decisions about the quantity of the goods and services it supplies on the relationship between its costs and its revenue. In this model, profits by definition are maximised when the difference between costs and revenue is greatest. Fourth, each firm has complete information about the market in which it operates.

Since in the hypothesised perfectly competitive market the revenue per unit generated by the sales of its product does not vary with its own level of production, the characteristics of the relationship between costs and volume of production determine the profit maximising level of supply for each firm. To generate an upwardly sloping supply curve for the totality of producers, two further assumptions are required namely that beyond a certain level of output average costs increase and the supply curve of the whole set of firms making up the industry can be obtained by adding up the supply forthcoming from each individual firm at the price established when the demand curve is determined.

Under this extensive set of assumptions Figure 4.1 represents the postulated cost/revenue relationships of the model for an individual firm. Note that the marginal cost curve is derived from the total and average cost curves since it measures the increase in total cost associated with an additional unit of output.

In neoclassical economics a distinction is made, following Marshall, between the short-term and the long-term. The former is defined by the period over which the variable costs can be changed whilst the latter is the period when costs which are fixed in the short-term can be varied. The representation of the cost curves is based on the short-term assumption.

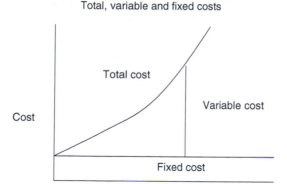

Figure 4.1   Cost Curves of a Firm under Perfect Competition (1)

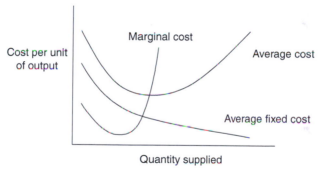

Figure 4.2   Cost Curves of a Firm under Perfect Competition (2)

The further development of the conventional supply theory of the firm under perfect competition is obtained by introducing the price of the product and hence the revenue generated by units of production. As Figure 4.2 indicates the profit maximising position of the firm is achieved where marginal cost equals the price per unit of the product. Since at every level of output average and marginal revenue are equal, the point of maximum profit occurs where marginal revenue equals marginal cost.

Beyond this point where the marginal cost is greater than marginal revenue the additional cost of supplying an extra unit is not met by the additional revenue generated. In the deployment of the factors of production, the profit maximising firm in Figure 4.3 also has to ensure that the input of each factor is such that the marginal revenue product is equal to the cost of employing the factor The marginal revenue product of labour, for example, is

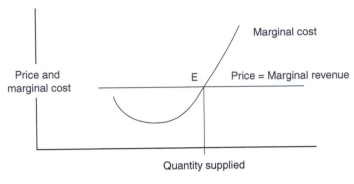

E = Equilibrium (Marginal cost = Marginal revenue)

Figure 4.3   Cost and Revenue under Perfect Competition

the additional revenue generated by the employment of an additional unit of labour.

The other important cost concept used by economists is that of opportunity cost. This measures the cost of an activity as the opportunity foregone to use the resources needed in an alternative activity. Thus a decision to invest a certain sum of money in capital equipment means that the opportunity to invest the same amount in a financial asset is foregone.

A further economic concept which looms large in neoclassical economics is that of equilibrium. This is the situation where the factors affecting the level of a given economic variable are in balance. Thus the price achieved by the intersection of demand and supply curves is regarded as the short-term equilibrium price since a different price, for example, at which supply is greater than demand, would lead to a reduction of supply to that which would restore the equilibrium price, according to the neoclassical model.

The assumptions of perfect competition

The reasons why each of the assumptions about the market may not be met have been set out in detail by Rice (1998a,b). The conditions for the existence of a perfectly competitive market are highly restrictive, especially the requirement that there be a large number of firms producing the same product which in turn implies that there are or have been no barriers to entry of new firms into the industry. Industries in which there are large numbers of small firms responsible for most production of the item are now unusual in developed countries, unlike the situation in England and elsewhere in the latter part of the nineteenth century when, as we have observed previously, the neoclassical theories were first formulated. Most industries are now dominated in terms of total output by a small number of very large firms.

Moreover, production of the same commodity by each firm ignores the increasingly common phenomenon of firms endeavouring to differentiate their products from similar ones by advertising and other means. In addition, the theory assumes that firms are able to estimate their costs and their relationship to the levels of production of the commodities. Generally good cost accounting systems are confined to large firms and even in these cases their capacity to derive estimates of marginal costs are very limited. Later in this chapter we present evidence that very few firms set prices using marginal cost.

The shape of the cost curves is also problematical. It is not clear why the average cost curve should continue to increase beyond a certain level of production. The usual explanation provided is that additional units of production beyond this point are achieved in the region where the productivity of additional inputs of variable factors, when applied to a fixed factor such as capital equipment, has declined. This is a reflection of the so-called law of diminishing returns. Even in contemporary economics texts it is usually illustrated by the likely results of additional units of labour being applied to a fixed plot of land. Here it is quite plausible that beyond a certain ratio additional units of labour will yield reduced outputs of the agricultural products of the land.

When the diminishing returns principle is applied to industrial production, however, this plausibility may evaporate. We mentioned in Chapter 2 the work of Sraffa (1926; 1960) who had argued persuasively that firms normally work with excess capital capacity so that even in the short run all postulated factors of production are variable, thus the reason postulated for diminishing returns may not apply. In addition, the increasing level of production may generate other economies in the production process; for example, the greater scope for specialisation of the labour force may promote improved levels of skills. It becomes then an empirical question as to the level of output at which the average cost curve increases. The existence in many industries of very large firms, as we noted above, suggests that the decreasing returns argument may only apply at very high output levels where organisational complexity and coordination costs, for example, may rise steeply.

In the process of expressing scepticism about the perfect market-based theory of the firm we would not wish to deny that some aspects of the theory may provide useful insights into how the performance of organisations may be improved by applying the concepts carefully to real world activities. In addition, the structure of incentives influencing the behaviour of production entities, which are emphasised in the conventional theory, may provide some guide as to how producers of goods and services may respond to different sets of these incentives. We return to this issue in later chapters, especially when dealing with the funding of health services.

Production functions, technical efficiency; economies of scale and scope

Further insight into the neoclassical supply model is obtained by introducing the notion of a production function. Such a relationship depicts the inputs to the production process in terms of categories for which the supplier incurs the costs as defined previously. The fixed costs, in the usual exposition, include the costs of capital equipment used in the production process. Variable costs include labour and materials costs, the level of which is assumed to be adjustable over short time periods based on the desired level of total production. We stress the importance of the production function perspective in health economics in Chapter 7 concerning health workforce issues, provided it is not interpreted too rigidly as a fixed mathematical relationship.

The notion of a relationship between the output of a firm or industry and its inputs of labour, materials and capital equipment allows the economist to highlight the fact that choices can be made by substituting one input for another. The substitution of capital equipment for labour, for example, may lead to greater efficiency in production, that is, more output being achieved without additional cost. Similarly, the substitution of cheaper forms of labour for more expensive ones may achieve the same outcome at lower costs. This result is referred to as greater technical efficiency. This may also be achieved where there are originally other sources of inefficiency, sometimes referred to as X-inefficiency, where the required resources in production are not being used in the best possible combinations, according to the neoclassical theory (Leibenstein, 1966; 1981).

Two further economic concepts present in neoclassical economics are those of economies of scale and of scope. Economies of scale, part of long run cost phenomena, are present when a given proportionate increase in each factor of production used by a firm generates a more than proportionate increase in output. Economies of scope may be present where the firm generates more than one product and cost economies are achieved by the process of production yielding a lower cost outcome than if the products were produced separately.

The other by-product of the production function approach is the creation of the isoquant, a graphical and hypothetical representation of how the same quantity of product may be achieved by varying the relative quantities of the factor inputs involved in the production process. The case of two factors of production is illustrated in Figure 4.4.

It is to be noted that the downward sloping shape of the isoquant is designed to reflect the assumption that diminished use of one factor is

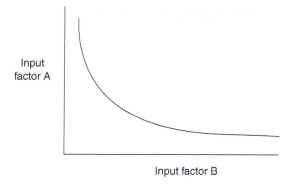

Figure 4.4 The Isoquant

associated with an additional requirement for the other to produce the same level of output in this two-factor model. The convexity to the origin of the isoquants occurs because increasing amounts of the second factor are required to compensate for a unit of reduction in the first factor in achieving the same level of output. This is a further application of the principle of diminishing returns which it will be recalled was the basis of the increase in the average cost curve for a single commodity beyond a certain level of production.

Is the neoclassical theory of production an idealised fiction?

In the light of the totality of the assumptions required to justify the neoclassical theory of supplier behaviour, based on the initial assumption of perfect competition in the market, the model is not likely to represent the actual behaviour of firms in an industrialised economy. The empirical evidence suggests that in critical areas such as marginal cost pricing private, supposedly profit maximising, firms for the most part do not set their prices where marginal cost is equal to marginal revenue (Eiteman and Guthrie, 1952). Their study of 1082 factory enterprises indicated that less than six per cent of firms set prices based on marginal cost equalling marginal revenue.

Nevertheless, there are aspects of the theory such as the production function and the technical efficiency concept that are capable of further development and applications. The use of neoclassical supply theory in health economics needs therefore to be assessed in the light of all the reservations about the theory, in addition to evaluating its potential contributions based on the special characteristics of health services and health.

Hospital production issues and models

The existence of economies of scale and scope in the hospital industry has been explored at length in a number of empirical studies. Studies on economies of scale, mainly undertaken in the United States, were designed originally to establish whether there was an optimum size for a hospital, that is, where it achieved a least cost outcome. The earlier studies suggested that diseconomies of scale started to emerge at relatively modest hospital sizes possibly of the order of 200 beds (Carr and Feldstein, P., 1967).

However, this research did not take adequate account of the fact that the types of patient who were treated in the larger hospitals, including the major teaching hospitals, were more complex and more costly (Evans, 1971). Later studies, where the casemix of the hospitals was taken into account, suggested that diseconomies of scale did not appear to arise until fairly large sizes were achieved. The use of casemix adjustment in hospital cost studies is described at length in Lave and Lave (1984) and Butler (1995).

In more recent times the interest of health economists in exploring the relationship between hospital output and cost in the form of a cost function seems to have waned in part as a result of the complexities of the factors contributing to costs that were explored in the two sources quoted in the previous paragraph. It is also possible that the objectives of the earlier studies were to provide a basis for the planning of hospital services, arising out of the Hill-Burton program of government funding of hospital development described in Chapter 5. With the increasing domination of conservative policies in the United States, and the ascendancy of neoclassical economics, the rationale for these studies has declined considerably in that country.

Hospital casemix

The casemix of a hospital is derived from the use of a classification of patients into categories which are relatively homogeneous in terms of the costs incurred. The most commonly used of these casemix classifications is that of diagnosis-related groups (DRGs). The variables used to define each DRG include the principal diagnosis, other additional diagnoses of the patient, and the surgical procedures performed. These factors are used to form more than 500 DRGs of which there are now several versions. The use of DRGs for funding hospitals in the United States and a number of other countries is discussed in Chapter 6.

The casemix of hospitals can be used as a method of conceptualising the output of the hospital as being the number of patients treated over all the categories of the classification. The relative cost of each patient category derived from the whole group of hospitals provides a measure of the quasi-price to be assigned to each unit of output where prices are not arrived at in a market but are administered ones set by the funding authority. This measure affords a basis for comparing the technical efficiency of individual or groups of hospitals.

In this conceptualisation it is important to note that the totality of treated patients serves as a measure of the performance of hospitals (Palmer, 1985). Those health economists who assert that the performance of hospitals should be assessed by their contribution to the health status of the populations for which they are responsible would disagree with this approach (Mooney et al., 1994). Implicitly they ignore the fact that unless the services achieve the optimum level of technical efficiency their contribution to health status improvement cannot be assessed from an economic efficiency standpoint. For example, a technically inefficient hospital might achieve good results in terms of health status improvement for the population which it serves but total hospital systems, allocative efficiency, might be increased by a transfer of resources from that hospital to those of greater technical efficiency.

The casemix approach also serves to enable the economic analysis of hospitals and their costs to be viewed from a multi-product perspective (Butler, 1995). Thus each of the DRGs may be regarded as a separate product when this system is used for categorising patients. One of the choices faced by hospitals is a result of their capacity to concentrate on the services required to treat patients of specified types. In the United States, this concentration has been a cause for concern because it could lead to some higher cost patients being ignored. The phenomenon has been described as 'cream skimming', that is, the process of deliberately concentrating on the most profitable patients. The existence of this process in some US hospitals has been well documented. However, in other countries it is unlikely to arise in any important way because of the greater government controls over hospital activities.

Production function issues

The production function concept enables us to state that services provided by institutions such as hospitals are one set of inputs into the generation of health status as one important output. However, the health status of populations, as our discussion of the health economics literature indicated, is influenced by many factors such as absolute and relative income (Fuchs, 2004b) and the position of individual members within existing occupational and other hierarchies (Marmot and Theorell, 1988; Marmot and Mustard, 1994).

Thus, it becomes extremely difficult, if not impossible, to measure the influence of the individual institutions and services on health status.

The potential for the substitution of one factor for another in the real world of hospitals has not been explored extensively in the literature. However, a few reservations need to be expressed. First, the substitution of other staff for medical staff is constrained in all health service systems by legal and licensing arrangements. These prescribe that certain activities, including the writing of prescriptions for medication, must be undertaken by medically qualified staff. The scope for the substitution of capital equipment for labour is also constrained by the fact that many of the tasks undertaken within hospitals are essentially based on a personal hands-on approach. Hospitals and other health services partly have the characteristics of a cottage industry as a number of writers have observed (Baumol, 1995).

When we turn our attention to health service suppliers, including hospitals, the application of neoclassical supply theory needs to take into account several aspects where the assumptions of the theory as just outlined are quite clearly violated. The most important of these is the assumption of private profit maximising organisations. Even in the United States, most hospital services continue to be provided in non-profit organisations, although there has been strong growth in the private-for-profit sector in recent times. In other developed countries, the typical hospital is a non-profit organisation, in some systems owned and controlled by governments or subject to many governmental regulations. Thus the profit maximising model of the unadorned theory has to be modified to take this fundamental difference into account.

If not profits what do hospitals maximise?

Health economists have thus been required to ask the question if non-profit hospitals are not profit maximisers what are the main determinants of their behaviour. In the United States, several different answers have been proposed, corresponding to the creation of different models of hospital behaviour (Newhouse, 1970; Pauly and Redisch, 1973; Jacobs, 1974). These turn on the postulated relationship between the three most influential groups within the US hospital – the medical staff, the management and the board of directors.

Key hospital groups in the United States and elsewhere

The first type of model accords the main role to the medical staff and what they wish to achieve. This model might be termed the model of the hospital as a doctors' cooperative. Doctors are assumed to influence the hospital to undertake those actions that will increase their earnings and esteem. In the

FFS context, which is the principal method of doctor payment in the United States, earnings and esteem are associated with the perceived attractiveness of the hospital to patients and referring medical staff. This attractiveness may be seen as reflecting the availability of specialised equipment, the range of services provided, the quality of nursing and other staff, and the amenities sought by patients. Doctors therefore seek to ensure that the quality of patient care and the perceptions thereof are augmented.

The models which emphasise the role of management may concentrate on the desire of senior management to increase the size of the hospital especially where there is a link between the size as measured by number of patients or total revenue and the earnings of senior executive staff. The board of directors may also wish to see the size of the hospital and its range of services increased. Their own prestige in the local community will be enhanced by these perceptions and possibly in some cases their own income.

In the United States, all these influences may be present to a lesser or greater extent. However, irrespective of which group is the most influential, the upshot is likely to be a system in which each hospital aspires to become bigger and 'better'. At the same time it must be recognised that in many communities more than one hospital may be in competition for patients and also for the services of medical staff. This competition may also be reflected in non-price competition in terms of quality of care and the range of medical and other services provided.

These proposed hospital models depart considerably from the neoclassical model of the firm. However, they represent a much better basis for drawing conclusion about how hospitals may respond to outside influences that are designed to affect their incentives and behaviour than those that are based on the profit maximising assumption. We have emphasised that the theoretical and empirical work of health economists on models of hospital behaviour is almost entirely based on US experience.

In countries such as Britain, where the central government plays a much more significant role in the provision and funding of health services, the models may require considerable modification, even though the same major actors are present. Clearly the ability of individual hospitals to act autonomously is much more restricted than in the United States by the government's responsibility for most of the funding and for the policy context in which the hospital system operates. Nevertheless, there are possibly similar influences in the NHS and other systems of public hospitals to expand their size and range of services offered as a result of the motivations of the same influential hospital groups.

In Chapter 10 we explore further the role of the medical staff in influencing hospital and other health services activities in countries with greatly varying arrangements for providing and funding the health sector, and differing methods of doctor remuneration. The influence of doctors in most hospital systems seems to be independent of their method of remuneration.

It is possible that in Britain and other European countries, where doctor payments other than FFS are often used, the role of the senior medical staff in influencing patient treatment policies may be even more important than in the United States. The influence of managers and hospital boards in some of these countries may be less well developed than in the American context. To a greater extent than in Britain and other European countries, the United States along with Canada and Australia have developed more intensive educational requirements so that most hospital managers in the larger institutions are expected to possess a masters degree in business or health administration.

Perceptions of the inadequacy of systems for monitoring the outcomes of patient treatments have been heightened in Britain by the deaths of young children at Bristol hospital. This has led in that country and elsewhere to an increased focus on clinical governance; that is how the activities of medical staff should be monitored and managed in ways that protect and enhance the quality of care provided to patients, but does not impinge unduly on the clinical autonomy of the doctors (Lugon and Secker-Walters, 1999)

Summary and conclusions

In this chapter we have presented a much abbreviated account of the conventional theory of the firm as a profit-maximising organisation. We have stressed the assumptions required to underpin the theory and the likelihood that these are often not likely to be met, as a number of economists have argued. We have noted that the models used are not simply abstractions from reality but may best be viewed as idealisations or limit types. These represent deformations of reality to produce an idea that is essentially a fiction. Nevertheless, it does not follow that all the concepts developed within this framework are lacking in usefulness if carefully interpreted. Nor should we discard the role of incentives of various kinds in influencing the behaviour of producing entities. These are often described as reflecting 'market forces' in the health economics literature.

When we moved on to deal with the applicability to hospitals of the theory, we noted that most hospitals operate as non-profit organisations and that it is necessary to seek other possibilities for what hospitals maximise. Models of hospital behaviour presented in the health economics literature stress the pressures from significant hospital groups, including the medical staff, to maximise the quantity and quality of services. These models are based on US studies but may have wider applicability.

We suggested that the notion of a production function showing the relationship between inputs of factors of production and the outputs of a product afforded a useful way of conceptualising health services activities including those of hospitals. The production function approach leads to an emphasis on the possibility of substituting one factor for another and of regarding the products of hospitals as one input into the output of health status. It can also provide the basis for measuring the technical efficiency of the individual hospitals.

The presence of economies of scale and scope has been explored extensively in the health economics literature with inconclusive results. The complexities associated with the study of hospital costs, including the role of casemix, were recognised increasingly. In addition, the studies in the 1970s were designed to provide information on such matters as the optimum size of a hospital when government intervention to plan or influence such matters was still considered to be feasible. More recently in the United States, under the domination of neoclassical economics and the rejection of planning principles, the literature reveals rather less interest amongst health economists in these studies.

FURTHER READING

The book by Steve Keen (2001) quoted earlier, *Debunking Economics: The Naked Emperor of the Social Sciences*, provides an excellent and well-documented account of the criticisms of neoclassical and other economic theories. Unlike some of the authors of other earlier 'radical' critiques, Keen, an Australian economist, displays a deep and comprehensive knowledge of conventional economic theory. Though clearly written, aspects of the work are not easy to digest, but it should be essential reading for anyone who wishes to obtain a comprehensive account of the limitations of contemporary economics and economists.

For a conventional account of microeconomics numerous texts are available. Two that are commonly used are Samuelson and Nordhaus (2005) *Economics*, which also includes a coverage of macroeconomics, and Stockman (1996) *Introduction to Microeconomics*.

Discussion questions

- What are the essential features of a model in economics?
- Why is the marginal cost curve depicted as U-shaped in the conventional theory? Be careful to define each of the characteristics of a firm's cost on which this proposition is based.

- Why is the supply schedule of a product always shown by economists as a smooth upward sloping curve? What are the assumptions used which lead to this outcome?
- The most important assumption on which the theory of supply is based is that of perfect competition. List the assumptions, in turn, required to establish the existence of a perfectly competitive market.
- What is the justification for studying the neoclassical theory of the firm if the assumptions, including perfect competition, and the deductions of the theory are regarded as 'idealisations' and 'fictions'?
- In criticising the neoclassical theory of production are we ignoring the fact that markets exist in which producers interact with consumers, and the 'invisible hand of the market' operates to produce coordinated outcomes of price and quantity setting? In other words should a distinction be made between the observed phenomena of economic relationships and the theory used to explain these relationships?
- Why do health economists face difficulties in applying the neoclassical theory of production to health service entities such as a hospital?
- What is meant by economists' use of the concept of a production function? In what ways may the concept be applied usefully to the activities of a hospital?
- What is meant by a hospital's casemix? Discuss the application of the concept to assessing the performance of hospitals.

The Tools of Economists as Applied to Health: The Demand Side

Background

In the light of the discussion of the assumptions required to justify the application of neoclassical theory to markets, with our initial emphasis being on supply characteristics and the theory of the firm, it is clear that the theory of consumer demand requires a similar treatment. Again, we present a brief summary of the main characteristics of neoclassical demand theory and the assumptions on which it is based. We then assess the implications of our analysis for the application of the theory to the health field. As we noted in earlier chapters the theory of consumer demand has been used extensively by health economists in the United States, in combination with the theory of welfare economics, to draw conclusions about health policy requirements.

The neoclassical model of consumer demand

One of the important principles, along with the assumption of perfect competition, which underlies the neoclassical theory of demand, is that of consumer sovereignty. This notion is based on the belief, or value judgement, that community satisfactions and welfare are maximised when the consumer is responsible for making his/her own decisions about the choices available. How true this might be is examined later in the context of welfare economics and the doctor/patient relationship.

Ordinal utility and indifference curves

The theory of consumer demand, as we noted in Chapter 2, has played a central role in neoclassical economic theory and the work of its developers up to the present time. In the Marshallian and earlier accounts, utility theory was based on the notion of utility as a concept that could be measured in absolute terms and hence could be compared in principle between different consumers. This cardinal conception of utility was subject to a number of criticisms, especially in terms of making interpersonal comparisons of utility. It was difficult to argue that the extra utility derived by a rich person for a given increase in income could be equated with what a poor person would derive from the same increase.

This led economists to reconceptualise utility as an ordinal concept and the development of the indifference curve approach. Demand theory using this construct is based only on the assumption of the ability of individual consumers to rank their preferences for combinations of goods and services. In the two commodity case it is assumed that the consumer can rank as equally desirable any set of quantities of the commodities. The indifference curve shown in the Figure 5.1 presents the usual neoclassical diagrammatic representation of this tool.

The way the indifference curves are shown as downward sloping and convex to the origin is based on the usual assumption of diminishing marginal utility of both commodities. At the higher levels of consumption of one commodity, lower levels of the other commodity are required to yield the same level of utility. This property is sometimes referred to in economics as the law of substitution.

When indifference curves are combined with information about the prices of the two commodities and the budget (income) available to the consumer, the point of maximum utility for the individual is achieved where the budget line is tangential to the highest indifference curve as Figure 5.2 indicates. A higher indifference curve cannot be reached with the available budget and a lower indifference curve would not exploit the full potential of the consumer's budget for this purpose.

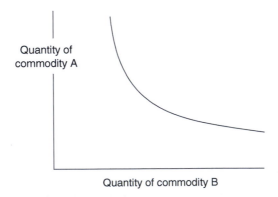

Quantity of commodity A

Quantity of commodity B

Figure 5.1   A consumer's indifference curve

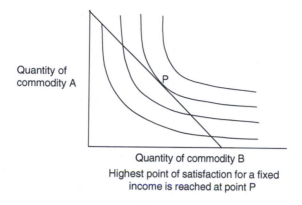

Highest point of satisfaction for a fixed
income is reached at point P

Figure 5.2   Indifference maps and consumer income

The whole set of possible indifference curves is referred to as the indifference map. Using indifference maps for sets of prices and quantities it is then possible in principle to derive a demand curve, setting out the hypothetical price/quantity relationships for the individual for the two commodities for a fixed level of income. Market demand for each commodity can then be derived, according to the theory, from aggregating across all consumers in the market.

Based on the assumptions of indifference curve analysis it becomes possible to draw conclusions about the response to both price changes of the two commodities and of income changes for the consumer. Health economists make extensive use of indifference curves in their work and have displayed considerable ingenuity in this endeavour. However, we need to stress again for our purposes the difficulties with the marginal utility concept which is fundamental to indifference curve analysis. Again it is of relevance to note that when we move away from the food examples which still pervade the microeconomics text books, the applicability of marginal utility theory to other commodities becomes dubious. Generally these problems are ignored in the applications that economists make of indifference curves.

A social indifference curve?

A further fundamental problem with the application of indifference curves arises when the attempt is made to generalise the two commodity one consumer model to many consumers and many commodities. This generalisation is required to derive an aggregate demand function and its properties from the original model. In addition it may provide the basis for the derivation of a social indifference curve. Such a curve would purport to show the preferences of all consumers and it could be used to demonstrate that a community of utility maximising individuals would also maximise social welfare. As we shall see, the field of welfare economics which plays a leading role in health economics is heavily dependent on the notion of a social welfare function.

However, as Keen and others have demonstrated the problem with endeavouring to generate a social indifference curve is that the distribution of income between individuals will vary with changes in prices (Keen, 2001). For the neoclassical economist any change in relative prices of commodities at the community level will redistribute income between the members of that community depending on their individual preferences as reflected in their indifference curves. Thus, the transition from the two commodity one consumer case to the social level can only be justified by introducing further assumptions. These are that all individuals have identical preferences and that incomes in aggregate differ only by a proportional factor (Chipman, 1974). These assumptions have quite rightly been derided as being out of touch with reality.

The elasticity of demand

For the moment we ignore the problems with the use of indifference curves to generate community demand schedules and a social welfare function, and approach the postulated downward sloping community demand curve as an empirical reality, the existence of which has been convincingly demonstrated. The question then arises as to whether there are aspects of the economic analysis of demand which are capable of potentially useful applications in health economics.

The first of these is the concept of the elasticity of demand, a term invented by Marshall. The price elasticity of demand is a measure of the responsiveness of the quantity demanded to a price change in a form which is independent of the units in which these variables are expressed. As usual it is assumed that all other influences on demand are held constant. The price elasticity of demand measures the proportionate change in demand divided by the proportionate change in price for the given commodity. In symbolic form:

E = % change in Q/ % change in P
where E denotes the elasticity measure, Q is the quantity and P the price.

Since an inverse relationship is postulated on the basis of the assumed negative relationship between price and quantity (the downward sloping demand curve) the value of the elasticity has a negative sign attached to it. However, it is preferable for ease of comprehension to discuss the magnitude of the elasticity in absolute terms, by ignoring the negative sign.

If the elasticity is greater than one in absolute values the demand can be described as elastic; a given change in price leads to a more than proportionate change in quantity demanded. Values of the elasticity of less than one represent inelastic demand, that is, a given percentage change in price is associated with a less than proportionate change in the quantity demanded. For a commodity with inelastic demand, an increase in price means that total expenditure (price multiplied by quantity) on the commodity will increase. The increased price is not offset by the less than proportionate decease in quantity. For inelastic demand a decrease in price leads to a decrease in total expenditure.

In principle, in markets where the assumptions of demand theory are met, the elasticity measure provides a potentially powerful tool for establishing the all important implications of price changes on the total expenditure variable. In the empirical quantification of demand curves the elasticity measure is one of the main and potentially useful outcomes of the work. As we emphasise, however, the 'market' for health care services almost universally is not one where these assumptions apply. In these circumstances the elasticity measure, where available, has to be interpreted with great caution.

The concept of elasticity can also be extended to a number of other demand relationships, for example, the income elasticity of demand shows the responsiveness of demand to a given change in income when prices remain constant. There is a long history of the attempts to measure the characteristics of demand curves using empirical data (Stigler, 1965). For our purposes it is sufficient to note that there are considerable difficulties associated with using data for this purpose, irrespective of whether the data are in the form of observations over time (time series) of price/quantity variables or of cross sectional data. The latter consist of observations for the same period based on different groups.

The demand for health and health services

A central issue for health economics is how much use can be made of demand theory and its applications in the health field. For this purpose we need to examine a number of the special characteristics of health and of the health services. The latter include the notion of supplier-induced demand (SID) and the nature of the relevant agency relationships. The differences between the concept of need and that of demand will also be examined.

What is different about health?

The special characteristics of health as a commodity have been reviewed extensively in the health economics literature (Klarman, 1965; Evans, 1984). In summary these include the observation that health, involving life and death issues, is associated with intense emotional reactions in all communities; that concerns about the health of fellow community members impinge on other members of the society; that for all of us the expected impact of disease is fraught with uncertainty; and most individuals lack knowledge of both their existing health status and of the technical interventions required to sustain or improve it.

Health economists with diverse perspectives have emphasised different aspects of these special characteristics and their implications for how the health services are or should be regulated and financed.

Health as a capital good and a consumer good

The 'demand' for health care has been interpreted in the model of Grossman (1972a, 2000) as having two characteristics, corresponding to what are usually classified as those of a consumption good and an investment (or capital) good. When applied to health the consumption good aspect relates to good health (healthy time) as a commodity which consumers wish to acquire because of its intrinsic characteristics in generating utility.

The capital good aspect claims that each person is born with a specific stock of health which depreciates over time with increasing age. The rate of depreciation over time can be influenced, according to the theory, by activities such as seeking medical attention and by undertaking other forms of behaviour such as exercise and dietary change. These activities are conceived as substitutes for one another and can only be achieved by incurring certain costs. In principle the theory is designed to make predictions about the behaviour of individuals; for example, a decrease in the cost of medical care to the person will lead to a reduction in the other healthy time promoting activities.

Grossman's theory represents an interesting example of an attempt to derive a more sophisticated approach to the demand for health than the simple demand function of conventional economics with the conceptualisation of health as being determined by the prices of the health services associated with the production of health. It represents a partial recognition of the different nature of health and health services from that of other commodities. However the theory retains the essential features of neoclassical economics with its emphasis on the behaviour of individual utility-maximising health consumers. In particular it ignores the role of doctors and other providers, and of community values in influencing the utilisation of their services.

Supplier-induced demand/utilisation (SID)

We noted in Chapter 3 that the idea of SID and its implications for health policy have been a subject of considerable discussion and research in health economics. The term contemplates the possibility that the suppliers of health services may be able to act in such a way that the demand for their services can be affected by them. Whilst the term SID has normally been applied to the situation where the inducement is to increase the utilisation of services, it can also be applied to a negative inducement, that is, where the doctor acts to reduce the utilisation of services, notably where medical staff are involved in the rationing of their services. It may be preferable to use the phrase 'supplier-influenced demand' to cover both sets of circumstances, but for our present purposes we shall retain the usual terminology.

There is a long history of empirical attempts to investigate SID in the health services. The classical study is that of Roemer (1961) who applied the idea to data on the utilisation of hospital services. He found a close relationship between the number of available hospital beds and the use of those beds when analysing data from all US states. Where the per capita number of beds in the state was high the use of the beds was also high. This led to the enunciation of the principle that a 'bed built was a bed that would be filled'.

Despite the difficulties in interpreting some of the data generated in the Roemer study, the results were supported strongly by the plausible reasons provided for why hospitals and their medical staffs might influence the 'demand' for hospital services. Many hospital admissions are discretionary in that alternative settings for treatment are available. It is the senior medical personnel who make these assessments but in this process they may be encouraged by management to adopt easier admission criteria in order to increase hospital revenue when beds are being under-used.

The influence on the use of hospital beds by the medical staff and the hospital administration should also be viewed from the perspective of the wide variations in medical practice in hospitals between areas and regions highlighted by Wennberg and Gittelsohn (1973, 1982a, b). These variations seemed to reflect differences in practice styles between medical communities when the influence of demographic factors and other patient characteristics is held constant. Further empirical studies on practice variation in the United States have recently been generated and these also point to the presence of SID (Fisher et al., 2003a, b). The studies of Fisher and his colleagues are discussed in Chapter 7.

The presence of SID in respect of hospital utilisation seems very plausible in the light of the role of doctors in admitting patients, especially in emergency circumstances, and the wide variation in admission rates between areas when the influence of measures of patients' characteristics are taken into account. However, in respect of general practitioner encounters it must be noted that it is patients who initiate the visit. However, the number and frequency of visits may often be influenced by the doctor.

The notion of SID has been extended to all medical encounters between doctors and patients. There are several reasons why doctors may be able to influence the use of their services in all circumstances. First, there is a major gap between the knowledge of the treating doctors and that of their patients; information asymmetry exists. Thus the idea of consumer sovereignty where a fully knowledgeable consumer interacts with the supplier based on comprehensive information in making choices about the quality and likely outcomes of his/her potential purchases is far from the realities of doctor–patient interaction.

Second, whilst doctors no longer have the capacity to call all the shots in these encounters it is probably still a reasonable generalisation that most patients will accept the advice of their medical practitioners about the frequency of their contacts and the recommended treatments. This is likely to be further influenced in the United States by the comprehensiveness of their health insurance. Those whose health insurance, normally paid for by their employer, provides complete coverage without the need to make any co-payment are likely to be the most receptive to accepting the advice of their medical practitioners where this is associated with a more costly deployment of services.

The FFS basis of most payments to doctors in the United States may also result in a conflict between their financial aspirations and their ethical commitment to meeting the needs of their patients. However, SID is also found in health systems that do not use FFS for doctor remuneration predominantly. Moreover, with the growth of managed care arrangements in the United States the role of doctors, some of whom may not be paid on a FFS basis, may be to exert a negative influence on the use of their services.

A further phenomenon that SID has been used to explain is the tendency of the fees charged by doctors to increase when the number of doctors in an area increases (Evans, 1974). How widespread this relationship might be is unknown. However, it is obviously inconsistent with competitive market theory where an increase in suppliers generates a decrease in the prices charged. As Jacobs (1997) pointed out, however, patients' utilisation of medical services is likely to be influenced by a number of factors other than prices and quantities, such as their incomes and their perceptions of their health status. The ordinary demand schedule assumes that these factors are held constant but in practice this may be difficult to achieve adequately. Thus direct empirical verification of SID is fraught with problems, and for this and other reasons has remained a contentious issue amongst health economists.

The search for empirical evidence of SID also possibly misses the point that its existence is conditional on a number of additional factors in the doctor–patient interaction some of which are not accessible using the available data, such as the patient's preferences about the treatment options and the doctor's motivations. Moreover, we have noted previously the limitations of marginal utility theory when applied to commodities in general. With health care it is inherently implausible that the patient is able to assess the satisfaction in terms of a desired improvement in health status of the options for the quantity and types of services required.

As we noted previously in the British NHS and similar financing systems in other countries, the implicit rationing of the medical services provided has been the responsibility of medical staff. In spite of the central provision of some guidelines about medical treatments, decisions about who might be candidates for the more expensive forms of treatment are normally left to senior hospital consultants. This may be one of the reasons for the much lower provision of dialysis services to aged patients in the United Kingdom as compared with the United States. Where implicit rationing of this kind is present a further reason exists for supplier-influenced utilisation.

A major problem for consumer demand theory as applied to the health services

The existence of SID in health care poses an important threat to the use of conventional market analysis where the separation and independence of these two determinants of price and quantity is a fundamental characteristic of neoclassical economic models. To rescue the market model from this dilemma it is necessary to assume that the doctor acts as a perfect agent for the patient in the doctor–patient relationship. In addition, market-oriented health economists in the United States have made ingenious theoretical attempts to refute the evidence for its presence.

The economists' concept of 'agency'

According to this principle the ethical position of the doctor is to act as a fully informed agent of the patient especially in the light of the state's willingness to afford special privileges to the group under licensing arrangements. In other words the doctor as agent should act in such a way that it is only the interests of the patients that enter into his/her decision-making. That is he/she should recommend the quantity and type of service required that would maximise the benefit to the patient. The benefit may be couched in terms of improvement in health status or more generally in respect of quality of life.

In this formulation of the problem several issues arise. First, does the doctor have sufficient information about the likely outcome of each possible option to indeed recommend that which would provide the maximum benefit? Second, in assessing the benefits, is the doctor in a position to know or find out the preferences of the patient for alternative outcomes? Third, to what extent may the doctor's decisions be influenced by his/her own preferences, for greater income or leisure, or for meeting other objectives of the system such as overall budget constraints?

There is also the problem for both doctors and patients of their lack of knowledge of the costs of the alternative treatments available. A fully informed perfect agent would need to take into account all the costs that fall on the patient. However, at least we can say that the notion of an autonomous demand for medical treatment by patients looks increasingly unrealistic, where either the patients or their providers lack crucial information, and the completeness, or otherwise, of the agency relationship is largely unknown.

As we noted above, in the usual formulation of SID the emphasis has been on the capacity of the doctor to increase the demand for his/her services beyond the point which the fully informed patient would prefer. This formulation has been based on the doctor's remuneration being met on a FFS basis. The more general formulation of the problem set out above covers the possibility that the SID may fall short of the patient's preferences where other doctor payment arrangements prevail.

The implications of imperfect agency

The application of the idea of a demand schedule in the neoclassical sense to the interaction between doctors and their patients is fraught with sufficient reservations to call into question its use as an analytical tool by health economists. However this does not mean that the nature of the agency relation between doctors and their patients should not be explored further. Whether economists are the disciplinary group best equipped to undertake such studies, rather than sociologists and psychologists, for example, is an open question. A multi-disciplinary approach to studies of this kind is likely to be the most fruitful.

Further perspectives on the concept of agency are presented in McGuire (2000). It might also be noted that other disciplinary groups, notably sociologists, use the term agency in a rather different sense from that of economists.

Welfare economics and its underpinnings

If the neoclassical theory of consumer demand cannot be applied to the health services, contrary to the beliefs of many health economists in the United States and elsewhere, where does this leave the discipline of health economics? First, it undermines the case for resorting to Paretian-based welfare economics as the underpinning of policy prescriptions about the health services. To an extent that may not be appreciated by some health economists, welfare economics provides the starting point for many of their prescriptions and predictions about changing financing and health insurance systems. This caveat may also apply to the basis of some evaluation methods such as cost-benefit and cost-effectiveness analysis.

Second, it leads to the tentative conclusion that the tools of economics may more profitably be applied to the supply side of health services (see Chapter 12). Third, if 'demand' functions exist as empirical realities is it useful to measure their characteristics, notably the elasticity of demand for specific services, even though we recognise that such a function reflects a mixture of patients' and doctors' behaviour and motivations?

Empirical studies of the demand for health services

The RAND study: Its implications and limitations

In the health field there have been a large number of attempts to measure demand functions, often for the purpose of assessing the implications of the diverse options for health insurance policies. In the United States, where many of the empirical studies on the demand for health care have been undertaken, the most ambitious study was that of the RAND Corporation based on a controlled experiment covering persons in six sites in the United States. The Health Insurance Experiment received substantial backing from the Federal government as a possible input into the design of health insurance policies.

In brief, this study divided the study populations sampled consisting of a total of 2,756 families into five groups, based on the type of health insurance option which they were offered (Newhouse et al., 1981, 1993; Manning et al., 1987). These ranged from insurance coverage of all health care costs, that is no co-insurance, to those with increasing levels of co-insurance, namely 25 per cent, 50 per cent and 95 per cent. In addition, each plan had a limit on out-of-pocket payments of either 5 per cent, 10 per cent or 15 per cent of household income, up to a maximum of $1000. Above these limits all the health care costs were met by each plan. A further group was offered a policy with free hospitalisation, but a 95 per cent co-payment for other medical services, with an annual limit of $150 for individuals or $450 for households. The expenditure of each group on health services was then determined over the next three to five years.

The results indicated that the number of patient encounters and the per capita cost of these encounters were substantially higher for the free group.

For example, the expenditure on the free plan was 45 per cent higher than where the 95 per cent co-insurance applied.

If the cost to the patient is treated as the price of the service the results demonstrate the expected relationship – the higher the price met by the patient the lower was his/her utilisation and expenditure on health services. The effect of other variables on health service utilisation and expenditure such as health status, income and the demographic characteristics of patients were as far as possible held constant.

Subject to the limitations of the demand model discussed above the results demonstrate the expected relationship of a downward sloping curve. The estimated 'demand' elasticity for the zero to 25 per cent co-insurance groups was –0.2. That is for these groups the provision of free or almost free care to the patients was associated with an increase in utilisation of 20 per cent. This result indicates that household utilisation of health services is relatively inelastic in respect of price changes but not zero.

The study is subject to the limitation that whilst the sample of families was no doubt representative of the communities included it covered only a small proportion of each community. Thus the responses of doctors in each area to the changes may have been quite different if the insurance rates were applied to everyone. Faced with a decline in demand for their services with higher insurance rates doctors in these circumstances might be more tempted to generate additional demand. Again SID may render questionable any model of patient demand and the empirical results which ignore this phenomenon. As noted by Donaldson and Gerard (2005), the presence of SID is assumed away in the RAND study, which is based on the conventional neoclassical approach.

The other problem highlighted by the results which included the types of services where the demand changed, and the income levels of participants, was that for low family income levels, health promotion and potentially preventive services were reduced relatively more at the higher co-payment levels (Lohr et al., 1986). This result raises important equity and health status concerns about the attempt to introduce large co-payments into health insurance systems. We discuss further distributional and equity issues and health policy in Chapter 10.

The demonstration of a downward sloping utilisation/price relationship in the case of health services in no sense can be regarded as a justification of the underlying neoclassical theory of demand based on marginal utility and its characteristics. Marginal utility theory remains subject to all the criticisms discussed in Chapter 2 and the specific problems in applying this theory to the health services just discussed. Nor does it demonstrate that a demand curve in the neoclassical sense with its assumed independence of supply and demand factors exists for health services. That families faced with higher costs of medical services in relation to other household budget items would necessarily reduce their use and expenditure on medical care only requires an assumption of rational behaviour on their part.

The elasticity of utilisation estimates derived from the study nevertheless do provide a measure of the responsiveness of families to the price changes. How much should results of this kind influence health insurance policies is explored further in the next chapter.

The 'need' for health services

Measurement for resource allocation

Disparities in the availability and provision of health services between regions and areas in the same country have led governments to institute policies designed to reduce these differences. A notable example was the Hill-Burton program introduced in the United States after the Second World War, which focused on hospital bed provision. In the light of the analysis of data dealing with hospital bed to population ratios, and the considerable differences in these ratios between the states, the federally funded program was designed to reduce or eliminate the disparities. The official rationale for the program was that the need for hospital services, subject to some demographic differences between the states, was roughly similar.

In a number of other countries, including Britain and Australia, differences between regions and states in the provision and expenditure on health services led to the creation of formula-based approaches to reducing the disparities. In England the Resource Allocation Working Party (RAWP) constructed a formula to allocate government funds between the regions into which the country was divided (Department of Health and Social Security, 1976). Similar methods were also adopted for Scotland and Wales.

The details of the complex formula devised mainly by operations researchers in the Department of Health are not relevant in the present context. In summary, however, the rationale underlying the formula was that the need for hospital and other NHS funded health services could be estimated largely based on population- and age-adjusted mortality rates, a substitute for morbidity rates which were not available. Adjustments were also made for inter-regional flows of patients and for teaching and research responsibilities. Separate population weightings, normally based on national usage by age/sex specific groups were derived for the different types of services categorised as inpatients, outpatients, psychiatric patients and community services patients. Separate targets for re-allocation were used for recurrent (revenue) and capital funding.

A modified version of the RAWP formula was adopted in the Australian state of New South Wales to allocate funding between the areas into which the state was divided for health administrative purposes.

Many of the details of the RAWP formula were criticised subsequently, especially the use of age specific mortality rates as a surrogate for morbidity rates (Buxton and Klein, 1978). In the English case it is clear that part of the opposition to RAWP reflected the large redistribution of funds the formula implied from the London area and the south east of England to the northern parts of the country. However, it seems to have largely achieved its objective in Britain by the time the approach was abandoned in the late 1990s after approximately 20 years of implementation. What is important is that the use of a formula of the RAWP kind is based on the attempt to measure health care needs, rather than demand, for planning and financial purposes on a geographical area specific basis. But what is meant by need?

Relationship between demand and need

The relationship between the 'demand' for health services and the need for them also requires examination. Generally, market-orientated health economists have supported the use of the consumer demand concept in drawing policy relevant conclusions. They have been critical of the notion of 'need' favoured by epidemiologists and doctors involved in planning and management decision-making about health care. We have noted the inherent limitations of the theory of consumer demand when applied to the health services, especially where these involve the critically important area of doctor/patient decision-making. However, it does not necessarily follow that the somewhat vague concept of need when applied to the health services provides a better basis for decision-making.

In respect of health there is a need for a service when a person falls ill or is injured, and the possibility exists of a treatment being provided which will cure the condition or relieve the pain and discomfort associated with the condition. However, as many economists and others have pointed out, meeting all population needs in this sense is unrealistic. Some rationing of health services is required to the extent that total needs, somehow defined, within the context of resource availability constraints, cannot be met.

In largely publicly funded systems such as the NHS the total funding available to provide hospital, medical and other services has to compete with the funding of other services which are the responsibility of government, notably defence, education and social welfare. Thus governments in centrally financed systems are faced with the making of choices about the funding of health services for which they are responsible, their other commitments and the assessment of priorities about the disposition of funding within the health sector. The amount of total government expenditure and the allocation to health services are essentially political decisions of governments.

The RAWP type formulas only attempt to address the relative needs between areas and obviously cannot determine the absolute needs of the different types of health service patients, for example, whether there are greater needs of psychiatric patients than other types of patients. To address this problem economists have enunciated the principle that a cost-benefit approach is required. At the margin the benefits derived from the allocation of funding should be related to the costs associated with achieving these benefits. That is, the funding required should reflect not only the meeting of the needs of different types of patients but also the costs of meeting the needs.

However, when we discuss evaluation methods in Chapter 8, it will become evident that the implementation of this logically impeccable principle is fraught with considerable difficulties of a conceptual and practical kind. Nevertheless, even in the absence of a competitive market and consumer price signals, and the pervasive intertwining of supply and demand factors, the insights derived by economists may prove to be important in framing health policy and planning decisions.

Conflicts between medicine and economics

An inherent conflict often arises between the needs of patients as perceived by medical and other health services staff, and the implications of the cost-benefit principle. This is not to say that doctors are only concerned with the meeting of patient needs irrespective of other considerations such as the age and other characteristics of patients, and the costs of meeting these needs. The role of medical staff in the implicit rationing of resources in the NHS and other similar systems, to which reference was made earlier, implies that their decision-making about which patient needs should be met and those that need not be met go beyond the medical assessment of needs. Nevertheless, as we noted when the work of Mooney was discussed, the ethical position of doctors favours the attempt to meet the needs of patients for whom they are responsible above cost and other matters. These matters are discussed further in Chapter 9.

Finally in this regard the variation between hospitals and doctors in the provision of specific services is considerable as we noted previously. It follows that the opinions and perceptions of medical staff about the needs of patients for these services are also highly variable. It cannot be said that there is any simple relationship between a given medical condition and diagnosis, and the treatment option undertaken. Medically interpreted need for services on a diagnostic specific basis emerges as an increasingly dubious concept.

Whilst the aggregate need for services based on mortality, morbidity, and the age and sex distributions of population, of the kind incorporated in the RAWP approach, may be a reasonable guide to broad resource allocation and planning decisions, the concept of need can do little to inform us about the priorities to be assigned to the different types of services. For this purpose it is necessary to resort to the evaluation methods to be described in Chapter 8.

The demand for medical and hospital services

Our emphasis on SID should not be taken as a claim that there is no influence of patients' preferences on their use of health services. In general, members of communities seek medical treatment for a variety of purposes, all of which have as their basis the belief that the services will generate health status benefits. In addition, people undoubtedly derive satisfaction even from their knowledge that hospitals and other health services are available when they require them. Moreover, the results of the RAND Study, despite its limitations, indicate that patients display some response to changes in the prices they pay for these services.

What we are querying in our criticisms of neoclassical demand theory, especially as applied to the health services, is the notion of an autonomous demand of patients displaying community sovereignty in which the price of the service is the most important factor in determining how much is used of the service. The abstraction from reality embodied in the theory of demand based on a schedule of possible price/quantity relationships may be useful for some commodities.

For all the reasons discussed above about the differences of health services and health from other commodities it should be clear that those who try to apply the theory to the health services are not abstracting from reality but inevitably grossly distorting it in an extreme case of idealisation, the concept we introduced in the previous chapter.

Flat of the curve medicine

It is a source of considerable illumination about the relation between consumer demand for medical services and health outcomes to consider the notion of flat of the curve medicine (Enthoven, 1980; Evans, 1984). Beyond a certain point in the provision of additional medical care no benefits to patients may accrue. It is also a reasonable hypothesis with some evidence to support it that beyond a certain level of medical treatment disutility occurs as iatrogenic and other aspects of poor quality services may emerge. For the great majority of members of communities, and for the medical profession, these possibilities are rarely considered either in individual cases or for the whole community. The demand for health services in the sense of the results of the interactions between medical decision-makers and patients may not lead to the best results in terms of maximising health benefits in relation to the resources deployed.

These issues are represented in Figure 5.3 with the downward sloping segment of the graph representing the negative effects. If the curve continued to slope upwards at all levels of medical care provision, it would be impossible to meet all potentially useful medical interventions and needs.

It must be emphasised that the presence of flat of the curve medicine may vary considerably for individual patient conditions and for aggregate provision in different communities. In practice the determination of where the flat of the curve provision cuts in may be extremely difficult. Nevertheless, in this particular case the theoretical construct provides a useful way of representing the possibilities. In what Evans has described as the Medico-Technical model, wherein patient needs can be defined and met with resort to the appropriate technology, the possibility of flat of the curve medicine is ignored.

Evans, it might be noted, was also scathing in his criticism about the application of the Naïve Economic model, whereby the health services are simply another commodity, and subject to the inexorable 'laws' of supply and demand. He went on to point out in regard to critiques by free market economists of health service institutions that they are:

> usually calling for freer entry, more competition, more reliance on prices, and less on subsidies or insurance. The adoption of such a framework as a basis for analysis necessarily imposes the strong, though implicit, assumption that the extensive and detailed structure of public and self-regulation and control which governs health care in every developed society is all a terrible mistake, the result of a nefarious conspiracy by suppliers imposed on an ignorant and gullible public, which should be dismantled as soon as possible. (Evans, 1984)

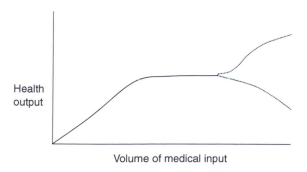

Volume of medical input

Figure 5.3   Flat of the curve medicine

Summary and conclusions

We again provide a summary account of some of the essentials of the neoclassical theory as applied to consumer demand, including the formal conditions for the generation of downward sloping demand curves and the use of indifference curves for this purpose, based on the theory of diminishing marginal utility. In the health field, the notion of the consumer as an independent utility maximising individual with comprehensive information on the available choices has been queried in the light of the role of the doctor in patient-medical interactions. This has led to a consideration of the possibility of supplier-induced demand and of the concept of an agency relationship in which ideally the doctor's actions are determined only by the interests of the patient.

The absence of a perfect agency relationship, that is where the doctors' own interests and that of governments affect the treatment, seems to be the most plausible situation in the light of the evidence. This leads to the conclusion that the utilisation of medical services is not solely dependent on the preferences of the patient. We have used the term in common usage, supplier-induced *demand*. However, it is highly questionable in our view whether the notion of 'demand' in the strict neoclassical sense is applicable at all in these circumstances. Marshallian price theory is based on the complete independence of supply and demand from each other. Nevertheless, some of the economic concepts regarding demand, notably that of elasticity, may be useful in measuring the responsiveness of health services utilisation to price and other changes.

The other important issue is the role of need as usually interpreted in the epidemiological and medical literature. We have concluded that its use in aggregate priority setting may be justified in some circumstances but it cannot be regarded as a substitute for the range of economic evaluation methods to be discussed in Chapter 8.

The preferences of patients for health services, as a reflection of their desire to protect or improve their health status, undoubtedly exist as does a limited degree of price sensitivity. However, the notion of an autonomous demand for health services, where prices are the main determinant of this demand, is best characterised as a fiction.

Finally, the concept of flat of the curve medicine provides a further perspective on a plausible relationship between the 'demand' for medical services and changes in health status. The concept calls into question the commonly held assumption of the general population that more medical care is always desirable.

─────────────────── **FURTHER READING** ───────────────────

The readings described in the previous chapter regarding microeconomics supply theory are relevant to the theory of consumer demand as well.

Many of the topics considered here are discussed at greater length and depth in Evans (1984) *Strained Mercy*.

Discussion questions

- In the light of our discussion of supply theory and other aspects of neoclassical economics as being idealisations or fictions, do you believe the theory of consumer demand should be regarded in the same way? If so, why?
- What does a demand curve for a consumer represent? What is the relationship between a demand curve and the prices and quantities actually observed in a market?
- In the conventional theory of consumer demand why are the indifference curves portrayed as being downward sloping and convex to the origin?
- The concept of diminishing marginal utility is an important element in the theory of consumer demand, and it was derived by the founders of neoclassical theory from introspection. Based on your own introspection how do you feel the theory applies to the consumption of chocolate, alcohol, cigarettes and automobiles, respectively?
- What is meant by an agency relationship in the sense that health economists apply the concept?
- Summarise the main reasons why a perfect agency relationship may not be present when doctors and their patients interact? What is the importance of this lack of perfection for applying the theory of consumer demand to the health services?

The Macroeconomics of Health Services: Health Expenditure, Financing and Utilisation

What is Macroeconomics?

Those aspects of economic theory and its applications that deal with aggregate economic entities such as gross domestic product (GDP), represent the main features of macroeconomics. It will be recalled from Chapter 2, Keynesian economics mainly dealt with aggregates of this kind, along with the reasons for the emergence of unemployment as an international problem in the 1930s.

The distinction between microeconomics of the kind discussed under the demand and supply aspects of the previous chapters and macroeconomics is never very clear cut. For example, welfare economics in the neoclassical sense finds its theoretical basis in microeconomics but the field is designed to inform policy-making for the whole society. Similarly, the economics of health insurance in the neoclassical tradition is firmly based on its impact on the demand functions and preferences of individuals, but for policy-making purposes the health insurance system must be regarded as an important aspect of the whole national economy. In this chapter we consider the measures for funding health services, and issues associated with health insurance and welfare economics, from a macroeconomics perspective.

In addition, we have included a brief review of the aggregate data relating to the health services and how this may be used especially for international comparative purposes to inform health policy-making. The Organisation for Economic Cooperation and Development (OECD), based in Paris, has produced regularly data for a large number of countries dealing with the types of macro-data to be discussed now. The OECD data-based comparisons of the health service characteristics of individual countries are discussed and applied in detail in Chapter 10.

The basis of the national economic accounts framework lies in the approach derived from Keynesian macroeconomics. This approach leads to a concentration on estimating broad descriptive aggregates of economic activity, notably total investment and total consumption expenditure along with GDP, the total money value of all goods and services produced in a country, normally over a period of a year or quarterly. It is one of the main components of the national accounts data published by most countries.

These data play a major role in economic policy-making, for example, to provide a measure of economic growth and the implications of changes in this growth for government or central bank intervention. It is useful, also, to calculate the value of GDP per head of population to provide a measure of the income of each country relative to other countries when the influence of population size is taken into account.

National health data

Whilst not all countries are able to produce data in the detail required, particularly developing countries, the work of the OECD has helped to produce general agreement about the format and classifications of national health data. The World Health Organisation (WHO) has also been involved in this process especially in regard to the creation of health accounting systems for developing countries (Mach and Abel-Smith, 1983; WHO, 2003).

The methods of funding health services are closely related to health insurance issues, including the economics of health insurance, along with the use of alternative methods for funding individual services, notably hospitals. Knowledge of the health funding and health insurance aspects of countries also provides the basis for categorising countries into broad groups based on these factors.

Basis, structure and applications

The national health accounting framework represents an extension of the national economic accounts to the health sector. It has a similar role to the general economic accounts in measuring aggregates which can be used for health economic policy-making and planning. For our purposes we do not need to consider the details of the fine classifications of type of health expenditure and of the sources of funding. These vary considerably from country to country and the accuracy of the data may be questionable in a number of cases. We concentrate in this chapter on the main aggregate relationships, in particular the proportion of gross GDP represented by total health expenditure, and the proportions of total health funding derived from private and public sources.

The ratio of total health expenditure to GDP provides a useful measure of the relative importance of health expenditure in the national economy. It also enables comparisons to be made between countries, highlighting those countries where the ratio is high or low compared with similar types of countries. These data are therefore a potentially important factor in health policy-making.

The major items of health expenditure include hospital expenditure, expenditure on non-hospital institutional care such as nursing homes, expenditure on medical services, that is, services provided by medically qualified personnel, expenditure on pharmaceutical products, expenditure related to other groups notably dentists and allied health professionals, and expenditure on public health and health promotion activities. The education of health personnel, research and development activities associated with health, and administrative costs in some cases may also be classified separately as part of health expenditure.

Total health expenditure can be shown either including or excluding capital expenditure, that is, expenditure on such items as hospital building and major items of capital equipment. The ratios of health expenditure to GDP are sometimes presented for recurrent expenditure only.

Examples of key data and their policy uses

Table 6.1 shows the ratio in percentage terms of health expenditure to GDP for all OECD countries for 2003, and earlier years.

It is noted that the US ratio is easily the highest with a value of 15 per cent whilst the United Kingdom and Japan have amongst the lowest ratios of 7.7 per cent and 7.9 per cent, respectively, for the more developed OECD economies. The reasons for these variations between countries are not well understood at present. At the aggregate level there is clearly a relationship between GDP per head and the proportion of GDP devoted to health expenditure, that is, the more affluent countries devote a relatively greater portion of their national income to health related services.

In a simple regression of the ratio of health expenditure to GDP and total national income the latter emerges as the most important explanatory variable. In this regression relationship the United States emerges as an outlier. It has a much higher ratio than the regression line based on other developed countries would predict. The reasons for the outlier status of the United States, including the higher prices of health services inputs in that country, are explored in Chapter 10.

Table 6.1 OECD Countries 1980–2003. Total expenditure on health percentage of GDP

	1980	1985	1990	1995	2000	2001	2002	2003
Australia	7.0	7.4	7.8	8.3	9.0	9.1	9.3	9.3^{-1}
Austria	7.4	6.4	7.0	8.5	7.5	7.4	7.5	7.5
Belgium	6.4	7.2	7.4	8.4	8.7	8.8	9.1	9.6
Canada	7.1	8.2	9.0	9.2	8.9	9.4	9.6	9.9
Denmark	9.1	8.7	8.5	8.2	8.4	8.6	8.8	9.0
Finland	6.4	7.2	7.8	7.5	6.7	6.9	7.2	7.4
France	7.1	8.2	8.6	9.5	9.3	9.4	9.7	10.1
Germany	8.7	9.0	8.5	10.6	10.6	10.8	10.9	11.1
Greece	6.6	7.4^{2}	7.4	9.6	9.9	10.2	9.8	9.9
Iceland	6.2	7.3	8.0	8.4	9.3	9.3	10	10.5
Ireland	8.4	7.6	6.1	6.8	6.3	6.9	7.3	7.4
Italy	..	7.7^{3}	7.9	7.3	8.1	8.2	8.4	8.4
Japan	6.5	6.7	5.9	6.8 b	7.6	7.8	7.9	7.9^{-1}
Luxembourg	5.9	5.9	6.1	6.4	6.0	6.5	7.2	6.9
Netherlands	7.5	7.4	8.0	8.4	8.3	8.7	9.3	9.8
New Zealand	5.9	5.2	6.9	7.2	7.8	7.9	8.2	8.1
Norway	70	6.6	7.7	7.9	8.5	8.9	9.9	10.3
Portugal	5.6	6.0	6.2	8.2 b	9.2	9.4	9.3	9.6
Spain	5.4	5.5	6.7	7.6	7.4	7.5	7.6	7.7
Sweden	9.1	8.7	8.4	8.1	8.4	8.8	9.2	9.4
Switzerland	7.4	7.8	8.3	9.7	10.4	10.9	11.1	11.5
United Kingdom	5.6	5.9	6.0	7.0	7.3	7.5	7.7	7.7^{-1}
United States	8.7	10.0	11.9	13.3	13.1	13.8	14.6	15.0

Source: OECD Health Data 2005 CDROM, October 05.

Notes:
a) −1, −2, −3, 1, 2, 3 shows that data refers to 1, 2 or 3 previous or following year(s).
b) For Germany, data prior to 1990 refer to West Germany.
c) 'b' means there is a break in the series for the given year.
d) Some OECD countries, with relatively low GDP, have been omitted.

The other focus of national accounting for the health services is the sources of the financing of health expenditure. In this case, the major categories have funding provided by governments at all levels; those associated with private health insurance, and other private funding. The proportion of expenditure financed by governments provides a basis for categorising countries into groups using their financing arrangements as we explore further in Chapter 10. Table 6.2 shows public expenditure on health as a percentage of total health expenditure for a selection of OECD countries. The proportion of private expenditure, not shown separately in this table, is of course 100 minus the public percentage.

Table 6.2 OECD Countries 1980–2003. Public expenditure on health, % total expenditure on health

	1980	1985	1990	1995	2000	2001	2002	2003
Australia	63.0	71.4	67.1	66.7	68.5	67.8	67.5	67.5^{-1}
Austria	68.8	76.1	73.5	69.7	68.2	67.0	67.8	67.6
Belgium	..	..	..	..	..	..	..	..
Canada	75.6	75.5	74.5	71.4	70.3	70.1	69.7	69.9
Denmark	87.8	85.6	82.7	82.5	82.4	82.7	82.9	83.0
Finland	79.0	78.6	80.9	75.6	75.1	75.9	76.3	76.5
France	80.1	78.5	76.6	76.3	75.8	75.9	76.1	76.3
Germany	78.7	77.4	76.2	80.5	78.6	78.4	78.6	78.2
Greece	55.6	59.9	53.7	52.0	52.6 b	54.2	51.6	51.3
Iceland	88.2	87.0	86.6	83.9	82.6	82.7	83.2	83.5
Ireland	81.6	75.7	71.9	71.6	73.3	75.6	75.2	78.0
Italy	..	77.6	79.1	71.9	73.5	75.8	75.4	75.1
Japan	71.3	70.7	77.6	83.0 b	81.3	81.7	81.5	81.5^{-1}
Luxembourg	92.8	89.2	93.1	92.4	89.3	87.9	90.3	89.9
Netherlands	69.4	70.8	67.1	71.0	63.1	62.8	62.5	62.4
New Zealand	88.0	87.0	82.4	77.2	78.0	76.4	77.9	78.7
Norway	85.1	85.8	82.8	84.2	82.5	83.6	83.5	83.7
Portugal	64.3	54.6	65.5	62.6 b	69.5	70.6	70.5	69.7
Spain	79.9	81.1	78.7	72.2	71.6	71.2	71.3	71.2
Sweden	92.5	90.4	89.9	86.6	84.9	84.9	85.1	85.2
Switzerland	..	50.3	52.4	53.8	55.6	57.1	57.9	58.5
United Kingdom	89.4	85.8	83.6	83.9	80.9	83.0	83.4	83.4^{-1}
United States	41.5	39.9	39.6	45.3	44.2	44.8	44.9	44.4

Source: OECD Health Data 2005 CDROM, October 05.

Notes:
a) −1, −2, −3, 1, 2, 3 shows that data refers to 1, 2 or 3 previous or following year(s).
b) For Germany, data prior to 1990 refer to West Germany.
c) "b" means there is a break in the series for the given year.

Again it is noticeable that the proportion of expenditure funded from public sources is lowest in the United States, 44 per cent, along with Switzerland, 58.5 per cent. Most of the more developed OECD countries with a few exceptions have over 70 per cent of public financing, with a correspondingly lower value for private sector financing.

As well as the use of these data for international comparative purposes the changes in the data over time are also a useful guide to how successfully broad health policy goals are being achieved. For example, in response to the perception that in the early 1970s a disproportionate amount of total health expenditure was associated with short stay hospitals and a relatively low proportion on public health, primary care and health promotion, a number of countries adopted policies designed to redress the balance.

In countries with a large public hospital sector primarily funded by the central or regional governments two strategies were adopted. The first was to reduce the number of hospital beds per thousand of population and the second was to put in place funding mechanisms designed to produce incentives for achieving greater technical efficiency, most noticeably the casemix-based methods described later in the chapter. In the British NHS a large number of indicators of hospital performance have been devised to enable comparisons between hospitals to be undertaken.

The considerable interest in containing the growth of health expenditure in most developed countries in the last 20 years was a consequence of the national health accounting data revealing a strong tendency for the ratio of this expenditure to GDP to increase as Table 6.1 indicates, often as in the Unites States at a rate which could be regarded as unsustainable in relation to the willingness of governments and individuals to fund the increases.

In the early 1990s in the US projections into the future of the trend in health expenditure to increase in the previous decade indicated that as much as 20 per cent of the GDP might be associated with health early in the next century. The encouragement and growth of managed care arrangements and tighter controls over government expenditure on health care served to slow down subsequently this rate of increase. In other developed countries a good deal of experimentation has been undertaken on separating the roles of the purchasers and providers of hospital and other health services. This process is discussed later in this chapter.

A further interesting example of the use of national health accounting data has been the recent policy decision of the British government to increase the ratio of health expenditure to GDP to the average value for the European Union countries (Klein, 2001). The planned expansion of NHS funding has been designed to reduce waiting lists and waiting time for hospital patients. These were regarded as becoming politically unacceptable in relation to the goals of the NHS. In Chapter 10 we explore in more detail the characteristics of the different types of health care financing and provision arrangements and how these may influence the overall efficiency and equity of the systems.

The challenge of financing reforms

The separation of the roles of purchasers and providers

Based on the work of the Dutch economist Alain Enthoven, now based at Stanford University in the United States, proposals to separate the roles of the purchasers and providers of health services were implemented, tested, or proposed in several countries in the 1980s (Enthoven, 1983). In developed countries where governments funded or subsidised a high proportion of health expenditure these roles were often combined in the same organisation.

In national health services with most of the funding of health services undertaken by governments, the latter normally were responsible for the ownership and management of large segments of health service provision, notably by hospitals. In other countries which relied heavily on health insurance, usually subsidised by governments, these governments also have had an important role in the provision of hospital and other services.

The underlying rationale for separating the two roles was that the financing organisations established would be obliged to seek out providers who could supply their services at the least cost for a specified quantity and quality of the services. In this way the providers would be placed in a competitive situation with one another and thus induced to achieve greater efficiency in their activities if they were to remain viable. Enthoven had noted that it was unrealistic to expect that governments with zero or heavily subsidised price arrangements for patients would introduce significant user charges to institute competitive incentives on the demand side (Enthoven, 1988, 1993). Thus the emphasis of his proposals was firmly on the supply side and changing the incentives for service providers.

A decade of British NHS funding and related reforms

In Britain, the Enthoven approach was embraced with enthusiasm by the then Prime Minister, Mrs Thatcher, and it formed the basis of the reforms of the NHS adopted in 1991. Mrs Thatcher had committed her government to retaining the fundamental features of the NHS, namely the absence of user charges for most hospital and medical services and the retention of taxation funding for the services. However, her conservative government argued that the lack of competition in the health care system produced inefficiencies in the production of services which the new funding and provider arrangements should rectify.

The District Health Authorities (DHAs) responsible for the areas into which the NHS regions at that time were divided undertook the role of purchasing of services whilst the individual hospitals in the areas were the principal providers. In the allocation of funding the DHAs were obliged to take into account the potential of each provider to ensure the services achieved 'health gains' for their populations.

The 1991 reforms also included the establishment of budgeting arrangements, on a voluntary basis, for groups of general practitioners (GPs). The groups were allocated budgets which could then be used in purchasing their patients' hospital requirements. This aspect of the reforms of the NHS was based on the principle that with fixed budgets the GPs would be more cautious about referring patients for hospital treatment. This initiative was also designed to place competitive pressures on hospitals to achieve greater efficiency.

The 1991 reforms of the NHS have been the subject of several evaluations by health economists and others in Britain (Klein, 1998; Le Grand, 1998; Le Grand et al., 1998). The details of the evaluations lie beyond the objectives of the current work. However, they came to the conclusion that there was little evidence that the NHS changes had led to greater efficiency in the hospital services. The reasons usually cited for this failure include the poor bargaining position of the purchasing authorities in relation to hospital providers. An aggressive approach to purchasing might have led to some hospitals closing, a politically unacceptable outcome, so that the preservation of the status quo in funding allocations emerged as the preferred option for purchasers.

It might be added that it was often extremely difficult for the purchasing authorities to access adequate information about the technical efficiency of each hospital to guide funding decisions. For this purpose detailed casemix information, including cost per case type, of the kind discussed below would have been needed. The criterion of ensuring health gain for populations based on the activities of the local hospitals is an extremely difficult if not impossible one to implement as we discuss further below when dealing with funding reforms.

The results of the evaluations were no doubt one factor leading to the abandonment of the purchaser–provider split using the DHA, and the purchasing role being based on a revised version of GP fund holding via a new and compulsory grouping into primary care groups (PCGs). The change also reflected the defeat of the conservative government in 1997 and the Labour party which replaced it being rather less wedded (so far) to competitive solutions. New policies were designed to reflect cooperative rather than competitive relationships according to official government pronouncements about the changes (Secretary of State for Health, 2000).

It was argued that since in the NHS referrals to hospitals (except for emergencies) are based on the GP as 'gate keeper', the financial incentive provided to PCGs as fund holders would promote greater caution in referrals. It is still too early to assess the impact of this last set of reforms to the NHS (Klein, 2006). We provide more details about the characteristics of the UK NHS, and the most recent reforms in Chapter 10.

Casemix hospital funding initiatives

In all OECD countries and elsewhere there has been a rapid development of interest in improving the methods that governments use in funding the hospital sector. Much of this interest arose out of the adoption in the United States of a new funding method for hospitals providing services for its Medicare patients, predominantly eligible persons aged 65 and over. The basis of the funding arrangement was the patient classification system of diagnosis-related groups (DRGs) which we mentioned in Chapter 5. The DRG classification originally used by Medicare consisted of 470 groups, but this number was subsequently increased to over 500. The groups were formed by using a combination of patient data, notably on the disease diagnoses and operating room procedures performed, where relevant. Additional variables used in the original classification were patient age, and discharge status, including death. The principal criteria used in the creation of DRGs were the relative cost homogeneity of the groups and their clinical meaningfulness or 'coherence' (Fetter et al., 1980).

The DRGs were developed by a team at Yale University headed by Professors Robert Fetter and John Thompson, and funded by the federal government. Fetter was an operations research and management expert, whilst Thompson held qualifications in nursing and public health. Mathematical, computing and medical personnel also contributed heavily to the work of the team. The method of devising the groups was to use a large database of patient records containing the requisite information on individual patient characteristics and then using computer software to review possible groupings to achieve those that best met the criteria (Fetter et al., 1980).

The DRGs for funding purposes were assigned cost weights using the extensive database of hospital charges which hospitals were required to report under the previous hospital cost reimbursement system for Medicare patients. These cost weights show the average charge for each DRG relative to the average charge across all patients. In essence, a price in money terms is set for each DRG by allocating the total budgeted amount each year for Medicare hospital patients between hospitals according to their DRG profile (casemix) for Medicare patients. A large number of other factors, such as the indirect teaching costs of the hospitals, and regional variations in wage and salary costs also influence the payments to hospitals (Averill, 1991).

Of considerable importance in the reform of hospital funding in the United States was that the data collected under the cost reimbursement regime revealed very large variations between hospitals in payments for the same diagnostic and procedure groups. It was perceived that a prospective payment system based on casemix would provide a strong incentive for the less efficient hospitals to become more efficient since Medicare payments provided over 40 per cent of hospital revenue.

The diffusion of the DRG technology and funding method spread fairly rapidly to other countries with a very mixed pattern of achievements. This diffusion, the reasons for it, and the requirements for its success have been adequately documented in several books and papers (de Pouvoirville and Kimberly, 1993; Roger France et al., 2001). The introduction of casemix payments in the United States had led a number of countries, universally concerned with hospital cost containment, to place DRGs on their health policy agendas.

It was realised that in countries with very different hospital financing methods from the United States, the DRG profiles of hospitals could be used to apportion a fixed total funding for hospitals between each of them according to their costed casemix profile (Palmer, 1986). The data from Australia also revealed that there were very large variations between hospitals in their funding, when account was taken of the types of patients they treated, under the global budgeting arrangements used in that country. By the late 1990s, 20 countries had responded to the invitation to report on their DRG developments in an international monograph on casemix (Roger France et al., 2001). The progress reported ranged from a comprehensive implementation of casemix hospital funding in Australia (Palmer, 2001) and Portugal to a few largely experimental pilot studies in others.

Since that time, comprehensive DRG-type funding has been undertaken in Germany, France, Denmark and Japan. There was initially a great deal of interest and research in England and Wales about DRGs, including the establishment of a casemix unit in the Health Department. More recently, a British version of casemix, Healthcare Resource Groups (HRGs), has been created. These follow the general structure of DRGs but give more emphasis to surgical procedures. The creation of HRGs seems to have reflected concerns that DRGs were not acceptable to British clinicians and others because of their US origins. It is understood that in the near future HRGs will be used extensively for setting 'tariffs' and determining hospital budgets in the United Kingdom.

Casemix funding, mythology and the economic rationale

Myths and misconceptions concerning the use of casemix funding for hospitals outside the United States have been widespread (Palmer, 1996). Most importantly, many medical personnel claimed that DRGs would not work in other countries because they were based on US clinical practice, and that practice procedures were different in these countries. This and other claims proved to be false or misguided when statistical analysis and clinical reviews of local data were conducted in a number of countries considering the introduction of casemix funding (Roger France et al., 2001).

The economic rationale for casemix funding is based on the premise that hospitals should be paid for the treatment of patients, taking into account that some patients were much more costly to treat than others. Existing methods of hospital funding were either based on cost reimbursement, which provided no incentives to achieve greater efficiency, or on very arbitrary global allocations of funds from governments or other payers.

As we indicated earlier casemix funding is designed to place pressures on the less technically efficient hospitals to improve their performance or face the risk of being unable to remain viable. The threat of this risk seems to have led to hospitals improving their performance even before the new funding method was fully implemented. Most countries using casemix funding have had a long lead in time or have phased in casemix funding over several years (Roger France et al., 2001).

Evaluations of casemix funding in the United States

Several evaluations of the prospective payments system have concluded that in the early years of its application considerable economies were achieved, although it is difficult to distinguish the various sources of the reduced payments relative to the preservation of the status quo (Russell, 1989; Lave, 1989). However, the data clearly showed that the main concern of economists, that hospital admissions would increase, was not borne out. Indeed hospital admissions for Medicare patients, along with their average lengths of stays, declined quite substantially.

It has been suggested that medical staff, often opposed to DRG-based payments for the hospitals and concerned about having to cope with the administrative requirements of the system for them, had transferred some suitable patients to their own offices. The powerful role of medical staff in influencing the use by patients of hospitals, a part of supplier influenced demand, had been ignored in the predictions of economists about the likely outcome of basing payments on average costs instead of marginal costs.

Health insurance: Public and private

Most of the theoretical and empirical studies of health insurance issues have again been US-based. This is not surprising in view of the lively political debate in that country about reforms to health insurance policy, especially in the light of the large number of people who lack any health insurance. Health economists in the United States have been interested principally in the demand for health insurance by individual consumers and the alleged welfare losses associated with the provision of health insurance, especially when funded by governments (Feldstein, M., 1973; Feldman and Dowd, 1991). They have also devised possible funding strategies to deal with the special problems of the uninsured population and its various components in the United States (Fuchs 1996; Feldstein, M. and Gruber, 1997).

All other developed countries have almost universal and compulsory health insurance. As we indicate in Chapter 10, the precise arrangements vary considerably from country to country. In some countries the government through its health agencies is the health insurer with taxation being the principal source of financing, whilst other countries rely heavily on not for profit or private organisations to provide much of the health insurance, subject to government regulations and tax funded subsidies.

The growth of government controlled and funded health insurance as part of social welfare policy has reflected the widespread belief that all members of resident populations are entitled to receive a basic level of coverage for medical and hospital services without meeting all or a large part of the costs. The special features associated with the growth of compulsory health insurance have included the need for financial protection against the unpredictable risks associated with disease and the responsibility assumed by governments to ensure that these risks do not lead to access to health services being restricted by financial considerations.

Terminology and concepts

To understand the literature on health insurance and the variety of health insurance schemes that exist between and within individual countries it is necessary to be familiar with some basic terminology and concepts:

Co-insurance applies where the amount of the health services charge is met in part by the patient and in part by the insurer.

Co-payment is the percentage of the charged price paid by the health care consumer with the remainder being met by the insurer.

Deductible refers to the amount of the charge which the patient must pay before any payment is made by the insuring organisation.

Full service coverage occurs where the insurance covers all the costs to the patient; that is, there are no co-payments or deductibles.

Moral hazard refers to the possibility that insurance coverage may lead to a greater probability that the event being insured against will occur than if no insurance contract existed.

Third party payment is the component of a charge met by an insurance agency, including the government.

Risk sharing refers to the underlying rationale for insurance that the risk of the event being insured against is spread across all the individuals who are at risk.

Welfare or dead weight cost is the alleged loss, using the criteria of welfare economics, to the community if an insurance arrangement is present.

Premium is the regular payment required by the insurer in respect of each person covered by the insurance contract.

Community rating refers to the principle that everyone in the covered population of the insurer pays the same premium irrespective of age, income and their other personal characteristics.

Experience rating means that the insurer varies the premiums charged according to the usage experience of the individuals covered or of the whole group in relation to other population groups.

Adverse selection occurs where the insurer is able to refuse insurance coverage to groups of high risk individuals, such as AIDS patients or others with chronic and expensive conditions.

Disease and service exclusions are additional devices used by insurers to insulate themselves from the impact of diseases and services which would generate high costs for them. These include psychiatric disorders which are often explicitly excluded in the United States from the list of service benefits covered in a health insurance contract.

The provision for co-payments and deductibles in health insurance contracts may be regarded as rationing devices, since their existence implies that the patient would experience a lower utilisation of health services than if these devices did not exist, that is if full service coverage applied, other factors influencing utilisation remaining constant.

The individual insurance contracts may contain provision for both a co-payment and a deductible. Where a national health insurance policy is present, for example, in Britain and Canada, all hospital and medical services may be free to the patient, that is, there is full service coverage and no co-payment or deductible applies. No health insurance premiums along with community rating are characteristics of this system. Where the principal source of funding is taxation revenue, the risks for meeting the health expenses of the population are being spread across all taxpayers. This type of health insurance is often referred to as being based on social insurance but the term is also applied to countries where health insurance is subsidised by governments without having the other characteristics of a national health service.

In a number of European countries and Australia the health insurance provided by the government may cover only the expenses incurred in public hospital stays. Private health insurance is available to meet the costs of private hospital usage or of treatment as a private patient in a public hospital where this option is provided.

The response to uncertainty; risk aversion

The American economist Arrow has written what is usually regarded as the seminal paper on the theory of health insurance, 'Uncertainty and the welfare economics of medical care' (Arrow, 1963). He emphasised that health insurance exists as a response to the uncertainty that surrounds illness, that is, it is unpredictable for individuals what their future needs for health services and the costs of these will be. He highlighted that a key factor in understanding the demand for health insurance was that of risk aversion. He pointed to circumstances where government intervention might be required to fill the gaps in insurance coverage and thereby promote greater community welfare.

The theory of health insurance takes into account the fact that the degree of risk aversion in a country where a number of health insurance options are available may vary considerably from person to person, depending on several factors including their current state of health, their age and income. Thus a highly risk averse person could be expected to choose a policy with low or zero co-payments and deductibles. It might also be noted that where a choice exists for insurance against different types of health expenditure, for example, hospital inpatient treatment and treatment for out of hospital care, the risk aversion characteristic for each type of service may also be variable for the one individual.

The notion of risk aversion is linked closely with the administrative costs and other outlays of the insurer. The existence of these costs means that the premium charged will inevitably be higher than the actuarially fair price (if it were possible to make this estimate with any degree of accuracy). The latter is obtained as the expected value of the probability of the risk occurring times the money cost of the outcome being insured against. For a purchaser of health insurance the degree of risk aversion, according to the theory, must be sufficient to overcome this gap.

Health insurance and welfare economics

Much of the US literature on health insurance goes into considerable detail on the implications for consumer behaviour and social welfare of the various options for health insurance available in that country. This literature is based generally on the application of utility maximisation theory, the competitive market model, and the demand for health insurance being treated as a further application of consumer demand theory. The normative conclusions of this theory include the desirability of the presence of deductibles and co-insurance in the health insurance contracts, the advantages from the theory of welfare standpoint of the existence of a number of health insurance options for each individual, and the disadvantages of full service coverage. The community rating principle, rather than experience rating, is also regarded unfavourably by most health economists in the United States (Jacobs, 1997; Feldstein. P, 1999).

However, a recent book on health insurance in the United States (Nyman, 2003) and several papers by the same author have raised considerable doubts about the existing welfare economics-based theories including the inefficiency of moral hazard (Nyman, 2004). Similar reservations were raised by Evans 10 years earlier (Evans, 1984).

Two other issues have been highlighted in this literature. First, some economists have ascribed the considerable growth in health expenditures in the United States after the Second World War to the extension of health insurance provision to larger numbers in the population such as those covered under the government subsidised Medicare and Medicaid schemes. Using a 12 equation econometric model Martin Feldstein concluded that about 80 per cent of the increases in hospital prices could be attributed to the extension of health insurance coverage (Feldstein, M., 1971). It is strange that the advocates of the coverage of health insurance as being a major determinant of the rise in health expenditure in the United States had not acknowledged that many European countries with almost complete insurance against health services expenditure had much lower levels of health expenditure, and slower or comparable growth rate over time as compared with the United States.

Second, economists have calculated the dead weight cost of health insurance, by estimating the difference between how much individuals would have been willing to pay for health services in a free market situation and the expenditure that had taken place in the light of the current health insurance arrangements. The deadweight loss of health insurance is then measured by the estimated additional health expenditure as compared with the free market situation in which patients would pay the market prices up to the point of usage at which these equate to their marginal utilities (Feldman and Dowd, 1991). Those health economists who calculate the dead weight loss are implicitly assuming that to maximise community welfare no health insurance should exist except for that which consumers would choose to purchase in a free market where the costs to each individual were borne solely by them.

Whilst the proponents of assessing the impact of health insurance in this way do not necessarily carry their argument to the logical conclusion that all health insurance should be abolished, it has led them to recommend forms of health insurance in which this covers only catastrophic events with very high costs (Feldstein, M. and Gruber, 1997). Again, the obvious income redistribution effects of such health policies, from the sick poor to the healthy affluent, are excluded from the analysis (Reinhardt, 1998).

Health economists in the United States have been critical, also, of the exemption from taxation of the benefit to the insured population of health insurance being paid for by employers, and of the tax deductibility of this expense for employers. The free market oriented economists see the main problem in the United States as being one of over-insurance for most of the population and have been active in advocating health insurance policies that would eliminate the tax deductibility incentive.

The 'over-use' of health services generated by health insurance is claimed to represent 'moral hazard' where the existence of insurance coverage against fire or burglary is said to increase the likelihood of these incidents occurring for illegal or careless reasons. The terminology when applied to health services carries a strong implication that increased usage of these services is also morally reprehensible.

The dead weight loss argument rests on several shaky foundations. Here is not the place to repeat the arguments about the inadequacies of the application of the neoclassical theory of demand to health services, including the role of supplier-induced demand. Yet it must be pointed out that the loss of welfare thesis is based on the assumption that the free market solution represents the optimum allocation of welfare. This conclusion ignores the likelihood that health insurance may promote better access to health services with this in turn increasing the health status of the covered population (Nyman, 1999a, b). It also ignores the role of health insurance in redistributing income to low income, high risk groups especially where the government subsidises the health insurance.

Outside the United States neither policy-makers nor health economists have been inhibited by the welfare loss argument from their extensive involvement in promoting the various health insurance programs that exist in developed countries. Amongst the arguments they have made for social insurance arrangements in some form, including the national health service variant, is that the administrative costs where there is only one insurer may be substantially less than if a multiplicity of private health insurers exists. These costs emerged as a major factor in comparisons of the costs of the Canadian system of universal health insurance funded and organised by the government, with the US situation of numerous for profit and not for profit health insurance agencies along with the federal and state governments (Himmelstein and Woolhandler, 1986; Woolhandler and Himmelstein, 1991; Redelmeier and Fuchs, 1993).

Comprehensive health insurance programs in developed countries have also been supported on the grounds that they promote social solidarity. It will be recalled, Chapter 3, that Gavin Mooney has made this point explicitly in describing the communitarianism justification for social welfare programs. The interests of the society benefit when there is a commitment by its members to protecting the well-being of the less fortunate members of the community.

A critique of the theory of welfare economics

A comprehensive review of the theory of welfare economics is outside the scope of this work since it would require a deep understanding of a number of complex theoretical issues. An extensive set of sources dealing with this material and the closely related problems of applying market-based reforms to health care is available (Rice, 1998a, b). Here we restrict the discussion to those aspects of welfare economics which are relevant to health insurance issues.

However, it is as well to note the observations of several other economists about the limitations of welfare theory as a guide to social policy. For example, Arrow (1963) indicated that any method of aggregating individual preferences into a social welfare function violates at least one reasonable and desirable ethical condition. Mishan who wrote extensively about welfare economics has concluded that 'it promises much but yields little' (Mishan, 1969). Two papers by Sen on the ethical limitations of welfare economics are also highly relevant to this critique (Sen, 1977, 1979).

It is clear from our discussion of health insurance and of our preliminary review of the contributions of individual health economists that the role, implications and validity of welfare economics has been an important theme in the controversies associated with health policies. We have observed previously that the neoclassical theory of welfare economics relies heavily on the notion devised by Pareto that a change in which some people gain greater welfare (increased utility) and no one is made worse off should be regarded as a desirable change. It was also noted that the application of this principle to policy changes is severely limited by the fact that most changes produce some losers.

A second version of the Pareto principle is that a policy is desirable if the winners could in principle compensate the losers. The important point about this principle is that compensation does not need to be paid by the winners. Reinhardt has referred to this approach in characteristically eloquent terms as the 'unrequited punch in the nose principle' (Reinhardt, 1998).

Limitations as a guide to health policy

The application of the weaker form of the Pareto principle potentially extends the coverage by welfare theory to many more policy initiatives. However, as Reinhardt and others have pointed out, it permits health economists wedded to the application of neoclassical economics to health policy to have further grounds for ignoring the impact of their health insurance proposals on the distribution of income between the likely losers and the rest of the society.

As Evans, Culyer and others have argued, the drawing of normative conclusions from positive economic analysis inevitably requires the imposition of a set of values, a welfare function, implicitly that of the person making the policy recommendations (Culyer and Evans, 1996; Evans, 1998). These values do not necessarily coincide with those of the community or of many policy-makers.

The extra-welfarist response

For this reason, as we noted in Chapter 3, Culyer has advocated an extra-welfarist approach to health economics. This approach concentrates on the use of health status as a measure of the performance of policy initiatives and the resort to ascertaining the values and preferences of the stakeholders in reviewing the policy options. Rather than devising and promoting policy changes using welfare economics criteria the health economist, according to this framework, is to act as a consultant to the research sponsor, who is usually the funding agency.

Health insurance, distribution and community values

This method leaves open the question of whether the values of the funding agency are consistent with that of the community to which the policies are directed. The heavy emphasis in Britain and elsewhere on the development of measures of health status, notably quality adjusted life years (QALYs), is consistent with the extra-welfarist method. In Chapter 8 we discuss QALYs and similar measures for health status measurement. Their rationale and the extent to which they are dependent on neoclassical demand theory are also considered in the chapter.

Summary and conclusions

In this chapter we have focused on a number of issues arising out of a macro-perspective on the health services. The data designed to provide a broad overview of the financial functioning of the health care systems are based on estimating the flows of funds between funders and providers of health services.

We have noted that the OECD has produced these data for all of its 30 member countries in a standard format which provides a basis for comparing countries on such measures as the proportion of GDP devoted to expenditure on the health services, the proportion of expenditure devoted to hospitals and other institutions and services, and the break down of financing between public and private sources. These data are drawn on extensively in Chapter 10 when we compare individual and broad categories of countries.

In recent years, in all OECD countries and others, there have been a number of attempts to reform the methods of funding the health services. These have included the separation of the roles of purchasers and providers of health services to generate a more competitive set of relationships on the supply side, the introduction of casemix funding of hospitals and proposals for changing health insurance arrangements.

These reforms have been generated by a number of factors including a widespread belief in policy circles that the efficiency of the health services could be improved considerably, and that increased efficiency might serve to reduce the rate of growth of health expenditure. The growth internationally of casemix funding for financing hospitals has primarily reflected the realisation that existing methods of hospital finance, based either on cost reimbursement or the establishment of aggregate budgets, were unsatisfactory. They provided no incentives to achieve greater efficiency and were often based on inadequate information about the activities undertaken by the hospitals.

The US proposals for reform of health insurance have usually been based on the application of neoclassical welfare economics to establish a rationale for greater patient co-payments and co-insurance in health insurance. To date they have had only a limited impact on health policy in that country. However, it is possible that they have influenced some countries to place a greater reliance on such measures, at the risk of affecting the equity of their systems.

An extra-welfarist approach has been advocated as an alternative to welfare economics. It concentrates on health status rather than utility as the goal of the health services and the application of the values of policy-makers to assess proposed changes.

FURTHER READING

A very comprehensive account of a large range of health care funding issues is provided in the book by Donaldson and Gerard (2005), including the reasons for market failure and the need for a 'visible hand', meaning government intervention. Funding reforms in a large number of countries, including those of the developing world, are also reviewed. A careful deployment of economic reasoning is featured in the book.

Two OECD publications, (OECD, 2005a, b) provide a great deal of useful information about the data which the organisation produces in the health area. Details, including a selection of tables, are provided at the OECD website, www.OECD.org.

Discussion questions

- What are the main components of national health accounts on both the expenditure side and the financing aspect?
- Describe two potential applications of the health accounts data as an input to national health policy-making.
- Separating the roles of purchasers and providers of health care in national health services has been an important initiative in the United Kingdom and elsewhere. Explain the rationale for implementing this reform. What have been the limitations of the reform in generating greater health services efficiency?
- A large number of countries have adopted the casemix method of funding their hospitals. What are the main reasons for implementing this reform? What have been the objections to the use of casemix for this purpose?
- Health economists, especially in the United States, have been critical of many aspects of health insurance arrangements in their country and elsewhere. In particular, they have argued that it leads to the over-use of health services, and a 'welfare loss' of considerable dimensions, especially where full service coverage applies. Do you agree with these claims?
- What do economists mean by the phrase 'moral hazard'?

The Economics and Planning of the Health Workforce

7

Background

This chapter is designed to present several key health policy and planning issues concerning the health workforce with some emphasis on an economics perspective. This is not a well-developed area in health economics possibly because most US health economists do not perceive that there is much scope for economic analysis from a neoclassical perspective. A notable exception is the pioneering work of Yett on the nursing workforce (Yett, 1975). Indeed with some exceptions most of the recent published material on the medical workforce in the United States has been produced by medically qualified personnel and organisations (Council on Graduate Medical Education, 1994, 2003a, b; Cooper, 1995, 2004; Goodman et al., 1996; Schroeder, 1996; Association of American Medical Colleges, 2002a, b; Cooper et al., 2002).

Of the material written by health economists on the workforce Chapter 13 of Evans's *Strained Mercy* (1984) provided perhaps the most comprehensive and insightful account. He has made the important point that policies about the workforce are treated by economists as an aspect of the development of human capital, which in turn represents an input into a production process. He emphasised, moreover, that in the health field the development of private human capital is heavily subsidised by governments as they allocate substantial funds to educational and training activities.

The Australian health economist Richard Scotton (1974, 1998) has also written extensively and cogently about the medical workforce policies and problems in that country. Amongst other health economists Alan Maynard and his colleagues' work on the topic in Britain is also of special interest (Bloor, Maynard et al., 2003; Maynard and Bloor, 2003; Walker and Maynard, 2003).

The need for workforce planning

The absence of a free market

The need for the planning of workforce stocks and requirements as normally undertaken is a product of the limitations of a free market approach to these matters. No country has been willing to leave these matters to the workings of a perfectly competitive market in which there were no barriers to entry either into educational programs or the activities undertaken by the practitioners, and in which the analysis of these markets would be predominantly based on the traditional supply and demand concepts.

The role and responsibility of government

The need for legislation to protect the public in regard to the quality of the services delivered has been of paramount importance in all matters relating to health workforce issues. However, the current health workforce planning studies have largely ignored the impact of economic factors in determining the inputs to and requirements for health personnel. This is not justified by the numerous reasons for the limitations of the free market model when applied to this complex area. An appropriate balance between the demographical and statistical exercises and relevant economic analysis should be a basic requirement.

As we have noted previously British health economists in general have been preoccupied with evaluation methods and policy issues, and have correspondingly displayed little interest in the health workforce, again with the important exceptions noted earlier. Planning exercises regarding the health workforce in the NHS appear to be the responsibility of the Department of Health in its oversight of the administration of the service. This includes inputs from health economists within the Department. Recent changes in the administration of the NHS have led to the devolution to local areas of greater responsibility for workforce planning, subject to broad central guidelines.

Scope for the application of economic insights

The potential for technical efficiency enhancement: the production function approach

Together with the basic questions about the existence of surpluses and shortages of key health service personnel that have dominated the studies of the health workforce to date, a number of other policy and planning issues also arise in this area. Some of these lend themselves directly to the use of an economics-based framework, especially the insights gained by the use of a production function approach. As we have indicated previously, the method raises the possibility of achieving increased technical efficiency by the substitution of one form of labour input for another or of the use of more (or less) capital inputs for labour. The increased use of nurses ('nurse practitioners') instead of medically qualified staff is the most notable example of a potential efficiency promoting labour input substitution.

Other topics concerning the health care workforce which may be fruitfully examined from an economics perspective include aspects of the quality of the educational inputs to health services personnel which may have a profound influence on the efficiency with which these services are delivered. Similar considerations apply to the closely related area of the traditional structures of the educational arrangements for the training of health services personnel, notably for postgraduate (specialist) medical education.

Regulatory and political obstacles

The extent to which these potential initiatives for achieving increased efficiency may be limited by legal regulations, health insurance legislation and licensing requirements is also an appropriate field for further study and research (Arrow, 1963; Cooper and Aiken, 2001). It might be noted, moreover, that there is a large literature on the economics of regulation which has rarely been drawn on by mainstream health economists, despite the fact that the health services field is dominated by regulatory requirements and mechanisms.

In this chapter we explore a number of these issues in varying degrees of detail. Our purpose here is not to provide a comprehensive review of all the topics listed but to stimulate thought and discussion about those matters that we regard as having been relatively neglected in the mainstream literature of health economics. Moreover, it will become evident from our review of health workforce planning studies and methods that inputs from demographical and statistical perspectives, as noted, have to date dominated the field. This may also explain the tendency in workforce planning studies for economic concepts such as supply and demand to be used very loosely and inaccurately in this context.

Supply and demand concepts

In the projections of the future size of health personnel numbers what is being estimated is the stock of workers at a future date, rather than supply in the economic sense which is a flow concept based on technical and economic factors in defined periods of time. The projections as we illustrate below are usually based on determining the size of the specified workforce at a base period and adding to this number the projected inputs from newly qualified personnel and other sources over the time period of the projection, less attrition from retirements and departures for other reasons from the occupational group. Economic demand factors such as the expected income returns from undertaking an educational program to qualify for the occupational group are of relevance in contributing to the size of the inputs in each year, but they have usually been neglected in the models of stock projections.

Similarly, the projections of the total workforce of a specified category required in the future are estimates of the expected stock of needs based on such factors as the forecasted age and morbidity experience of the population. The extent to which these needs might be met will reflect economic demand determinants such as the willingness and capacity of governments to pay for them but again with a few notable exceptions (see next section) these have not been incorporated in the projections of future workforce requirements.

Definitions and measurement of surpluses and shortages

Economic and other criteria

The presence of surpluses and shortages in the components of the health workforce have dominated health policies in most countries. Yet both these outcomes are difficult to define operationally. In purely economic, free market terms a shortage would exist at a point in time if the numbersof personnel at the current rates of remuneration were insufficient to meet the demand from consumers for their services.

In the light of our earlier discussions of the inappropriateness of applying these concepts to the health services it is clear that this definition has very limited application. For this reason other methods of defining shortages and surpluses, often with a flawed conceptual basis, have been used in the general literature of workforce studies. However, as we argue later, it would be unwise to neglect the possibility that inadequate rates of remuneration especially for nurses may contribute to the perceived problem of a shortage, and thus point to one possibility for alleviating the problem.

In this chapter we concentrate on surpluses, shortages, planning and related issues dealing with medical and nursing staff. These are the two most important workforce groups in the health services because of their influence on the health care system and their numerical magnitude. Most of the theoretical and empirical work on the health workforce has been undertaken regarding these groups. There has been a limited amount of study of other health workforce groups such as dentists and physiotherapists but the methods used are very similar to those we describe concerning doctors and nurses.

International comparisons

The OECD data

The OECD data which we discussed in Chapter 6 also include details of the number of physicians and nurses per thousand of population in all OECD countries. We defer the discussion of these data until Chapter 10 in the context of our international comparisons of the health care systems of a number of OECD countries.

Definitional problems

In the making of international comparisons of workforce data we need to be conscious of the possibility that the definitions used by each country of health services staff may differ considerably. The medical workforce may sometimes be expressed as full-time equivalents and in other cases include all personnel who possess medical qualifications and work in the health services. In respect of the nursing workforce some countries include all persons who perform nursing duties, whereas others may distinguish between types of nurses, with the emphasis being on 'registered' nurses, that is, those possessing higher qualifications. Detailed studies of the health workforce in different countries should endeavour to clarify what precisely is meant by the terminology adopted in each case.

The medical workforce

The key role and influence of medical personnel

In our previous chapters we have stressed frequently the key role that doctors play in a number of activities such as influencing the utilisation of their own services, and according to some models of hospital behaviour exerting the predominant influence amongst all the groups in these institutions. Political scientists have put forward the hypothesis that the financing and other health care arrangements of each country mainly reflect the preferences of the medical profession (Marmor, 1983). Governments in a democracy may wish to avoid a confrontation of a potentially very damaging kind with a powerful adversary.

However, in some circumstances governments have been able to undertake health services reforms despite the strong opposition of organised medicine. A case in point is the changeover from a voluntary health insurance system to a universal, taxation funded one in Australia in the mid-1970s. The unpopularity of the former system, operated under a conservative government, a well-documented critique of it by two health economists, Richard Scotton and John Deeble, and a carefully constructed compulsory health insurance program funded from general taxation, proved to be politically popular and contributed to the success of the Australian Labor party at the federal election held in 1972 (Scotton and Macdonald, 1993).

Supplier-induced demand once again

The assessment of the requirements for the number of doctors is closely bound up with whether account is taken of the capacity of doctors to influence the utilisation of their own services, that is, of supplier-induced demand (SID). Those who accept the potential for this phenomenon to be present are inclined to question the wisdom of adding to the number of doctors being trained to overcome perceptions of a shortage of medical staff. The effect of an increase in the number of doctors may simply be to increase the utilisation of their services without any significant gains in the access of many patients to medical care, or on the fees charged. We explore this issue later in our discussion of planning methods and outcomes.

Those economists who are unfamiliar with the workings of the medical market, sometimes found in Treasury Departments, may advocate an increase in the number of doctors to place additional competitive pressures on the profession, to restrain fee increases and to overcome the perceived shortage. This approach is consistent with the application of free market, neoclassical principles, to the hypothesised market for medical services, but it falls well short of a balanced approach to medical workforce planning.

Geographic mal-distribution

The perceptions of a shortage may in some cases reflect a mal-distribution of the medical workforce, especially where many medical personnel are reluctant to work in the more unattractive locations such as remote rural areas or the more economically depressed sections of cities. In these circumstances, politically active groups may lobby governments to improve the supply of doctors even though there may be relative surpluses in other areas and regions.

Planning policies that involve the establishment of additional medical schools or increases in the student intake to existing schools may do little to relieve the underlying problem if new graduates display the same geographical preferences as their predecessors. We do not know of any democratic country which has the power to direct doctors to work in a given area. However, as we note later on, countries may have available to them a range of financial incentives to increase the desirability of practising in certain areas.

Levers for government intervention

In all developed countries, including the United States, medical education is heavily supported by governments, either as part of a general subsidy of university activities or as a result of specific allocations associated with the training of doctors. Thus governments in these countries are able to influence the supply of doctors by financial means of a variety of kinds even where they do not have explicit health workforce planning policies. These funding mechanisms may include financial support to universities for the establishment of new medical schools or the provision of scholarship support for students, which is some times conditional on their agreement to work for a period of time after qualification in an under-serviced area.

Distribution between types of practitioners

The other important medical workforce issue is the distribution of the medically qualified between the various specialties, including general or family practice. Thus it is possible for shortages, somehow defined, to exist for certain specialist areas, such as orthopaedic surgery or psychiatry, when the overall supply of medical graduates is adequate. These possible shortages may reflect the intakes into the specialist training programs, often controlled by the specialist group or College, being restricted, inadequate funding by governments of the requisite training places which are usually hospital-based, or a lesser degree of attractiveness of the medical specialty to new graduates.

The possible methods of medical workforce policy ideally need then to address both the optimum total size and the distribution of the total amongst all specialties. In the latter respect it has been argued that the domination of American medicine by specialists may have contributed to the higher costs of health expenditure in the United States as compared with Britain and other OECD countries where general or family practitioners play the role of 'gatekeeper' (Grumbach, 2002a, b).

However, the tools currently available for establishing the optimum size and composition of the medical workforce are surprisingly limited and generally inadequate in relation to the importance of being able to get the numbers right, bearing in mind both the economic and patient welfare implications. It hardly needs to be emphasised that the size of the medical workforce is one of the most important determinants of total health care expenditure and of the satisfaction that the populations serviced have in their health care systems. (However, the work of Cooper has pointed to the opposite link between health care expenditure and the size of the health care workforce, as we discuss below.)

Rapid shifts between perceived shortages and surpluses

In many countries recently there have been considerable shifts in health workforce planning policies based on what has been a changed perception that no large surpluses but shortages of medical personnel exist. These changes may reflect a number of factors including the diversity of methods used for defining and measuring these concepts, the greater availability of the basic statistics required for determining the existing size of the workforce, and unexpected shifts in the composition of this workforce.

An important aspect of the latter is the greatly increased proportion of women entering and graduating from medical schools which seems to have been common in all developed countries in recent times. Many women choose to work for long periods on a part-time basis after becoming qualified. In addition, it may be the case that male doctors are also choosing to work fewer hours.

The United States

In the United States, conclusions drawn about the future trends in the size of the medical workforce up to the mid-nineteen nineties from health workforce planning studies were that an increased surplus of doctors would soon emerge (Cooper, 2004). The paper by Cooper, an MD, reviewing the American situation described how in that country for two decades health planners had 'forecasted impending physician surpluses and policy decisions related to medical schools and residency programs have been based on such expectations'. Indeed, in a paper Cooper himself published in 1995 he forecast a surplus of 31,000 doctors in the United States by the year 2000 and 62,000 in 2010 (Cooper, 1995).

Similarly, Goodman and his colleagues using a benchmarking approach had concluded that a surplus of doctors existed in most regions of the United States (Goodman et al., 1996). This position was supported by an editorial in the same issue of the journal by Schroeder who quoted a number of 'common sense' indicators pointing to an over-provision of doctors in the United States in 1996. These included incomes falling after decades of steady growth, a decline in job advertisements for specialists, poor job satisfaction and newly trained physicians finding it difficult to secure full-time employment (Schroeder, 1996).

In his 2004 paper Cooper indicated that the problem for the United States had become a looming shortage of doctors. He forecast that by 2020 this shortage would be about 200,000 in the absence of remedial measures. His more recent forecasts were based on the use of a different method of projecting the 'demand' for medical services using explicit economic criteria. (The various methods used in forecasting requirements for medical services and their limitations are discussed in more detail later.)

Cooper asserted, moreover, that there had been several reasons why the earlier estimates in the United States of a surplus of doctors had not been borne out including in his view the inappropriate methods used to make the estimates, notably the benchmarking method, the increased feminisation of the workforce and reductions in the working hours of doctors. Some physician organisations in the United States in their later reviews of the medical workforce have also concluded that the more recent evidence pointed to a growing shortage (Council on Graduate Medical Education, 2003a, b).

Australia

In Australia, where the federal and state governments have taken a more active role in forecasting medical workforce requirements than their counterparts in the United States, a similar reversal of earlier concerns about the growth of a surplus has occurred in the last 10 years. Policies up to the mid 1990s had focused on methods of reducing the size of the medical workforce with the politically easiest option being to limit the number of overseas graduates allowed to practice (Australian Medical Workforce Advisory Committee, 1996). Reducing the number of medical schools or restricting the intakes into these schools were not viewed as politically feasible options in that period.

Not surprisingly the Deans of medical schools had bitterly opposed the Federal government's proposals put forward in 1995 to cut intakes. In this period Australian health economists and senior government officials had achieved a broad consensus about the existence of SID, and the thrust to restrict the number of doctors was seen as a potentially useful device for containing health expenditure increases.

By 2003, however, the Australian Medical Workforce Advisory Committee (AMWAC, 2003) had concluded that fewer doctors were available than were needed and a number of new medical schools were established or foreshadowed with substantial federal government financial assistance. The shift in official policy may have been related to the change in federal government in

1996 from a social democratic (Labor) government to a conservative government which was less inclined to give credence to the role of SID in health care issues. The composition of AMWAC also changed considerably in the post 1996 period with more emphasis being given to medical advisors.

A great deal of useful data on the characteristics of the Australian medical workforce has been published by the Australian Institute of Health and Welfare (2004). As we indicate in our international review of health services data in Chapter 10 (Table 10.8), the latest value of the ratio in Australia of 2.5 practising physicians per thousand of population is somewhat lower than the median OECD value of approximately 3 but slightly higher than the comparable US and UK values.

Britain and other countries

The NHS Medical Workforce Standing Advisory Committee in its Report (1997) emphasised the rise in health care demand, and rising expectations from the public for the quantity and quality of medical services. The Report also referred to reduced working hours for junior doctors mandated by the European Working Time Directive which sets a limit of 48 hours to the working week of doctors in training in the European Union (EU). The directive is to be implemented in the NHS by 2009.

Recent NHS policies have had the objective of increasing the size of the medical workforce along with total expenditure on health care (Maynard and Walker, 1997; Walker and Maynard, 2003) following on the belief in the early 1990s that there was a surplus of medical personnel. Maynard and Walker pointed to the changes in the NHS medical workforce from one in which there was a predominance of males in full time positions until retirement at 65 years of age or more to one in which part time employment and early retirement were increasing. Consistent with the pattern in other countries more female doctors contributed to the medical workforce with the number of male and female medical students having become approximately equal by the mid 1990s. Maynard and Walker stated that NHS policy was based on the view that there was a shortage of doctors and an increased intake of medical students had commenced.

Walker and Maynard's work is also of considerable interest in deploring the reliance in medical workforce planning on mechanistic forecasting and ignoring economic determinants. They emphasised the need in planning the size of the medical workforce, in the context of international shortages of doctors, to reduce practice variations, and generate outcome improvements and skill-mix changes as essential ingredients in the process.

In 2000 a report of the Department of Health on the NHS improvement plan, the workforce contribution was envisaged as being based on a 'bottom up' approach. This will involve a move away from centrally prescribed national targets on medical and nursing numbers to rely on credible local plans that maximise the capacity to support delivery. However, the Department of Health would continue to provide national assumptions and models that can be adapted to local circumstances (Department of Health, 2000).

In Britain the number of doctors per 1000 of population has been substantially lower than in most other developed European countries, with the latest value recorded being 2.2 as compared with the median OECD figure previously quoted of about 3 per 1000 of population. Whether the reliance on salaried service and capitation rather than FFS as the predominant method of doctor remuneration has contributed to this outcome remains an open question.

In other EU countries there has appeared to be a mixed picture of surpluses and shortages of the medical workforce. In the late 1990s it was reported that surpluses as reflected in unemployment had emerged in several European countries, including Italy, Austria, Germany, Spain and the Netherlands.

In Canada concerns had been expressed about the uneven distribution of the medical workforce between metropolitan and the far-flung rural areas of that country. The report of two health economists, Barer and Stoddart (1991), to the Federal/Provincial/Territorial Conference of Deputy Ministers of Health recommended a number of measures to stabilise the physician supply in relation to the growth of the population. Their recommendation to cut the intake of medical school students was acted upon with a reduction of 10 per cent in the intake in 1993–94. However, in 1999 the Canadian Medical Association called for a substantial increase in intakes to all medical schools.

In responding to this request Stoddart and Barer accepted that there were serious problems in the availability of doctors and that these shortages now extended to medium-sized cities (Stoddart and Barer, 1999). They denied, however, that the cuts in intakes in the earlier period that they had recommended were the main cause of the shortages. They criticised the associations of doctors for their reluctance to embrace new models of care that had the potential to reduce the need for medically qualified personnel. These included a greater use of nurse practitioners, the creation of multi-professional health centres and alternatives to FFS doctor remuneration.

They claimed that an exclusive focus on increased medical school enrolments was unlikely to resolve the problems without an evaluation of all aspects of medical services issues. They also made the important point that an increase in medical school enrolments is not reflected in an increase in the stock of doctors until about eight years later.

Reasons for the shifting perceptions

It is evident that judgements about the existence of current shortages and surpluses of medical personnel have often relied partly on the subjective perceptions of health management staff, policy advisors and medical associations. In these circumstances anecdotal evidence capable of varying interpretations may be an important driver of policy, and the rapid shifts in perceptions that we have emphasised have taken place in many countries in relatively recent years. In the absence of further hard evidence we can only speculate about the influence of political and financial forces in the changes in judgements of governments and of medical associations.

In countries such as Britain, Canada and Australia where many aspects of the health care system are the direct financial responsibility of governments, it may be possible to link the shift from the notion of a surplus to a shortage of doctors to wider issues of the fiscal performance and policies of the economies in question. Following on the periods of concern with the avoidance of budget deficits that characterised the 1980s and the earlier 1990s, leading to an emphasis on cost containment regarding all public sector expenditure including health, the more buoyant budgetary situation of recent years may have led to greater priority being given to augmenting public sector services.

A greater voice for consumers in health matters has been fostered by governments in the 2000s and this may have had the possibly unexpected consequence of bringing to bear additional pressures to overcome perceived inadequacies in the health care systems, including those of medical services, of many countries.

The priorities of medical associations

The apparent changes in the priorities of medical associations are also of considerable interest in an under-researched area. In the earlier period the limited amount of evidence from several countries, notably the United States, Canada, Australia and Britain suggests that these associations were happy at least to acquiesce in restricting the number of students entering medical schools, or undertaking specialist training programs, as a consequence of being concerned to protect the economic interests of their membership. However, what appears to have been a surprisingly rapid shift in this position in the mid to late 1990s does not lend itself to any simple interpretation. Our purpose in spelling out all these difficulties, and unresolved issues, is not to deny the possibility of adequate and relatively objective and evidence-based medical workforce planning in what is obviously a complex area. However, they point to important reasons why the results differ considerably from one study to another over time in the same country, or between different countries. They also underscore the reasons why some analysts have sought better methods of undertaking health workforce planning exercises than those that have existed in the past.

Planning methods

Benchmarking and doctor-to-population ratios

Either implicitly or explicitly in the studies of the existing state of the medical workforce, that is, whether a surplus or deficit exists, the current numbers are related to a standard for the requirements for doctors. In the various reports on medical workforce planning it is clear that most countries have relied in the past on what has been described as the benchmarking approach to the estimation of requirements. The use of different methods, as we suggested previously, has no doubt contributed to the varying results about the existence of surpluses and shortages in the workforce.

In summary, benchmarking is based on the use of a standard ratio of doctors to population and the application of this standard to the population and doctor numbers in the country or area which is the focus of attention. However, even using this broad method there is scope for differing results and conclusions to be derived. The objective of studies may be to analyse the countrywide situation, or that of specific geographical regions, notably metropolitan and rural areas. In addition, studies may be undertaken to draw conclusions about medical workforce categories, for example, specialist and primary care or general practitioners. Underlying all these uses is the problem of what are the criteria and methods to be deployed in setting the standard.

Sources of the standards and applications

In setting the standards two approaches have been adopted. One is to review the evidence from other countries about the ratio of total medical personnel to population numbers where there is evidence that the values reflect a desirable relationship between 'supply' and 'demand' as perceived in that country. Population numbers need to be adjusted or standardised to reflect any differences in the age and sex distributions between the two countries. Alternatively, the existing ratio in the home country, or in certain areas and systems, may be taken as reflecting a desirable benchmark, and the focus then is on projecting the current numbers into the future.

Cooper has argued that in the past what he has described as time and task projections have been used frequently to establish these standards, and to forecast future requirements (Cooper, 2004). The time and task projections have been taken over from industrial applications where studies of the processes used in manufacturing have been applied by measuring the activities that need to be undertaken to achieve specific tasks, and then aligning these with the time taken by the workforce members to perform the tasks.

As Cooper pointed out, however, medical tasks are too complex to make the approach feasible in medical workforce studies. With a multiplicity of diseases and of types of patients and medical personnel the scope for errors is undoubtedly considerable. In more recent years, prior to Cooper's criticisms, the method seems to have fallen into disfavour amongst medical workforce planners.

Goodman and his colleagues (1996) have used a different approach to benchmarking in which the standards are set by reference to the doctor to population ratios in selected contexts, notably those in specific areas where Health Maintenance Organisations (HMOs) operate, or other areas where the stock of doctors is relatively modest, without any detrimental effects on the populations served being detectable. Cooper's criticisms of benchmarking do not appear to extend to this method.

Projections of the size of the medical workforce

The projections of the size of the medical workforce, as undertaken in most countries, take the existing level and estimate the number of doctors becoming qualified each year, attrition as a result of retirements, net gains or losses from migration to and from other countries, and changes in the working hours of physicians. Projections of population numbers are also of critical importance to determine future ratios of doctors to population. These projections may then be related to the standards for requirements that are judged to be relevant at a future date.

As we indicated previously, this approach represents the application to the medical workforce of the most popular model of health workforce planning studies. It is evident that from this perspective medical workforce planning becomes largely a statistical exercise where an awareness of traditional economic criteria and models is of limited relevance. This may provide a further explanation of the relative neglect of health workforce planning by most health economists.

Statistical requirements

It is clear that a good deal of judgement must be exercised in each workforce projection scenario. Moreover, an adequate set of statistics and definitions must be available to establish the baseline doctor and population numbers.

The availability of this basic data varies widely from country to country, and a good deal of preliminary effort may need to be devoted to acquiring or generating the statistical data. The censuses of the population normally conducted regularly in most countries usually cover items such as occupation and industry, but the results are often reported in insufficient detail for workforce planning purposes.

Registration requirements for medical and other personnel are the best source of accessible data for workforce planning but these may need to be supplemented by special surveys, in particular to determine whether those who are registered are actively practising medicine, and in what capacity.

It has also been notorious in the past that population projections, an essential item in planning for the future, may be very inaccurate when sudden shifts in fertility experience take place. The requirements for workforce planning obviously become even more demanding where the estimates are used on an area or a medical workforce type-specific basis or a combination of both.

The 'facilitation' of workforce size by economic variables

The most important new development in methods has been creation of a model of the determinants of medical workforce requirements that relies heavily on economic indicators and projections. As we indicated above the recent work by Cooper illustrates this new method (Cooper, 2004; Cooper et al., 2002). In outline it is assumed that the main determinant of workforce requirements is the capacity of the economy to meet the costs of the given stock of physicians. Thus the level and changes in GDP are seen as central to each country's ability to provide additional health care services.

The international empirical evidence to support this hypothesis is compelling when account is taken of the lagged nature of the response of the workforce size to the changes in the economy (Reinhardt et al., 2004). The evidence of the relationship between the size of GDP and how much is devoted to the health services in individual countries is also consistent with the hypothesis. Part of the reason for the lagged response of the medical workforce to the expansion of the economy is the time lapse between the training of additional physicians and the contributions they make to the medical workforce.

Cooper argues that the relationship between the size of the economy and that of the medical workforce should be interpreted as a 'permissive' one rather than implying a direct causal relationship. From this perspective the 'demand' for medical services is seen as being almost insatiable, driven by technological developments and consumer demand, and the constraint on this is determined by the size of the economy and the willingness of governments and others to support the provision of health services. Thus the projections of the required size of the medical workforce should be based on projections of the future trends in the economy as measured by GDP.

He recognises that the waning desire of members of the medical workforce to commit themselves to full time hours and the age at which they retire, together with the increasing proportion of female graduates will impinge on the projected shortage of doctors via a diminution of the effective stock of medical practitioners. An effect of an opposite nature is the extent to which other health services personnel, notably nurses, may take over some of the current roles of the medically qualified.

The model of the economic factors setting an upper limit to the size of the medical workforce is subject to important qualifications as a guide to policy-making. In particular, it ignores the issue of whether the number of medical staff facilitated by the size of the economy is conducive to achieving an optimum allocation of resources from a social welfare perspective, for example, when account is taken of SID.

Moreover, Grumbach (2002a, b) has criticised the approach of Cooper for potentially perpetuating the unhealthy domination of American medicine by specialists. Reinhardt (2002) pointed to the possible confusion of cause and effect in the Cooper model, and emphasised the daunting task of estimating surpluses or shortages one or two decades into the future. However, he commended the work of Cooper and his colleagues as a welcome contribution to a long dormant debate.

The overall approach by Cooper of basing workforce planning on the projected growth of the economy, with some adjustments, appears to us to provide a better starting point for policy interventions than the attempt to base them on arbitrary standards and projections normally derived from past experience.

It should also be noted that the emergence in the United States and elsewhere of a projected shortage of medical staff which flows from the Cooper model is consistent with the information derived from other sources such as the perceptions of medical school deans and of medical organisations. Despite the biases in these perceptions to which we have referred above they cannot be wholly discounted in policy-planning exercises.

Flat of the curve Medicine and SID

It has long been recognised that the provision of extra medical services beyond a certain point may lead to little or no improvement in the health status of the population being serviced. This phenomenon, which we discussed in Chapter 5, is referred to as flat of the curve medicine. In the context of planning the size of the medical workforce it is relevant to examine whether this possibility may set a limit to future expansions in doctor numbers.

The basing of medical workforce policies on the Cooper-type projections also ignores the role of SID, leading to the same result of the provision of additional medical services that do no more than augment the aggregate incomes of doctors, especially as we have noted previously where FFS is the predominant method of remuneration. Further evidence on both these phenomena is provided in the study of Fisher and his colleagues as reported below.

Cooper recognised these potential objections to basing medical workforce planning on estimates of the future growth of the economy and is at some pains to downplay the importance of SID, possibly based on a somewhat biased account of the evidence for this phenomenon.

New US evidence on practice variations and SID

As we indicated earlier, of relevance to medical workforce planning are the relationships between the size and other characteristics of the medical workforce, health expenditure and measures of health care use, and quality and outcomes. For Medicare patients in the United States with diagnoses for colorectal cancer, hip fractures, and acute myocardial infarction, these relationships have been studied by Fisher and his colleagues (Fisher et al., 2003a, b).

In this carefully conducted multi-disciplinary study using regional data they were able to establish that patients in Medicare higher-spending regions received 60 per cent more services. Adjustments were made for differences in the health status of the patients and in the price of services between the regions. The increased utilisation in the higher spending regions was associated with more frequent doctor visits, especially in the inpatient setting, more frequent tests and minor (but not major) procedures as well as increased use of specialists. Quality of care, access to care and outcomes in the higher spending regions were no better on most measures (Fisher et al., 2003b).

The results of this study lend further support for both the SID hypothesis and the 'flat of the curve' relationship between increased provision of medical services and health outcomes. Their implications for medical workforce planning are potentially considerable. As Fisher and his colleagues pointed out, a reduction in the utilisation and expenditure of the higher expenditure regions to those of the lower ones has the capacity to produce enormous savings for the Medicare budget. However, a distinction needs to be drawn between the shorter term and longer term implications for workforce planning.

In the shorter term, which in this context might be 10–20 years, it is unlikely that any substantial changes in physician and hospital behaviour that would reduce utilisation in the high expenditure areas might take place. Overall shortages as defined and measured in the Cooper studies are likely to persist and require remedial action to alleviate. In the longer term the pressures to constrain cost increases may again become overwhelming and information of the kind generated by the Fisher study may gain favour amongst all the stakeholders and policy-makers.

Implications for other countries

The implications of the Fisher study for other countries are several. First, the attempt should be made to replicate the research elsewhere, including in those countries where FFS is not the predominant method of doctor remuneration. Second, the data used in the study might serve as a guide to organising and augmenting the information being generated in other countries about the quality and costs of health services. Third, it would be desirable to extend the diagnoses and procedures examined to others, and to extend the coverage of patient ages beyond the 65 years and over group who make up the great majority of the US Medicare population. The latter process may be more feasible in those countries, such as Canada, that have a single insurer and complete coverage of the whole population.

Doctor remuneration

The methods of doctor remuneration have important implications for medical workforce planning and for many of the characteristics of the health care systems across countries. The predominant method of payment may influence considerably the incentives faced by doctors in treating patients. For example, some payment arrangements may lead to medical practitioners working longer or shorter hours and spending more or less time with individual patients. The relative attractiveness of medicine as a profession, and hence the quality and quantity of practitioners likely to become available, may also be affected in principle by the payment mechanism.

As a consequence, the desirable and achievable size of the medical workforce is likely to be influenced in any individual country by the predominant method of doctor remuneration. In this section we review the various methods and the advantages and disadvantages of each, how the fees and other forms of remuneration are set under the different service provision and financial arrangements. The incentives for doctor behaviour and the consequences of these for the production of medical services are of central importance in the context of this chapter.

The emergence of the predominant method in each country seems to be a product of a number of historical circumstances in which the preferences of governments, the medical profession and the populations interact. In no cases would it appear that the most common method is the product of some rational and objective process of evaluation unhindered by political and other constraints. We explore further in Chapter 10 how these and other factors combine to determine the style of health care delivery, health insurance and financing that characterise each country.

The methods of paying doctors: advantages and disadvantages

The three most common means of paying for medical services worldwide are salaried, capitation and FFS. In all countries some doctors are remunerated on a salaried basis, especially in areas such as public health, teaching, research and in managerial roles. However, the role of salaried medical service may also extend to direct patient care especially for junior medical staff in hospitals where other methods of payment for these services may prevail elsewhere in the country. The doctor is being paid for his time which may be provided on a part-time or full-time basis. The rate of payment per unit of time may be determined in a number of ways which are dependent on the overall system of industrial relations prevailing in each country. These may include collective bargaining or individual workplace contracts.

For the employer the use of salaried medical staff has the advantage of making budgeting predictable and of affording a measure of control over the quantity and quality of the services provided. There are advantages for the medical staff also in that fringe benefits such as superannuation and leave entitlements are normally included in the employment contract. Perhaps more importantly, the doctor is relieved of many of the administrative and financial responsibilities and their associated risks faced by his colleagues in other modes of practice.

For doctors with direct patient care roles the salaried mode, where his/her income is usually not related to the volume of patients treated, the risk of supplier-induced demand is minimised but not necessarily eliminated – there may be other incentives for the doctor to treat more patients such as professional standing with colleagues. However, there may be an incentive in salaried service for the under-provision of patient care, especially where the level of demand is high. It is probably the case that a shift to the greater use of salaried direct patient care would be associated with fewer patient contacts and costs, than the alternative modes of doctor remuneration. The implications for the quality of care are unclear. More care does not necessarily produce better outcomes as Fisher's work clearly established for the United States.

The second method of doctor remuneration for direct patient care is that of capitation. In this method medical services are paid for according to the total number of patients for whom the doctor is responsible. In this situation the medical staff act as independent contractors to governments or insurance companies and the payment per patient is fixed, normally collectively, by negotiation with the funding agency. In the pure capitation model there is no relationship between the number of patients actually treated and the total income of the doctors in any period. Thus the incentives for a lower provision of medical services to the patient population are much the same as in the salaried mode. The retention of their role as independent contractors will be perceived as an advantage as compared with salaried payment by some medical staff.

The most important example of the use of capitation applies to the payment of general practitioners in the British NHS where each practice has a list number assigned which determines the capitation size for payment purposes. However, this mode has been combined in the NHS with some FFS payments designed to provide incentives for the provision of preventive and similar services.

The third principal payment method is FFS where each type of service is charged for based on a fee scale. The latter is designed to correspond with the nature and complexity of the medical service provided. However, in different countries there is considerable variation in how the fee scales are determined and the requirements, if any, for medical practitioners to adhere to the scale. In Canada, for example, with provincial and federal government taxation funded health insurance program there is a legal obligation on doctors not to charge above the governmentally determined fee schedule for all services reimbursed under the program. In Canada most inpatient and out-of-hospital medical services are paid for using FFS.

In Australia, where the government-funded health insurance scheme drew on elements of the Canadian system in its design, there is no requirement of doctors to adopt the fee structure determined by the Federal government agency for health insurance purposes. Further details of the Australian and Canadian payment systems are set out in Chapter 10.

Where doctors have had a choice they have strongly favoured the FFS method of remuneration. This preference is coupled with the fact that it is almost exclusively combined with doctors retaining the right to operate as individual entrepreneurs, and often to set their fees with a minimum of health insurance or governmental intervention. A further advantage claimed for the FFS mode is that it facilitates the acquisition of greater rewards for the more highly skilled members of the profession and those who may be prepared to work harder than their colleagues. However, it might be noted that in the British NHS, where specialists in hospitals are employed on a salaried basis, additional payments are made to those who are assessed as possessing special skills.

From the perspectives of governments and patients the main disadvantage lies in the greater potential for SID as compared with the other options for doctor remuneration. Moreover, FFS is usually associated with higher incomes for doctors, especially for procedural specialists, but the international evidence for this is patchy especially since FFS is the most common method of doctor remuneration in the majority of comparable developed countries.

In respect of medical workforce issues, FFS, and the expected high incomes on qualifying, serves to make a career in medicine an attractive option for those embarking on university studies, who are able to meet the usually demanding entry requirements. The supply of doctors is not constrained by a shortage of people who aspire to enter the career in all or most countries.

A comprehensive review of the issues associated with the various methods of paying doctors was provided by Donaldson and Gerard (2005) and Robinson (2001). They stressed the point that a mixture of methods in each country may represent the best set of arrangements, since each type of remuneration, with its different incentives, may be relevant where the circumstances and the policy objectives vary. For example, FFS may be less compatible with cooperative relationships between doctors and the fostering of evidence-based medicine, than capitation.

Fee schedules and their bases

It is evident that in FFS systems the fees charged by medical practitioners are of critical importance in determining their incomes, the differentials in income between the various specialties and the costs to insurers, governments and patients. All of these factors, in turn, are likely to have important implications for the supply of doctors, especially on a specialist-specific basis. High fees and incomes for procedural specialists relative to general practitioners are likely to contribute to shortages of the latter group and the possible over-provision of services by the former group. In the context of the Cooper model relatively high medical fees may reduce the economic capacity of countries to support increases in the stock of medical practitioners.

The practices about fee setting vary considerably from country to country according to local government legislation, and arrangements established largely by convention such as negotiation processes between medical associations and insurers. For health insurance purposes in government-funded systems a fee schedule is normally established which determines the rate of reimbursement of each specific medical charge.

We know of no international study dealing with the bases and origins of fee schedules in a number of different countries. In Australia in the early seventies, in a major revision of the (private) health insurance arrangements that previously existed, a system of 'common fees' was instituted. As the name indicates the fees charged by practitioners were surveyed and for each item identified in a classification of medical consultations and surgical interventions, the most commonly occurring fee was set as the amount to be reimbursed by the government agency under the then prevailing health insurance system.

Major adjustments in areas such as pathology or laboratory medicine were implemented subsequently where automated procedures had clearly rendered the earlier fees outmoded. There has also been provision in the Australian system for the annual updating of the average fee levels. However, it is our perception that the *relativities* between the fees have remained largely unchanged in the last 35 years. We suspect that similar origins of fee schedules may exist in other countries.

Resource-based relative value scales

In the United States, disquiet about the fee relativities, especially the much greater rewards for procedural specialists as compared with other doctors and the possible consequences of this situation for the optimum distribution of the medical workforce between the various branches of the profession, led to the search for a more rational and acceptable basis for fee setting than currently existed. Relative value scales had been developed in the United States by state medical societies as a guide for their memberships about the fees they might charge. However, the major initiative in this area was initiated in connection with the federally funded Medicare program for the aged in that country.

The studies to establish a resource-based relative value scale (RBRVS) in the United States, with federal government funding, were undertaken by a team led by Hsiao and his colleagues from Harvard University (Hsiao and Stason, 1979; Hsiao, 1987; Hsiao and Braun, 1988). In essence, the method consisted of surveying medical practitioners about their estimates of the relative intensity and complexity of a number of medical and surgical activities, procedures and other doctor/patient interactions.

Careful analysis and interpretation of the results led to a consensus amongst stakeholders that the relative value scale that emerged could form an improved basis for the federal government setting its fees for reimbursement of the doctors for services rendered to patients who were eligible for Medicare benefits. The use of the RBRVS commenced in 1992 and was subsequently phased in slowly.

The nursing workforce

Nurses form the largest single group in the health services workforce in all countries which are able to provide these data. Shortage of nurses which surface regularly in most countries pose special problems especially for hospitals where the majority of nurses are employed. The surplus and shortage status of the nursing workforce until very recently has been much less seriously researched than that of the medical workforce, and much of the published information is derived from US sources.

It is of interest to note that the classical article on nursing workforce issues was produced by a health economist (Yett, 1970). Yett was concerned with the shortage of nurses in the United States that had emerged in the 60s and earlier. He examined the possible definitions of a shortage from an economics standpoint, and the work on workforce issues undertaken by other economists, including the differing interpretations of the meaning of a shortage.

Since Yett's work was undertaken, there does not seem to have been much interest amongst economists in the nursing workforce. There are, however, welcome signs that this lack of interest is in the process of changing as the material quoted below indicates.

Special problems associated with nursing

Several characteristics of the nursing workforce are relevant to the planning of nursing requirements. First, there has been in most developed countries a relatively rapid change in the education of 'registered' nurses from the apprenticeship mode and in-service training in hospitals to a requirement for the acquisition of a tertiary educational qualification. It should be noted, however, in interpreting the international literature on the nursing workforce that the terminology concerning the types of nurses and their required educational standards varies considerably from country to country.

Second, the upgrading of the educational requirements for registered nurses has gone hand in hand with a lesser degree of influence of medical personnel on the content of the educational programs. In addition, the improved education of nurses has contributed to their no longer being contented as a group with their traditional role as the 'handmaidens' of the doctors. At the same time as the career opportunities for women have expanded dramatically in most countries the recruitment into nursing, traditionally a largely female occupation, has had to compete with occupations, including medicine and allied health services such as physiotherapy, opening up for women and other occupations outside health.

Third, there are more opportunities for the substitution of nurses with lower educational requirements for the more highly trained registered nurses, increasingly with degree level qualifications. The existence of several streams of nurses is a reflection of the fact that the job tasks of nurses can be segmented into those requiring greater skills, such as those meeting the needs of patients in intensive care and cardiac units in acute hospitals, and those responsible for the lesser skilled tasks of caring, for example, for many chronically ill and aged patients in nursing homes.

However, an under-researched area in studies of the nursing workforce is the determination of the optimum skill mix in the various venues where nurses are employed. The possibility of substituting nurses for medical staff in some activities, subject to quality of care safeguards, should also be noted in this regard.

Fourth, a constant theme in the more detailed analytical studies of the nursing workforce in several countries is the ageing of the population of nurses as we indicate in the summary of these studies we present later.

Fifth, the reliance of many developed countries on the importing of qualified nurses from other countries, including those recruited from the underdeveloped world to meet shortages, poses troubling ethical and possibly quality of care issues. It might be noted that similar concerns apply to the recruitment of medical staff from these countries.

Recent workforce studies

The United States

The US research literature has dealt with such issues as the use of benchmarking to plan the number of nurses required in individual states and regions based on the use of national ratios of nurses to population (Malloch et al., 2003), and the dissatisfaction of nurses with their roles and treatment contributing to their exit from the workforce and exacerbating shortages (Mills and Blaesing, 2000). The paper by Mills and Blaesing is of interest in that it highlights the cyclical nature of the emergence of shortages and surpluses in the nursing workforce, based on recent US experience. However, they were not able to offer an explanation of the causes of the cycles except to note that these are 'complex and multidimensional'.

The most important recent workforce study emanating from the United States is that of Buerhaus and his colleagues (Buerhaus et al., 2000). This carefully conducted multi-disciplinary study involved the co-operation of a team led by a professor of nursing, which also included an economist and a health policy analyst. The research focused on trends in the age of the nursing workforce and the implications of these trends for the effective size of this workforce in the future.

The data they presented showed that the average age of working registered nurses (RNs) in terms of full-time equivalents in the United States had increased from 37.4 years to 41.9 years between 1983 and 1998. Even more striking was that over the same time period the proportion of the RN workforce younger than 30 years declined from 30.3 per cent to 12.1 per cent. They noted several possible reasons for these changed age characteristics of RNs, including the factors referred to earlier such as increased opportunities for women undertaking other careers which had depleted the number of young women entering nursing programs on completion of secondary education.

The model used in the study was based on three factors, namely: the numbers in the total population born in a given year who had reached a specified age, the propensity of individuals in the population and age groups (cohorts) to work as RNs and the relative propensity of RNs to work at a given age. The parameters of the model were then estimated based on data from a variety of sources for 1973–98. Using these estimated parameters and population projections, the size of the RN workforce in the United States was projected for each year from 2001 to 2020. The results suggested that the number of RNs per capita will peak in 2007 but then decline over time.

The authors of the report indicated that the method of projecting the number of nurses was based on the assumption that in the future nurses will enter and leave the profession at the set rates incorporated in the estimation based on past experience. A further assumption was that economy-wide factors, such as the ability to support higher salaries for nurses, will not change in such a way as to make nursing relatively more attractive as an occupation.

Finally, the paper related the projected estimates to those of future requirements for RNs as established by the Federal government's Health Resources and Services Administration. These comparisons indicated that by 2020 the projected size of the registered nursing workforce would be 20 per cent lower than the projected requirements. Up to 2007 there would be an approximate matching of supply and requirements.

In the latter regard it is of interest to note that in a recent paper Buerhaus (2005) has recognised the existence of a shortage of RNs in the United States since 1998. The difference in the estimated shortages and the timing of their occurrences reflect, in part, the fact that a new and increased set of projected nursing requirements had been established by the US Health Resources and Services Administration.

Australia

There has been a multiplicity of studies recently from a number of countries which have concluded that shortages of nursing staff would worsen in the absence of appropriate policy changes. In Australia, the reports of four national nursing workforce investigations have been summarised recently by the AHWAC. Despite the fact that different methods were used in each study to determine both projected requirements and the size of the nursing workforce a consensus emerged that a shortage of nursing staff currently existed and that this would increase in the future (AHWAC, 2004a, b).

In its report on these and other studies from states and territories AHWAC (2004a) has provided a useful review of the methods and models of projecting the size of the nursing workforce and with projecting the requirements for nursing personnel. In common with other health workforce studies, the terms 'supply' and 'demand' are applied to what we have indicated above should be regarded as the stock of nurses and the requirement or need for nurses.

Comprehensive statistics about the nursing workforce in Australia are compiled by the Australian Institute of Health and Welfare (2003). These are up-dated regularly and can form the basis for more detailed analysis of current issues and problems.

Other countries

Similarities between the shortage situation in Canada and Australia have been discussed in a paper by Duffield and O'Brien-Pallas (2002). Buchan (2002) in an editorial in the *British Medical Journal* has summarised the international situation as indicating a global shortage of nurses. He states that 'The United States, United Kingdom, Australia and Canada and other countries have an ageing nursing workforce, caring for increasing numbers of elderly people.' In this paper he has reported also that in October 2001 government chief nurses and other delegates from 66 countries had discussed how to deal with a common problem, the global growth of nursing shortages.

Buchan and Caiman (2004) provided additional information on the global shortage of nurses and its implications for changing policy frameworks as the problems pose major challenges for all health care systems.

From an economics perspective, as we noted above, when an increased supply of new entrants to an occupation is sought, an increase in the income returns to the group, the salaries paid, is required. It is of interest to note that this solution does not appear in the four initiatives, according to Buchan, that policy-makers are adopting to solve the nursing shortage problem. These are: improving the retention of nurses by providing a more favourable working environment; broadening the recruitment base from a narrow range of younger women to other groups; attracting back those qualified as nurses who have left this workforce, for example by scholarship support for retraining programs; and importing nurses from other countries.

Buchan regards these strategies as being limited in so far as they focus on nursing as the problem. He rightly regards the shortages as symptoms of wider health systems problems, including the likelihood that health systems do not function to enable nurses to use their skills effectively. However, whilst he mentions salary-related matters such as nurses expecting to be fairly rewarded, the use of salary rewards as an incentive to help retain nurses and to attract qualified nurses to return to the profession are not referred to as part of a system-wide solution.

The main employers of nursing staff in the United Kingdom are the hospital trusts of the NHS but the wages are set centrally as part of a collective bargaining approach. Since the government has to meet the substantial costs of nursing salaries it is not surprising that increased salaries for nurses have not loomed large in official policy options to overcome shortages of nursing staff in the United Kingdom.

A more central role for the use of incentives for greater efficiency in the clinical labour market has been advocated by the health economists Maynard and Bloor (Bloor and Maynard, 1998, 2003; Maynard and Bloor, 2003). Most of Maynard's recent work has been about the medical workforce in the British NHS including the questionable use of distinction awards for specialist consultants. However, the 1998 editorial in the *British Medical Journal* has important implications for nurses and other non-medical clinical staff.

Bloor and Maynard's argument was that since health services personnel are expected to work as a team, the rewards for distinguished performance should go to the whole team. They suggested that clinical teams could be given clinical and other targets, and that team members be jointly rewarded. Such a process would also provide an incentive for team members to monitor one another's performance.

The application of such a pay reform in countries where the returns to medical staff are based on fee schedules would pose difficulties, and it does not appear that the approach has received official support to date in the NHS. Nevertheless the principle of linking salary payments to performance for non-medical clinicians has much to commend it as a way of achieving greater efficiency in the 'market' for health services.

International study of the perceptions of nurses

An important international nursing study has surveyed more than 43,000 nurses working in 711 hospitals in the United States, Canada, England, Scotland and Germany (Aiken et al., 2001). The study was designed to elicit information about the perceptions of nursing staff about their working environment and the quality of care they delivered together with their job satisfaction, career plans and feelings of 'job burnout'. Information on all these matters has considerable relevance for workforce planning in that it casts light on the reasons for attrition from the nursing workforce and on measures that might be taken to render the profession more attractive.

Low morale and discontent

A consistent feature of the results was the reporting of low morale in all countries with the possible exception of Germany. The percentages of nurses reporting that they were dissatisfied with their present job were 41.0 per cent in the United States, 32.9 per cent in Canada, 36.1 per cent in England, 37.7 per cent in Scotland and 17.4 per cent in Germany.

Especially troubling was the high percentage of nurses who expressed their dissatisfaction with staffing levels, including support services, and their relations with workforce management. Nurses from all countries reported that they performed non-nursing tasks such as delivering and retrieving food trays and other housekeeping duties but that numerous nursing tasks were left undone. Many nurses especially in the North American countries reported their perceptions that the quality of care provided had deteriorated in the previous year.

With regard to the adequacy of salaries there was a good deal of variation between the countries surveyed. For England and Scotland fewer than one in four nurses agreed that their salaries were adequate whilst the corresponding percentages for the United States and Canada were 57 per cent and 69 per cent, respectively. These variations probably reflect higher salary levels in the North American countries relative to those in the NHS. The results also suggest that increases in nurses' salaries in the NHS may have a greater impact in retaining nurses and encouraging new entrants than in North America where, as the authors of the report argue, a restructuring of work tasks and improved human resource management may be of key importance.

Policies to solve the shortage problem

The results of the survey support the proposition that strategies and policies to reduce the shortage of nurses may require several approaches, involving both economic and non-economic incentives, with the emphasis to be given to each set varying from country to country. There is clearly a need for other countries to undertake similar surveys in regard to their own nursing staff to guide future policies. Anecdotal evidence in Australia suggests that similar results would be obtained if the survey were repeated in that country. Our perception is that the Australian results would represent an amalgam of those from North America and Europe.

Statistical requirements for nursing workforce planning

It is evident from the studies we have summarised here that nursing workforce planning exercises require a great deal of statistical data to provide the basis for the drawing of conclusions about the subjects being explored.

The requirements are not unlike those for the medical workforce, discussed earlier, but there are several distinctive features of the nursing workforce that must be emphasised. These include the need to determine attrition rates by age group which we have noted are an important problem for planning exercises about nursing.

In the light of the varying definitions and required qualifications of nursing personnel, there also needs to be more emphasis than in medicine on establishing the categories of nurses, the qualifications required for each category and what arrangements may be present for moving from one category to another. Special surveys of a variety of educational institutions will normally be needed to ascertain the number of newly qualifying personnel of each kind entering the workforce. These surveys would also need to determine what provisions are made for nurses to upgrade their education qualifications.

The type of institution, for example, acute hospital, nursing home or community care, where each person works and its location, metropolitan or rural, will also be relevant for many workforce planning studies of nursing.

Summary and conclusions

In the absence of a free market for members of the workforce, planning the numbers by governments and other stakeholders becomes imperative. The objective of planning is to ensure that population requirements for health services personnel in the future are met by the number of new recruits to the field after taking account of attrition from the workforce. Governments in most countries have the ability via their heavy involvement in funding tertiary education to adjust the number of new entrants to ensure that the appropriate balance is achieved.

For the nursing workforce, a reduction in movements of qualified nurses into non-nursing positions and the possibility of retaining more staff in nursing roles provide other opportunities for augmenting the number of these essential personnel.

However, adjustments to overcome shortages may take a considerable amount of time to achieve this objective in the case of the medical workforce. Planning exercises in this area, moreover, have been complicated considerably by unforeseen changes in the gender composition of the workforce and a general tendency for medical personnel of both sexes to work shorter hours. In addition, projecting workforce numbers and requirements into the future is a difficult process because of errors in the associated population projections.

The setting of standards for workforce numbers, especially for medical personnel, has been based on several different approaches and there is currently a lack of consensus on the best method to apply.

The performance of workforce planning exercises to date has not been impressive in so far as perceptions and estimates of surpluses and shortages of staff in the relevant categories have often changed very rapidly. In recent years, however, concerted efforts have been made in a number of countries to improve the quality of the health workforce data and that of the planning methods.

We also observed that with some important exceptions health economists have not been active in researching this area, and the construction of most of the planning models and their implementation have become the responsibility of other professional groups. These groups have given less emphasis to the use of economic variables, for example, in the case of nursing – improved salary conditions, to overcome existing shortages. Economists have contributed greatly to workforce planning endeavours in other areas of economic activity and undoubtedly have much to offer in the future to health workforce planning endeavours.

FURTHER READING

There is a dearth of suitable material in this field, in spite of the very large number of reports we have quoted. The report of the [Australian] Productivity Commission (2005) on Australia's Health Workforce provides a good summary of the policy, educational and related issues associated with the health workforce, including the need to improve the productivity of the workforce and to overcome existing shortages.

We again recommend the perusal of Chapter 13 of Evans work, *Strained Mercy*, as representing one of the few readily available accounts of the health workforce from an economics perspective.

Discussion questions

- Why do governments and others need to plan the size and distribution of the health workforce rather than leaving these matters to the workings of the market?
- What is meant when the current situation is described as representing a surplus or a shortage of a specific health occupational group?
- Both the medical workforce and the nursing workforce have been perceived recently as shifting rapidly from a surplus to a shortage in many countries. Examine the factors which may have contributed to these perceptions?

- What are the most commonly used methods of projecting the size of a health workforce component into the future? What are the principal limitations of these methods?
- In examining the number of medical and nursing personnel in several countries what factors do we need to take into account to make the comparisons as valid as possible?
- Summarise the methods that might be used to overcome a shortage of nursing personnel where this exists in a given country.

Economic Methods in Health Services Evaluation

8

Background

The need to establish priorities for the provision of health services constantly arises, especially in respect of the funding of health services by governments. Decisions have to be made about which projects and programs should be supported or rejected, in the light of ever present budgetary constraints. In the past these decisions have often been determined by politicians and bureaucrats using guess work, or an undue emphasis on the expected political impact of each proposal. In all countries the results have often led to a considerable waste of resources in the health care sector.

As the costs of health care have escalated governments have been under increased pressure to achieve greater efficiency in their funding of the health services. As we have noted previously they have looked to economists for guidance to establish more objective bases for setting priorities for their expenditure commitments. Economists have been regarded as the best placed disciplinary group from whom advice and analysis could be sought in the devising of policies to resolve these problems of limited resources and increasing demands.

Again our objective in this chapter is not to provide a comprehensive literature review on a field which has grown exponentially in importance in the last ten years, but to highlight those aspects of health economics evaluation which we believe are of greatest relevance, especially for students, managers and clinicians. Our material is designed to highlight both the strengths and weaknesses of current economic evaluation methods and the extent to which they may have influenced policy and decision-making. We recognise, however, that some of the material in this chapter, especially regarding quality adjusted life years (QALYs), is at a somewhat more difficult conceptual level than the discussion in other chapters.

The upsurge in economic evaluations of the health services

Information provided in a recent paper by Neumann and his colleagues, from Harvard University's School of Public Health, indicated the very large expansion of studies in this area (Neumann et al., 2005). In the period from 1998 to 2001 their survey of the literature revealed that 305 articles were published. In the period from 1976 to 1997 only 228 papers were identified.

Their paper also provided evidence that the quality of the studies reported from the most recent period was generally better than those from the earlier years. More cases were published where the costs and quality adjusted life years were discounted to present values and where incremental cost-utility ratios were reported. The authors believed that the improvement reflects in part the recommendations made by the US Panel on Cost-Effectiveness in Health and Medicine to improve the standards for the reporting of studies, especially those using cost-utility analysis (Russell et al., 1996; Weinstein et al., 1996). This panel made very specific and detailed recommendations covering the methods of estimation for all the costs and effectiveness measures used in the cost-effectiveness approach to economic evaluation.

British contributions

It was pointed out in a previous chapter that much of the work of health economists in some countries, notably Britain, has concentrated on project and program evaluation including the devising of methods to improve the available evaluation techniques. A pioneering study from Britain was described in the paper by Alan Williams (1985), referred to in Chapter 3, on the economics of coronary artery bypass grafting (CABG). This study was designed to provide information on whether there was a case for increasing, decreasing or leaving unchanged the rate of performance of CABG in the National Health Service (NHS). The recent literature on evaluation describing current applications has revealed a focus on the evaluation of pharmaceutical drugs, on other clinical treatments and on technology assessment.

Professor Michael Drummond, a leading British health economist, together with a colleague, Alastair McGuire, have edited a comprehensive monograph on economic evaluation (Drummond and McGuire, 2001). Drummond has also played a leading role in the recent establishment of a European network of health economics evaluation databases covering 17 countries (de Pouvourville et al., 2005). These include an existing British database developed at the University of York and available on the internet which summarises recent published reports and also includes comments on the degree to which the studies adhere to desirable reporting principles.

Issues associated with the measurement of health-related quality of life have been reviewed in considerable detail in a chapter by Dolan (2000) in the *Handbook of Health Economics*.

Economic evaluation in clinical areas

In the United States, where some of the ideas for economic evaluation in health and clinical issues originated (Weinstein and Stason, 1982), a recent development has been the active engagement of medical clinicians with economic evaluation in a number of clinical areas. These are documented below.

The changing attitudes to the use of economic evaluation methods in the increasingly important area of mental health have been reviewed by Knapp (1999) who is based in London. It is of interest to note that in a comprehensive review of economics and mental health by Frank and McGuire (1999, 2000) from the United States National Bureau of Economic Research, very little attention was paid to economic evaluation studies as distinct from health insurance issues and the impact of the special characteristics of the mentally ill.

The phases of economic evaluation: clinician and managerial attitudes

The paper by Knapp is also of interest in its conceptualisation of the four stages of historical development which the application of economics to health systems has passed through. His comments are directed at the mental health field but they appear to us to possess a more general relevance to economic evaluation of health services. They provide additional insights into the problems that have been faced in this increasingly important but controversial area.

Knapp identified the first phase as that of 'blissful ignorance'. The fact of scarcity was not recognised; budgetary growth from year to year was assumed to deal with any increases in the demand for resources and perceived shortages. In this stage expenditure data were collected but little effort was undertaken to convert these data into credible cost estimates. Outcome data were also sparse. It is difficult to disagree with Knapp's view that the inevitable result was inefficiency and wasted resources.

In the second stage of unbridled criticism, economics when applied to health issues was aggressively rejected. The prevailing attitude amongst clinicians and managers was that life and health are priceless, and the involvement of economists is to be opposed in all attempts to evaluate health service activities. In this stage where evaluations were undertaken, outcome measures were used exclusively, and resources were allocated according to which group or institution 'shouted loudest' or who indulged in the most vigorous 'shroud waving'. The anti-economics sentiment amongst health professionals in this phase, according to Knapp, may have been stimulated by confusing cost cutting measures by conservative governments, such as the Thatcher administration in Britain, with the aspirations of economists to achieve greater relative cost-effectiveness and efficiency in health service provision.

The next phase according to Knapp's typology was that of undiscriminating utilisation in which the importance of economics is recognised and there is a search for cost information. However, many flawed studies were commissioned, management consultancy firms discovered new profit-making opportunities and decisions about resource allocation were often based on inadequate data and analysis. The studies with an economic component although labelled as 'cost-benefit analysis' incorporated conceptually inappropriate measures of both costs and benefits.

The final phase is that of constructive development in which the mistakes of previous years are recognised, and the standards for economic evaluation are improved to the extent that greater confidence can be accorded to the results and recommendations. There is also a greater likelihood that the design of the evaluation studies is integrated with the policy or clinical evaluations at an early stage. Most importantly, the use of data rather than armchair-based assumptions becomes more widespread with outcome measures being improved to include health-related quality of life and with more comprehensive measures of costs being generated.

The degree to which each of these phases has been encountered, and their timing, in different countries cannot be ascertained with any degree of certainty and it should be borne in mind that Knapp's observations were no doubt conditioned heavily by his experience with the British NHS. Even in the United Kingdom where health economists have been more influential in promoting and undertaking evaluation studies than in other countries there remain important weaknesses which cast some doubt on how much of the constructive development phase has already been achieved. The nature of these weaknesses will emerge as we discuss the contributions that recent health economic evaluation studies have made to the achievement of greater efficiency and improved health policy-making.

Equity in resource allocation and community preferences

The health economics literature originating in Britain and Australia has also contained several papers which analysed the methods of evaluation from the perspective of their implications for the achievement of equity in resource allocation, and their consistency with community preferences (Nord et al., 1995a, b; Coast, 2004). The article by Coast in the *British Medical Journal* contained a useful summary of the existing methods of economic evaluation and a thoughtful account of their assumptions and limitations.

The methods of economic evaluation 1

Cost-benefit analysis

Cost-benefit analysis (CBA) has a long history of applications in investment decision-making in areas which lie outside the ordinary workings of markets. These decisions are often those undertaken by governments where the measurement of the costs and the benefits associated with a project cannot be based on those observed in a market.

Examples of the application of CBA in the public sector have included decisions about the site of an additional airport, alternative strategies for the construction of dams and whether additional investment in road construction is warranted in a particular area. In each case the benefits cannot be quantified by reference to private sector investment criteria such as profit maximisation since the benefits may include positive environmental impacts, the reduction in road traffic accidents and deaths, and other contributions to community welfare.

Similarly, the costs to be taken into account may include the loss of sites of great natural beauty in the dam construction case, as well as the financial costs of the options being evaluated. In all cases accurate estimates of both the costs and benefits are usually very difficult to make. However, even very rough measures may be sufficient to indicate that a project should or should not be undertaken.

The applications of CBA have been designed to reflect the same economic theoretical underpinnings that have been derived for private investment decision-making. These include the need to discount both costs and benefits to present values using an appropriate rate of interest where these accrue over more than one year. This procedure provides the basis for comparing options where both the benefits and costs may be generated over different periods of time. Where the (discounted) benefit to cost ratio is greater than one, the investment should be undertaken if no other considerations are relevant. This formulation of CBA also implies that all costs and benefits can be expressed in money terms.

One of the other considerations is that some of the options may differentially benefit some individuals relative to others. It is this possibility that provides the connection between CBA and welfare economics. For example, the option of the government allocating additional funding to road construction in an accident-prone area will benefit only the users and potential users of the road. All tax payers who do not use the road will be worse off by virtue either of the payment of additional taxes or of the reduction in the capacity of the government to fund activities which would have provided direct benefits to them. It will be recalled from our previous discussion of welfare economics that the application of the Pareto principle even in its weak form (that the beneficiaries could compensate the losers in principle) provides a flawed basis for decision-making.

In the conceptualisation of conventional microeconomics the welfare economics approach leads to the enunciation of the general principle that a program should be undertaken up to the point where the marginal social benefit equals the marginal social cost. This principle is subject to the limitations we noted in Chapter 5 about the postulated shape of marginal utility and marginal cost curves, and the problems of deducing a social welfare function from the preferences of individuals.

Distributional and other problems with CBA

In the health field the most important difficulty with applying CBA, even in the straightforward benefit to cost ratio form, has been the need to express the benefit in terms of lives saved in monetary terms. Two methods of making these estimates of benefits are those of the willingness of individuals to pay for a potentially life saving or morbidity reducing treatment, and the value of the expected future earnings of individuals which would result from life saving and morbidity reduction interventions.

Both these methods introduce distributional issues into the analysis. The willingness to pay for treatments may reflect the resources available to each individual that is the ability to pay – persons on higher incomes may be prepared to pay a higher price than those on lower incomes. Thus surveys of individuals to determine their willingness to pay for specified therapeutic interventions will be highly sensitive to the income and possibly the capital resources of those selected to supply the information. Similar reservations apply to the expected future earnings approach. However, the move towards other options for economic evaluation methods has probably been driven mainly by the aggressive opposition by health professionals and others to the notion of valuing a human life.

Cost-effectiveness analysis

Cost-effectiveness analysis (CEA) avoids the need to quantify benefits in money terms by resorting to the more modest approach of seeking the least cost method of achieving a defined benefit. The defined benefit may be a rate of cure achieved by a pharmaceutical product: the most cost-effective pharmaceutical when several are compared is the one that achieves this specified rate at least cost.

It should be noted that cost-effectiveness should always be specified in relative terms. It makes no sense to state that an intervention or procedure is 'cost-effective' since effectiveness and cost are measured in non-comparable terms. This error often appears in the literature where the writer really means he/she assumes that the intervention is efficient – the benefit to cost ratio in money terms (if this could be measured) is greater than one. Moreover, even in the comparison of pharmaceutical products where CEA has been applied most usefully, many products designed to treat specific conditions may have varying side effects which are difficult to incorporate into comparable measures of effectiveness for the drugs being compared.

The limitations of CEA

It must be emphasised that the most cost-effective intervention is not necessarily efficient using the benefit cost ratio criterion of efficiency. In the drug example, the ranking of the options does not provide information on the more fundamental objective of establishing whether the cost of each drug is warranted by the effects it generates.

It is also important to bear in mind that CEA, as we have defined it here, is of limited application when health service interventions are being compared, where the benefits differ from one activity or project to another. For this reason in recent years there has been a tendency to distinguish cost utility analysis, using health gain as the effectiveness criterion for all interventions, from CEA. However, some writers on economic evaluation continue to apply the term CEA to the method used where an aggregate indicator of health gain measures effectiveness.

The methods of economic evaluation 2

Cost-utility analysis and QALYs

Cost-utility analysis (CUA) has come to be identified with the use of a specific aggregate measure of health gain, the QALY as the indicator of effectiveness which in principle is designed to ensure comparability between different health services interventions. As the name indicates there are two components of the QALY; the additional life expectancy estimated to be generated by the intervention and the estimated quality of the additional years of life. The term CUA is used because the health gain is designed to reflect the additional utility to the consumer or patient generated by the intervention.

Additional life expectancy is regarded as generating satisfaction for individuals but these additional years are discounted by the quality of the life likely to be experienced by the patient in each of the additional years.

The quality of life component is typically measured on a scale from zero to one in which zero corresponds to death and one to perfect health. The construction of the scale may be derived from surveying groups of people in which they are asked to provide a ranking of possible states of health or ill health, including such characteristics as blindness, inability to feed one's self, chronic severe pain, and minor discomfort. However, two other methods of deriving the quality component have been favoured by economists, the time trade-off and the standard gamble (Torrance, 1986).

Methods of quantifying QALYs

The time trade-off (TTO) method is based on each respondent in the calibration study being asked to assess how long a period in a specified state of health would be regarded as equivalent to a different period in another state of health. It is assumed that the higher is the specified state of health ranked the shorter is the period of life expectancy the individual would be prepared to trade for it as compared with a state of health with a lower ranking. For a condition associated with minor discomfort being compared with one generating severe pain the respondent could be expected to require a longer period of life expectancy to compensate for this more painful state than for the less painful condition.

The standard gamble (SG) approach requires each respondent in the study to estimate the certainty equivalent of an uncertain health outcome facing an individual. The usual example given is the situation being faced where the respondent is asked to choose between remaining in a poor state of health with certainty, and facing the risk of death from a surgical intervention which would restore full health if successful. If the assigned probability of being restored to full health is varied, the standard gamble approach is designed to establish where the person will be indifferent between the postulated continuing poor health status and the gamble involved with surgery.

It is assumed that the less satisfactory is the poor health status the greater will be the risk of death from surgery that the respondent would accept. Again a basis is established for ranking the poorer health conditions on the QALY scale between one and zero. The standard gamble method has been described as providing a basis for linking the QALY rankings of utility with welfare theory (Butler, 1990). Estimates of expected utility based on the assignment of probabilities to utility outcomes was the foundation of the attempt by von Neumann and Morgenstern (1944) to measure utility in absolute (cardinal) terms. It has been claimed, however, that respondents find the standard gamble approach more difficult to apply than the TTO method (Bowling, 1997).

Butler in the paper quoted above has argued that the QALYs derived from SG rankings represent rankings of the willingness to pay (WTP) which underlie CBA. However, the conversion of the WTP to a scale between zero and one eliminates the potentially objectionable link between the resources of the individual and the absolute value of the WTP. Nevertheless, the relationship between QALYs and willingness to pay remains a controversial topic in the health economics literature (Dolan and Edlin, 2002; Donaldson et al., 2002).

The CUA facilitates the measurement of effectiveness for different therapeutic interventions which is not possible using CEA. As we have noted previously, it does not permit projects and programs in health to be compared with those in non-health activities.

Criticisms of QALYs

The methods of generating QALYs and their theoretical underpinnings have been subjected to a good deal of criticism by both economists and others. It has been noted that the respondents in the studies designed to obtain the quality rankings are not normally those patients and others with the diagnoses and problems that are being assessed. They are typically health professionals and students. Their responses to the hypothetical states they are being asked to evaluate may then differ considerably from the responses that would have been obtained from those of patients or potential patients. For example, very elderly patients may feel that a painful condition is more valuable to them than a younger and healthy person would assess it to be (Carr-Hill, 1989; Bowling, 1997).

It has also been argued that the conceptual basis of QALYs and the methods used to determine them is difficult for clinicians and other non-economists to understand, leading to scepticism about CUA amongst those people whose behaviour and policy applications economic evaluation is designed to influence (Coast, 2004). In a recent paper two Norwegian economists, Arnesen and Norheim (2003) have produced a comprehensive conceptual critique of QALYs when based on the time trade-off method. They question whether the method derives results which are related more to attitudes about death than to quality of life.

Other sources of utility

The use of health status as the principal driver of consumer utility has been queried by some health economists in that it ignores other sources of utility.

These include such matters as the perceived fairness of the health service arrangements, where members of the community may favour measures that benefit some people with special problems.

The departures from utility maximisation in the individualist sense are referred to as representing externalities; it is a source of utility to persons that the more vulnerable members of the society are protected by the health services provision and funding arrangements. This, in turn, is the basis of the solidarity principle which provides the rationale for social health insurance in many European countries, as we discuss in Chapter 10. Other sources of utility may reflect what has been termed 'process' utility. For example, persons with the same health status outcomes following hospitalisation may have very different perceptions of such matters as the quality and empathy of the nursing services process (Coast, 2004).

Limitations in priority setting

The translation of measures of QALYs based on individuals to establishing the priorities for ranking resource allocations within the health services introduces further difficulties. Where QALY maximisation is the accepted goal of health service provision, in principle it is the total number of QALYs generated by each intervention or project times the number of people who are exposed to the intervention or project.

This formulation implies that the social benefit of a service is a product of the years of life gained, the quality of those years and the total number of service recipients. After a comprehensive review of the literature Dolan and his colleagues concluded that social value does not bear a linear relationship to length of life and quality of life, but social value diminishes in marginal increments of both (Dolan et al., 2005). Empirical studies of community attitudes in Australia have also revealed that the single objective of maximising health gains would not be the basis on which communities would wish to allocate their health care resources (Nord et al., 1995b).

A further problem with the translation of CUA into a basis for establishing priorities for health services planning is that it requires addressing the issue, after the cost and QALY estimates have been established in respect of the options, of where a cut-off point will be determined for the acceptable cost per additional QALY. This problem reflects the distinction between CUA and CBA where in principle only CBA can be used directly to choose between different projects.

Using CUA for this purpose then requires the decision-maker to specify the acceptable cost per additional QALY to draw the line between those proposed projects which will be funded and those that will not be funded. In the NHS decision-makers from the National Institute for Clinical Excellence (NICE) seem to have based their cut-off point at £25,000 per additional QALY

(Maynard, 2005b), but the basis of this value does not appear to have been published. This procedure places the burden on the decision-maker to inter-pret the meaning of QALYs when it is claimed that most decision-makers' knowledge of them is very limited (Drummond et al., 2003). In these circum-stances there is a risk that resource allocation decisions are taken which do not reflect social priorities.

It will be recalled that the QALY method of measuring the impact of clinical interventions was designed to avoid the problems of CBA, especially the use of willingness to pay as the benefit measure, and the limitations of CEA that it did not permit comparisons between different therapeutic inter-ventions. Those amongst health economists who support the use of QALYs are sometimes referred to as operating within an extra-welfarist framework. This is in contrast to the traditional application of the cost-benefit approach derived from a welfarist framework with its reliance on the quantification of benefits of health interventions and projects in money terms, based largely on the willingness-to-pay method.

The extra-welfarist framework, as we discussed in Chapter 3, is also perceived as embodying the principle that the state of health is the only or at least the most important measure of the effectiveness of health services interventions (Culyer, 1998). As a further development of the extra-welfarist framework, Culyer has argued that the role of a health economist should be to avoid the introduction of his/her values into the analysis and recommen-dations, and essentially act as a consultant to the funding agency. The implica-tions of the values of the agency for the policy options and recommendations are to be established by the health economist.

The construction and application of QALYs as measures of health status has absorbed the attention of many health economists, especially in Britain where policy-makers have generally accepted the use of QALYs and have funded their development. The approach has been consistent with the gen-eral philosophy of the NHS that the achievement of health gains is the fundamental objective of the service.

One may query, however, whether the focus on QALYs as a measure of effectiveness and utility generation has led to a relative neglect of the improvement of the methods of measurement of the costs of interventions, projects and programs. This issue is taken up further in Chapter 12 when we provide an overview on the priorities of health economics and how these might be changed productively in the future.

Controversies about economic evaluation

The literature on economic evaluation of health services, using CUA and QALYs, reveals a state of health economics in which many divergent views coexist. These vary from an unquestioning acceptance of the use of CUA based on QALYs for resource allocation with further refinements being based on dealing with uncertainty about the estimates, and to the search for alternatives to CUA such as cost consequences analysis (Coast, 2004). This proposed technique would detail in tabular form all the possible outcomes of specific interventions and all the relevant costs. It would then be the responsibility of the decision-maker to impute these costs and the values of the various health-related outcomes to arrive at a decision about resource allocation.

How values might be assigned to the costs and benefits remains unclear. It is difficult to see how guesses about costs, in particular, could achieve consistency and reliability in view of the complexity of the task when any of the available costing methods for patient types are implemented.

The recent French Guidelines for the Economic Evaluation of Health Care Technologies have also adopted a cautious approach to the use of QALYs and, in particular, to the creation of league tables of incremental costs per QALY (Collège des Économistes de la Santé, 2004).

A strident criticism of CUA has come from Professor Cam Donaldson and his colleagues (Donaldson et al., 2002). Donaldson, a well-known Scottish health economist, has argued that the reliance on incremental cost-effectiveness ratios in the setting of health service priorities is theoretically flawed. Where a new intervention is compared with an existing one if the new procedure is both more costly and more effective, a decision is required about whether the additional effectiveness is warranted by the additional cost, that is, whether allocative efficiency has been achieved.

The determination of allocative efficiency must be based on CBA since the additional effectiveness and the additional cost need to be measured in comparable money values to resolve the allocative efficiency question. Donaldson's principal criticism of the CUA approach is that practitioners claim too much for it if they regard the procedure as giving a list of options in order of priority about how resources should be allocated. We observed in our earlier descriptions of CBA, CEA and CUA that CUA could not be regarded as a substitute for CBA since it did not lead to a set of priorities based on the relative efficiency of the procedures being compared.

QALY league tables

At the present stage of development of CUA, policy-makers, managers and clinicians are perhaps best advised to treat all results about desirable resource allocations based on QALYs with considerable caution. In this regard the advice contained in the paper by Mason, Drummond and Torrance (1993) is well worth noting. Their attention was focused on the production and interpretation of league tables in the health economics literature setting out comparisons of a variety of health service interventions on a cost per QALY basis. However, the problems they encountered in examining one such table touch on many of the issues we have discussed.

The most important points Mason and his colleagues made were that published league tables are often derived from data with differing years of origin. This is relevant because each study will represent the state of knowledge at that time of costs and benefits. Technological developments including those resulting in changed relative prices of the different interventions will affect the comparability of the rankings of costs and benefits.

In addition, they noted that different methods of estimating the health states affect the results so that in reporting the results of QALY studies researchers should take care to set out in detail the specific method used for quantification. They were especially concerned that there were inadequate details provided about the methods of costing in many of the studies they reviewed. Generally, only direct health care costs were included in the estimates included in the cost per QALY values. In all except one study patient costs were excluded.

Mason and his colleagues also pointed to the additional difficulties encountered when the studies included in the league table are drawn from different countries. Adjustments for converting the costs reported to a common currency value should include an adjustment for purchasing power parity, ideally for medical goods and services. Differences in clinical practice between the countries, and in the relative prices of other options for interventions, may also need to be taken into account before any policy conclusions should be drawn from CUA studies embracing more than one country.

The authors concluded that whilst QALY-based league tables need to be treated with considerable caution as a guide to action by decision-makers, the evidence they provide is likely to be better than informal assessments of relative cost-effectiveness which may be made in any case.

Reponses to the controversies

What conclusions can then be drawn about the attitude that should be adopted in regard to economic evaluation as it has evolved over the last 20 years? In the light of our previous review of the limitations and problems of applying the theory of welfare economics to health services evaluation the move away from CBA to CEA and CUA should be regarded as a step forward. The extra-welfarist approach of regarding health as the main ultimate objective of the health services and the main source of consumer utility, along with the achievement of equity in the provision and financing arrangements, has a good deal of intuitive appeal.

The problems with CUA as described in the literature arise out of the QALY approach of relying on a single measure of quality of life, along with gains in life expectancy, as the measure of health. In our view the criticisms of QALYs that point to difficulties with the existing methods of ranking states of health and how these are derived are compelling. We agree that the somewhat nebulous phrase 'quality of life' is inherently not capable of being encapsulated with any degree of accuracy in a single numerical value.

Nevertheless, the point made by Mason and his colleagues that it is better to use CUA, despite its flaws, than rely on ill-informed guesses and politically biased hunches to establish funding priorities. This last point represents what appears to be a reasonable response to the whole CUA endeavour as it currently stands. Greater standardisation of the methods of estimating the QALYs, together with further refinement of the costing procedures, and a more transparent reporting of the details of how the results were derived are clearly required before the league tables and other applications of CUA achieve a high degree of face validity.

Further work on the weighting of QALYs differentially, for example, giving greater weight to those generated by services directed at the disadvantaged, would afford an improved basis for incorporating equity concerns into the decision-making framework (Williams, 1998a; Dowie, 2001).

Applications of economic evaluation

In recent years a good deal of attention has been devoted by health economists to the application of CEA and CUA to the assessment of pharmaceutical products, to technology assessment and to different techniques of surgical and medical interventions. A comprehensive review of these studies has recently been published by Drummond and Sculpher (2005). This review emphasised a number of flaws in the methods used especially in conjunction with clinical trials involving pharmaceutical products. They are very critical of the costing methods and the possibility of biases when the studies are sponsored by the industry. The limitations of costing studies as undertaken by economists form a topic we return to in Chapter 12.

Pharmaceutical appraisal

The use of CEA in the evaluation of pharmaceutical products has a long history. The Australian Department of Health in 1990 introduced the requirement that submissions by pharmaceutical companies for the listing of new products as part of the government's Pharmaceutical Benefits Scheme (PBS) must be accompanied by a CEA (Dickson et al., 2003). The PBS heavily subsidises from central government funding the drug costs met by consumers in the Australian health care financing arrangements. Since 1993 sponsors of all new drugs for listing in the PBS have needed to 'demonstrate cost-effectiveness'. However, the interpretation of CEA has included what are cost minimisation studies; where a new drug has been assessed as equally clinically efficacious as an existing one the comparison made is between the cost of each.

Since the early 1990s several other countries, including Britain and Canada, have required drug manufacturers to demonstrate the relative cost-effectiveness of their products as well as their clinical effectiveness. (Canadian Co-ordinating Office for Health Technology Assessment, 1997). The use of pharmacoeconomic information has been reviewed in depth by Drummond and his colleagues in their report of the task force set up to explore this issue (Drummond et al., 2003). One of the important points made in this report was, yet again, that decision-makers find the basis of QALYs difficult to understand in the reporting of CUA studies. Many of the studies on the relative cost-effectiveness of pharmaceuticals are published in the journal *Pharmacoeconomics*.

Technology assessment

In the process of technology assessment the decision-making is similar to that involved with pharmaceuticals; indeed the latter might be regarded as a special case of technology assessment. In practice, however, technology assessment in the health services has tended to concentrate on the 'big ticket' items with high individual costs. These include imaging devices such as Computerised axial tomography (CAT) and Magnetic resonance imaging (MRI).

An extensive review of the issues associated with MRI, including guidelines about the numbers and location of facilities was provided by an Australian Committee (Australian Health Technology Advisory Committee, 1996). In the British NHS where the numbers and distribution of these devices is tightly controlled, the results of these assessments may have a profound influence on the use and availability of the services. A journal, *The International Journal of Health Technology Assessment*, contains reports of many of the CEA and CUA studies incorporated in technology assessment.

Medical and surgical treatments

There has been a proliferation of studies reviewing the relative cost-effectiveness of a variety of medical and surgical treatments including a large number originating in the United States. Recent examples of CEA and CUA studies have covered mental health (Andrews et al., 2004; Pirraglia et al., 2004), ophthalmology (Brown et al., 2004; Hopley et al., 2004) and cardiology (Walker et al., 2003). Details of most of these studies with critical comments are provided at the NHS/University of York website (NHS EED).

In the United States the recent interest in clinically based studies using CEA and CUA has been a by-product of the universal drive to shift to an evidence-basis for medicine. Those clinicians who have participated in economic evaluation studies have no doubt realised that evidence about the clinical effectiveness of therapeutic interventions needs to be supplemented by cost information evidence before final decisions are made about the most appropriate procedure to be used.

However, a more pessimistic attitude to the influence of CEA on governments and clinicians has been expressed in a recent book by Neumann (2005). He made a strong case for the greater use of CEA in the United States especially in regard to its potential application in informing decisions about technologies for reimbursement under the US Medicare program. He argued, however, that the introduction of CEA into the US health care system has been impeded by 'political opposition and cultural factors'.

Evaluation of the achievement of equity goals

A further important evaluation issue is the extent to which the achievement of equity goals has been met by the methods of health systems funding. This type of evaluation becomes especially important when the attempt is made to assess the implications of the widely divergent methods of health services funding which exist internationally. Two health economists, van Doorslaer from Belgium and Wagstaff from England, have explored this area extensively and elegantly in a number of studies (Wagstaff and van Doorslaer, 1997, 1999, 2000; van Doorslaer and Wagstaff et al., 1999, 2000; van Doorslaer and Masserid, 2004).

International comparisons and methods

In the publications quoted above van Doorslaer and Wagstaff explained the evaluation methods used in the ECuity Project, funded by the European Union. This project was designed to study equity in a number of European countries and the United States. It was mainly based on the concepts of horizontal and vertical equity and the extent to which these were achieved in each country. Horizontal equity is defined as the principle which requires that households with a similar ability to pay should make similar payments for health care. The vertical equity principle requires that better off households should make larger payments than those households that are worse off. The value judgement that payments should be related to the ability to pay, according to the authors, is deeply ingrained in the mainly publicly funded European health care systems.

The methods used by van Doorslaer and Wagstaff to assess horizontal and vertical equity are mathematically and statistically complex. They are described briefly in Chapter 10. The authors were able to demonstrate that in countries where most of the health services are funded by a progressive income tax, horizontal and vertical equity are likely to be achieved. Where a progressive tax scale applies, individuals on higher incomes pay a proportionately higher (marginal) tax rate. At the other extreme where private payments for private health insurance and out-of-pocket payments by patients predominate, neither horizontal nor vertical equity will be present.

We return to the equity issue when we discuss the financing arrangements and measures of health services performance in a number of countries in the next chapter. The ECuity Project is of considerable importance in emphasising that the measures of relative cost-effectiveness and efficiency we have discussed in this chapter are not the only perspective from which health services evaluation should be viewed. It might be argued that the achievement of equity in the financing methods and in the meeting of health needs, are of even greater relevance to the overall welfare of the populations of countries.

Other economic evaluation methods

The most important method of economic evaluation not discussed in this chapter is that of program budgeting and marginal analysis (PBMA) (Mitton and Donaldson, 2003; Mitton et al., 2003). Whilst the method is based on economic principles, of the CBA type, the main innovation of the procedure is its attempt to address the problem of having economic evaluation integrated with managerial and clinical objectives within organisations. For this reason we include a discussion of PBMA in the next chapter in the context of translating economic evidence into practice.

Summary and conclusions

In this chapter we have reviewed the role of economic evaluation of health services with an emphasis on the theoretical bases of the various techniques developed, and the controversies within the health economist community about the appropriateness of the methods and techniques that are currently in use. The criticisms of important elements of economic evaluation, notably the use of QALYs in CUA, have not as yet led to health economists with an interest in evaluation to abandon this approach.

Whilst most British health economists have abandoned the integration of welfare economics with health services evaluation and adopted the so-called extra-welfarist position, others have argued for a return to CBA and the use of willingness to pay as a measure of the benefits derived from clinical and health project interventions.

In the United States there appears to have been a greater interest amongst clinicians than amongst health economists in assessing the economic implications of alternative treatment options. Varying views have also been expressed about why there has not been more incorporation of CAE and CUA in government programs.

We have noted that the critical issue of the impact of economic evaluation on clinical and health policy decision-making is not yet clear. Some health economists have argued that the difficulty of understanding the theoretical basis of CUA may lead to decision-makers using the results of the studies inappropriately, especially in regard to the establishment of priorities for health resource allocation. It is also possible that these difficulties may lead to decision-makers ignoring the studies.

The creation of a European database of economic evaluation studies under the co-ordinating role of the French College of Health Economists, drawing on the existing NHS database and foreshadowing the extension to separate databases in several other European countries, is a very promising development in this area. The ability via the internet to access these databases provides an excellent basis for the dissemination of this information and a greater standardisation of the methods used.

A very interesting development of the last decade has been the attempt to measure the equity of the health services funding arrangements deployed in a number of OECD countries in the ECuity project. The results confirm the expectation that those countries which emphasise payments by individuals for health services fail to achieve horizontal and vertical equity. It is noted that these studies embody a different approach to economic evaluation from the usual methods.

In considering economic evaluation of health service activities we should not lose sight of the fact that the assessment of the performance of individual countries in this area needs to take into account a range of attributes that lie beyond the scope of health economics as it is usually defined. These include the degree of satisfaction that the populations express about the workings of their health care systems, case fatality rates associated with individual diseases and interventions, and other measures of outcomes and the quality of clinical services. A useful review of the measurement of the performance of OECD health systems has been published by the OECD following on an international conference in Canada on this topic (OECD, 2002).

===================== FURTHER READING =====================

As we indicated previously, the article by Coast (2004) in the *British Medical Journal* provides a good summary of the methods of economic evaluation. Most importantly she stresses the limitations of the methods and the difficulties of having the results used by managers and clinicians.

Amongst the numerous other sources of information about economic evaluation, the book by McDonald (2002), *Using Health Economics in Health Services: Rationing Rationally?*, is worthy of special mention. This work also emphasises the problems of getting health services personnel to apply the results of the evaluations conducted by health economists.

The paper by Drummond and Sculpher (2005), 'Common methodological flaws in economic evaluations' in the journal *Medical Care*, provides a thorough analysis of the problems they perceive are present in many evaluation studies, and they include many recommendations for improvements. As we noted earlier they are very critical of the costing methods used, especially in the evaluation of pharmaceutical products.

Discussion questions

- What are the main reasons that there has been an escalation of economic evaluations in the health services in recent years?
- Summarise the principal characteristics of CBA, CEA and CUA.
- Why do you think that in the United Kingdom and elsewhere there has been a tendency to use CUA rather than CBA in health services evaluations?
- Is it possible and/or desirable to place a value on human life?
- Explain the principles involved in the construction and estimation of QALYs. Summarise the criticisms that have been made of this evaluation technique by health economists and others.
- Explain the meaning of horizontal and vertical equity? What value judgements are made in deciding that these concepts should form part of the evaluation of health care systems?
- What may be some of the problems likely to be experienced in getting policy-makers and politicians to use the results of the ECuity study in their own countries?

Translating Health Economic Evidence into Policy and Practice

9

Background

This chapter outlines the role of and associated challenges faced by health economists in guiding the decisions made by clinicians and health services managers. Health economics seeks to influence the directions of policies affecting clinical practice and management. However, a number of practical difficulties arise in translating evidence into policy and practice. The impetus for this chapter arose from a general sense of a stark division between the evaluation of health outcomes undertaken by clinicians, the estimation of costs gathered by health service managers and the measurement of values and preferences by health economists.

The focus of this chapter is on the contribution of health economics to clinical practice and management. It begins by examining the differing perspectives on the nature of evidence taken by clinicians from the biomedical sciences and health economists and managers from the social sciences. It summarises key points of potential conflict between clinicians, managers and health economists.

The contribution of health economists to making the best use of insights gained from these disparate disciplines is discussed, including debates on the effectiveness of the applications of economic methods to health care delivery and policy. The chapter concludes by considering how economic thinking has responded to the challenges of multi-disciplinary practice and evaluation with reference to program budgeting and marginal analysis (PBMA).

The role of economics in clinical practice and management

Health economists are skilled at identifying the necessity for making value judgements and spelling out the nature of the value judgements that are needed (Culyer, 2001). Such value judgements relate mainly to the objectives of the health care system, to distributive justice and to devising ways to resolve possible conflicts between efficiency and equity objectives. In practice, the major areas in which health economists engage with clinicians and health service managers in decision-making are in economic evaluation of alternative ways of delivering health care, planning, budgeting and monitoring health care.

As discussed in previous chapters, health economics, at least in the United Kingdom and Europe, has become predominantly a system of measurement, with a preoccupation with techniques of establishing planning priorities through such tools as the quality adjusted life year (QALY) and other measures within existing patterns of service. We have also noted in earlier chapters that health economists in the United States have been primarily interested in health insurance issues.

According to Bosanquet (2001), the discipline has contributed rather little either to the *management* task of using limited resources to improve efficiency or to the *policy* challenges of using incentives to reduce social costs. Often, the involvement of economists is initiated when a clinical trial of an intervention has shown the intervention to be clinically effective, and the clinicians and policy-makers then call upon the health economist to address the question of whether the intervention is relatively cost-effective. This separation and distinction between clinical effectiveness for clinical purposes on the one hand, and cost-effectiveness for policy purposes on the other hand, has, according to Dowie (2001), greatly exacerbated the difficulty of conducting a meaningful debate in the health care context.

Differences in perspectives of clinicians and health economists

How has this conflict between evaluation for scientific and clinical purposes and evaluation for decision-making purposes arisen? It is useful to explore the disparities in the theoretical approaches which characterise the frameworks within which clinicians function, and those within which policy-makers and their advisers such as health economists interpret evidence, to suggest ways and means by which the two groups might achieve a meaningful and collaborative discourse. This analysis is designed to suggest how the differing perspectives of the groups might be reconciled.

The source of the conflict was typified by Dowie (2001) in the following manner. There are two key differences which crucially affect how outcomes are defined and assessed in health care. The first difference is the reliance in conventional 'scientific' research, including clinical trials, upon avoiding a type one error (not rejecting a false hypothesis) at all costs, as compared with a type two error (rejecting a true one). The aim is to minimise, by statistical methods, the chance at a set level of statistical probability, that the intervention is seen as effective when it is not. The cost of the intervention does not surface for the clinical researchers as an issue in their pursuit of the 'truth'. In decision-making for policy purposes the health economist is concerned with the costs associated with interventions, as well as other aspects.

Second, science takes no account of time in the pursuit of knowledge – hence the absence of any consideration of time discounting, in marked contrast to economists and policy-makers who must always consider the time period of expected costs and consequences. Clinicians, in general, often fail to understand the theoretical basis of the pre-occupation of economists with this procedure, that people discount satisfactions in the future as compared with those immediately available.

Dowie postulated that the clinician's approach to an evaluative framework is intuitively ethical – that it is not possible to value life or health in a human being, and that no amount of analysis can measure and weight ethical standards of behaviour and care. Diametrically opposing this stance is the view by health economists that the assessment of equity and efficiency should be transparent, supported by the required standards of analysis – in other words, making explicit and open to inspection what is implicit to intuitively driven clinicians.

To provide further insight into how these varying approaches might apply to the clinical setting, Dowie (2001) took the case of the outcomes of a clinical drug trial. There are two possible and relevant outcomes: one is the effect of the drug on the patients and the second is the effect on other patients who did not receive the treatment they might have had if the resources had not been used to pay for the drug, the opportunity cost. These two separate outcomes lead to the scientific basis of drug effectiveness being left to the clinicians, and the cost-effectiveness and opportunity cost issues being assigned to the policy-makers and health economists.

Clinicians, managers and health economists – the divide

Health service managers and clinical staff increasingly need the most recent evidence and techniques in evidence-based clinical practice and management. Inevitably this calls for the development of skills for improving the evidentiary basis of clinical work to achieve improved quality, effectiveness and technical efficiency, in the context of managing clinical work within a multi-disciplinary team. The complex nature of health care delivery in large multi-disciplinary health care settings requires the use of 'good' evidence in clinical decision-making, and the management of clinical work (Degeling et al., 2000).

The difficulties encountered in the discourse in the use of health economics evidence to inform both medical practice and health services management are presented here, based on Maxwell and Ho (2004). The first issue arises out of philosophical debates concerning 'evidence-based' approaches to health care and clinical management. There are different beliefs about the nature of knowledge (positivistic, phenomenological/social construction and critical) and these impinge on the fundamental question of what can be considered as 'evidence'. The difficulties of decision-making in a pluralistic work place, and the problems that this poses for defining issues and work processes in clinical settings must also be considered.

Much literature has been published in recent years encouraging practitioners of all clinical disciplines to adopt an evidence-based approach to care as a basic tenet of their practice. Clinicians' responses to such encouragement are frequently acrimonious. This is not surprising since many clinicians interpret an exhortation to use evidence-based methods as an allegation that they have no sound rationale for their current conduct of care. Clinicians and managers who request some evidentiary basis for the care delivered to patients therefore will commonly hear rejoinders such as "What about evidence for evidence-based practice?" and "How about evidence-based management?"

Clinical management and evidence

There are various ways of interpreting the term 'clinical management'. Clinical management can mean simply the management of individual patients' clinical signs and symptoms. It can be a very broad term for the management of the overall clinical load of a health care setting that is determining the services provided, managing access, bed usage, resource distribution across departments, staff ratios, and so on. This chapter assumes that clinical management encompasses all these possible meanings. It also uses clinical management in a manner not common in the existing literature, namely, the management of all aspects of care delivery for an identified group of patients.

'Evidence' can take many different forms and also has several different meanings or interpretations. Depending on the combination of players and purposes in the decision-making arena, the nature and meaning of 'evidence' may be disputed, 'manufactured', manipulated or simply unavailable. Nevertheless, the complex nature of health care service delivery, particularly in large, multi-disciplinary health care settings, necessitates the use of 'good' evidence in clinical decision-making and the management of clinical work.

Effective management of clinical work requires that staff: can identify the clinical evidence they require, have access to available evidence, are trained to critically appraise it and can successfully devise and implement strategies based on that evidence. A significant part of this approach therefore covers the basics of an evidence-based approach to clinical decision-making (Dawes et al., 2000). Although this approach focuses upon randomised controlled trials and meta-analysis, case studies and peer reviews, data generated within one's own professional experience and the expert advice of opinion leaders do have a place in an evidence-based approach to clinical work. Though growing in support, 'evidence-based' clinical practice (especially evidence-based medicine) is still somewhat contentious in its content, emphasis, methods, breadth of coverage and applied ethics. Controversies continue even amongst its supporters (Charlton, 1997; Kerridge et al., 1998; Isaacs and Fitzgerald, 2000; Strauss and McAlister, 2000).

Effective management of clinical work also requires the development of processes that bring the various players to a common purpose in a manner which allows for their various values and objectives. It should enable clinicians and clinical managers to generate data immediately relevant to their own work; and understand the organisational context within which clinical work is conducted and managed.

The evidence that may be required for effective clinical management can therefore relate to any and/or all of the various personal, professional and organisational dimensions of clinical service delivery:

- Individual patient's needs.
- The common needs of patients with a specific condition as a 'user or client group'.
- Clinical standards and guidelines.
- Occupational responsibilities and 'territory'.
- Consumables.
- Usage of other resources.
- Bed occupancy.
- Professional colleges' standards.
- Legal obligations including statutory reporting requirements.
- Budget limitations.
- Interpersonal relationships.
- Personal goals and needs.
- Personal accountability and autonomy.
- Organisational authority.

Evidence relevant to clinical management may therefore include economic analyses, accounting reports, patient complaint summaries and case studies in organisational behaviour (Jones et al., 1999).

Many health professionals lack the relevant inter-disciplinary knowledge and skills to assess adequately evidence across disciplines. It is not necessary for health professionals to become experts in research methodology. However, they need the ability to identify the required evidence, access available evidence and possess the skills to appraise critically that evidence (or at least recognise when to seek expert assistance in searching for the evidence). A basic understanding of qualitative methodologies often used for gathering evidence in managerial disciplines, especially organisational behaviour, as well as the more familiar clinical research techniques, is therefore essential (Punch, 2005).

When appraising such evidence, knowledge of research techniques needs to be complemented by an ability to identify where professionals from other disciplinary backgrounds are 'coming from'. Every clinical, managerial and organisational discipline has its own vocabulary (used by specific occupations and disciplines), values (frequently implicit) and policy agendas. Every individual views the world through his/her pre-existing knowledge (gained through the education system), pre-existing professional values (learnt through professional culture), pre-existing organisational values (communicated in the past behaviour within the health institution) as well as their personal values (adopted through one's personal history and beliefs).

No two individuals will have identical knowledge and experiences and therefore each individual practitioner and manager understands and knows the world according to his/her own ontology (pre-existing classification system of 'reality'). Embodied within his/her 'reality' will be specific beliefs about the nature of knowledge and evidence (epistemology). These beliefs enable each individual to think more or less cohesively about his/her place in the world and his/her work. It also defines what will and will not be accepted as 'valid' within that person's world view and hence his/her views about acceptable 'evidence' (Harmon and Meyer, 1986).

Within groups of individuals with similar ontological and epistemological systems (generally people with similar social backgrounds, education, professional cultures and/or political standings), agreement about appropriate clinical care, management strategies and priorities may be easily achieved. Conflict about the appropriate types and use of evidence within groups of similar backgrounds may be negligible. Indeed, agreement about such matters may be so pervasive and taken for granted that suggestions favouring the introduction of an evidentiary basis into clinical management decision-making may be widely regarded as unnecessary.

However within a group of decision-makers from dissimilar backgrounds, professions and/or experience, the values may be so different that generating a consensus may well seem impossible (Degeling et al., 2000). This may be an especially daunting problem when health economists form part of the decision-making group.

As an example, in reviewing a paper on economic evaluation, one would ask first, 'How valid is this paper as a piece of economic evidence?' Second, 'Whose voice is being heard in the arguments in this paper? Whose voice(s) is/are not being heard? What values are being espoused here? How do these values differ from those of doctors?'

Whether it is clinical or non-clinical data, the underlying assumptions, research methodology, method of analysis, manner of presentation and con-clusions drawn from a piece of research can be, and frequently are, disputed. (Harmon and Mayer, 1986). Clinicians often feel that managers will not accept their evidence about clinical practice. Conversely, managers fre-quently feel clinicians will not accept their evidence about organisational survival and success (Ferlie et al., 2001).

This is not surprising given that individuals commonly seek to find and/or generate information that enables them to 'do their job well', 'make the most appropriate decision' and, depending on the work climate, 'prove' their case by disproving others. (Proponents of alternative or opposing views seek to do likewise.)

The evidence deemed most appropriate and/or relevant to each person's situation will depend not only on each person's world view but also on what they believe will best support their case politically. The volatility of the decision arena and audience, that is those participating in management decision-making, shifts from day to day, meeting to meeting, even moment to moment – complicating the choice and use of evidence. In this environment, evidence will have various interpretations and fluctuate in credibility as people attempt to use 'evidence' to reinforce or disturb the biases of those with power and authority or, alternatively, to redistribute power in their favour (Morgan, 1997).

Economic logic and medical ethics

The medical profession has criticised economic analysis on the basis of perceived threats to professional autonomy (Loewy, 1980) and quality of patient care (MacDonald, 1993). In his summaries of the relationship between medical ethics and economic logic, Williams (1988, 1992) argued strongly against the proposition that cost considerations compromise medical ethics, and defends the assumptions made in cost-effectiveness studies.

A common tenet of medical ethics is the obligation of doctors to have equal respect of individuals' autonomy in all dealings with patients (Stanley,

1989). Culyer (2001) pointed out that medical ethics has traditionally been devised for micro purposes, that is, at the level of the doctor–patient relationship. Accordingly, it is clearly inadequate to determine the equitable and efficient distribution of resources between programs, clinical specialties, hospitals and geographical areas. Indeed, while one doctor might be well placed to judge the needs of his/her own patient, doctors will rarely be in an objective position to weigh either the rival claims of other doctors who make demands on behalf of their patients, or the strength of their own claims vis-à-vis others.

Clinicians have traditionally avoided any concern with allocative efficiency – how indeed can doctors fulfil their obligations to their individual patients whilst having responsibilities for the finite pool of resources? (It should be recalled that the various definitions of efficiency from an economics perspective were discussed in Chapter 3.) Hiatt (1975) used Hardin's *The Tragedy of the Commons* (1968) to liken doctors to herdsmen who allowed their patients, as the herdsmen allowed their cattle, to use health services (graze the commons) to the limit of available resources. In such a scenario, Weinstein (2001) posed the question: if there is general agreement that resources should be allocated to maximise aggregate health benefits and who is responsible for the allocation of resources?

Taking the perspectives of patients, consumers and doctors in turn, Weinstein concluded that: patients were unlikely to be sufficiently knowledgeable to allocate resources and limit care due to their dependence on doctors in the agency relationship which has been discussed in earlier chapters. As consumers, rather than as patients, people behave differently: while people expect their doctors to do everything possible when they are ill, they are unhappy when faced with higher collective costs such as rising insurance premiums or increased taxes. Consumers, in contrast to patients, are conscious of costs.

From the doctor's perspective, doctors have the responsibility to patients to make decisions on their behalf in their best interests. Clearly, doctors are often placed in situations where they must consider the rival claims of different patients, such as the selection of organ recipients. From a societal point of view, Weinstein thus poses the question: should doctors be expected to make decisions allocating resources to one patient at the expense of other unnamed patients? In other words, and in terms familiar to health economists, should doctors recognise that resources are limited and consider the relative cost-effectiveness of all the clinical decisions they make? Indeed, is it their job to protect the medical commons? Our earlier discussion of the work of Dowie suggests that they are highly unlikely to accept this responsibility unless more emphasis is placed on organisational and cultural changes.

Who should determine resource allocation priorities?

Who then should make these judgements about the allocation of scarce resources between competing demands for health care services? Debate continues as to the legitimacy and primacy of clinician, policy-maker and community preferences with regard to priority setting.

According to Culyer (2001) in relation to judgements about needs, 'Ultimately, it ought to be policy-makers accountable to the public, because the principles and priorities they select are quintessentially political matters of public policy. But the concept of need has one crucial ingredient, the effectiveness of health care, and about this factor top-level policy-makers may be expected to know little. Conversely, those who know a lot about effectiveness are ill-suited, through lack of accountability and training, to make the value judgements required in trading off the rival claims of articulate and powerful provider interests within the health care system. It is clear that judgements about meeting needs at the macro level have to be made in a multi-disciplinary fashion and given their significance for public policy, in a publicly accountable way.'

It is clear, however, that this viewpoint is highly contested. Australian studies reveal that the public overwhelmingly want their preferences to be used to inform priority setting decisions in health care (Wiseman et al., 2003), particularly when these decisions involve broad health programs and affect different population groups. In this study, preferences of clinicians and health service managers were rated most highly in relation to prioritisation of different treatments and medical procedures. Mooney (2000) argued that no one is better placed to judge the good of health care than the community and that the direction and objectives of health care should be enshrined in what he terms a 'communitarian constitution'. His communitarian perspective, it will be recalled, was discussed at some length in Chapter 3.

Economic logic and clinical management

Health service managers face multiple and often unpredictable concerns and priorities: staying within budget for many different programs each with its own unexpected developments and over-expenditure; monitoring and maintaining safe quality patient care; establishing and supporting the supervision and training of staff; establishing consensus on changes in service patterns; meeting policy demands from above as well as meeting community and patient group expectations and concerns.

Whilst there is now a general agreement that decisions made concerning clinical practice and health care delivery should be based on evidence to a greater extent than they have been in the past, this recognition has not necessarily led to the implementation of knowledge based on sound research for improved effectiveness, safety and acceptability of health care.

It is often difficult to implement research evidence within clinical practice and health services management and policy. The literature abounds with examples of the failure or delay in the implementation of research findings. Examples include inadequate use of prophylactic anticoagulants in people undergoing orthopaedic surgery (Laverick et al., 1991), widespread failure to give steroids to women in premature labour despite evidence of their benefits in decreasing the incidence of foetal respiratory distress (Donaldson, 1992) and the failure to use anti-thrombotics, aspirin and beta-blockers following acute myocardial infarction (Ketley and Woods, 1993; Woods et al., 1998).

Degeling and his colleagues (2000) noted that recent health care reform typified by the institution of practices such as clinical pathways within multi-disciplinary hospital teams assumed that, due to its expert and scientific nature, Cochrane-style findings would ensure their incorporation into evidence-based practice. There is increasing awareness in the literature that these kinds of assumptions do not adequately take into account the range of organisational and professional factors that affect the dissemination and the willingness of staff to adopt the recommended changes.

Health policy-makers and clinician managers are increasingly concerned with the delays and failures in changing clinical behaviour, and the failure of management and organisations to implement decisions based on critically appraised evidence, including the results of economic evaluations.

Grol and Grimshaw (1999) noted that research into the effectiveness of different strategies to promote change in clinical behaviour, and the difficulty in the uptake of research findings into health care services and management is a distinct area of health services research. There has been a lack of investment in implementation research, which is bedevilled by its own characteristic problems. These include difficulties in accessing the relevant literature that is scattered across multiple disciplines (epidemiology, economics and behavioural sciences, management and organisational theory). The studies have many methodological problems when they are appraised using the guidelines of evidence-based practice as conducted by the Cochrane Effective Practice and Organisation of Care (EPOC).

The cultural divide

Empirical studies on the extent to which it is possible to change clinical practice refer to a 'cultural divide' (Haines and Jones, 1994). This cultural divide separates researchers in the field, clinical practitioners and managers who operate within a heterogeneous framework concerning the types of evidence needed, the degrees of evidence required and the implementation strategies most favoured. Wood et al. (1998) noted that biomedical research prides itself on its objectivity and rationality of knowledge. Thus, in this framework, transfer of this irrefutable knowledge as 'hard' facts to inform and change 'soft' intuitive knowledge of clinical practice separates and objectifies research evidence. This approach does not take into consideration individual values and attitudes, nor does it consider the many organisational factors, which affect the acceptance of changing practices.

An alternative framework, which takes the organisational factors into account, suggests that science and scientific information are socially constructed. Implementation must incorporate professional and social interests as well as political power within the existing institutional and financial arrangements. This type of approach is much more useful in analysing why certain strategies for implementation either fail or are not maintained in organisations.

The implementation process

In the context of the interconnection between politics, science and technology, the relationships between the chief stakeholders in the implementation process are key factors. Significant barriers to change may simply be overlooked unless the 'political' nature of scientific evidence is considered. 'Much of what is called evidence is, in fact, a contested domain, constituted in the debates and controversies of opposing viewpoints in search of ever compelling arguments' (Wood et al., 1998).

The existing literature does not provide sufficiently coherent and conclusive evidence on effective implementation strategies. There are no magic bullets (Oxman et al., 1995). This is not surprising given the inherent complexities of the decision drivers underlying clinical management. There is a diversity of values, attitudes and meanings attached to what is presented as 'evidence' by individuals in a multi-disciplinary team. The view that 'hard' facts from scientific evidence can be incorporated *into* 'soft' clinical experiential work assumes a linear transfer of knowledge into practice. This view is problematic in that empirical work does not support it, nor does it allow for alternative approaches.

What is needed is the appropriate rigorous evaluation of changes in health services management and organisation along the lines followed in industries outside the health sector. Such an approach allows useful insights into the individual, social and organisational factors, which influence uptake and acceptance. There is an increasing body of literature grounded in organisational and management theory that examines the diffusion and uptake of socially constructed scientific evidence, and implementation as a complex and contested process dominated by particular professional groups (Ferlie et al., 2000).

Within this framework, implementation is regarded as a political process: barriers to and facilitators of implementation need to be identified in terms of differences in the acceptability of different forms of evidence by individuals and groups. Negotiation with key stakeholders, together with the collection of sound and comprehensive information, is required to reach agreement on the most suitable approach. Any changes should be designed in such a way as to allow proper evaluation and feedback, in order to ensure sustainable change even after the departure of the champions of the innovation. In this approach, implementation should be rightly regarded as the cultural process of managing change.

Management and economic tools

This final section deals with the practical implications for getting health economics evidence into policy and practice with reference to program budgeting and marginal analysis (PBMA). In practice, how can economic approaches to resource management properly consider the practical challenges faced by clinicians and managers when they need to make rational priority setting decisions?

The remedy lies in some form of collective action. Doctors, as Hardin's parable suggests, can only save the commons by agreeing and adhering to mutually acceptable covenants or guidelines which restrict their use of the common resources (Weinstein, 2001). Weinstein advocates collective action which constrains rather than regulates the choices that clinicians make. Such constraints would force clinicians to consider the limited collective resources – the opportunity costs of each clinical decision. He suggests that doctors need to play active roles in developing and interpreting evidence on effectiveness and costs in medical decisions. They need to set constraints within which they practice and develop guidelines on the allocation of the resources they oversee. According to some studies, clinicians will accept and incorporate cost-effectiveness information into clinical guidelines as long as they participate in the formulation and have some control of the end-product (Kuntz et al., 1999). There is, however, evidence of poor uptake of results of economic evaluations at the local level in the NHS, as we indicated in the previous chapter (McDonald, 2002).

Program budgeting and marginal analysis

The most important application of economic evidence to clinical practice and management, PBMA, is reviewed by Ruta et al. (2005) as a potential means of aligning the goals of doctors and managers. The PBMA devised by health economists, directly incorporates economic constructs into the technique. Economists set priorities for resource allocation by considering the costs and benefits of health services, using the principles of opportunity costs and marginal analysis (Mooney et al., 1992; Mitton and Donaldson, 2003; Mitton et al., 2003).

Briefly, PBMA requires the identification of a set of programs competing for funding, with data on resource inputs and outputs – program budgeting, and the process of shifting resources across programs to those yielding the highest marginal gain per dollar. The PBMA has mooted advantages of transparency in relation to historical funding mechanisms, and the objective of efficiency when compared to other funding approaches.

Program budgeting and marginal analysis differs from other types of economic evaluation in that whilst it shares the same economic principles of opportunity costs and marginal analysis, that is the cost-benefit framework in economic evaluation, it incorporates these into a management process.

Whilst the PBMA framework has been widely used in over 60 organisations in Australia, New Zealand, Canada and the United Kingdom, there are challenges to its application (Peacock, 1998). There is a growing body of literature that highlights the importance of paying attention to organisational context and behaviour (Peacock et al., 2006). Factors affecting the success of PBMA include relative organisational stability, relative coherence in long-term strategies, achievable stated objectives (Peacock et al., 2006), together with carefully constituted and well-functioning advisory panels (Peacock, 1998; Mitton et al., 2003; Murtagh and Cresswell, 2003; Mitton and Donaldson, 2004).

Arising from these experiences with PBMA and the observed limited impact on policy (Jan, 2000), there is interest in the application of an institutionalist framework to recognise the importance of the organisational environment in which the allocation of health service resources occurs (Jan, 1998). Jan notes that the institutionalist approach seeks to extend economic development and growth beyond the individual improvements in income and welfare to the broader context of institutional and structural change. This is in sharp contrast to the reductionist approach of neoclassical economics which assumes that *ceteris paribus* holds and thus enables the isolation of factors under study. This emphasis on cultural and community contexts has particular importance and relevance to the evaluation of programs aimed at Australian Aboriginal and Torres Strait Islanders (Mobbs, 1991; Freeman, 1994; Gray et al., 1995).

Williamson (1999) noted that the use of PBMA in public sector transactions involves the redistribution of resources across competing programs and is thus heavily dependent for its successful implementation on the goodwill of managers and clinicians in providing realistic assessments of expected benefits. It is thus essential to gain insights from the organisational as well as economic literature to understand better the characteristics of different institutions and organisations.

According to Jan, one way of dealing with these contextual differences is to consider both transactions and administrative costs, and measure the relative technical efficiency of different institutional arrangements in terms of aggregate output as a ratio over the sum of production, transactions and administrative costs. This approach posits a broader version of the more traditional economic evaluation and requires a framework that goes beyond conventional economic theory (Jan, 2000; Jan, 2003b; Jan et al., 2003).

It should also be borne in mind in assessing PBMA that the method inevitably shares the problems and limitations of CBA as applied to the health services, including its foundations in welfare economics and the valuation of life, which we discussed in the previous chapter.

Summary and conclusions

In considering the contentious area of the relationship between economics and medical and other clinicians it is of considerable importance to emphasise the different perspectives adopted by these groups and others about the nature of evidence. Evidence-based medicine has developed around clinical trials designed to determine the effectiveness of alternative therapeutic interventions for specific types of patients. Economists seek to provide evidence of a variety of kinds, including deductive reasoning, about broad resource allocation issues, notably the establishment of priorities for publicly funded programs using cost-benefit analysis, cost-effectiveness analysis and the other evaluation techniques discussed in Chapter 8. The ethical position of doctors leads to the tendency to do one's best for individual patients and not to consider the costs incurred, including the opportunity costs implicit in their decisions.

These different perspectives lead to considerable problems for both groups in relating to each other. Clinicians regard economists as being pre-occupied with costs and as seeking to restrict their clinical autonomy by emphasising in some cases the large expenditure, especially of public funds, required to sustain their clinical practice. Economists tend to criticise medical practitioners for ignoring the costs of their interventions and the implications of these costs for the overall efficiency of the health care system and community welfare.

It has been recognised by many people, including medically qualified personnel, that resource allocation decisions would be improved by a multi-disciplinary approach bringing to bear the insights, knowledge base and values of these and other groups, including community preferences. To date no country or organisation has achieved this objective. However, some of the recent clinical evaluation studies discussed in Chapter 8, including the interest of distinguished physicians in the United States in CEA, drawing on economic expertise, may suggest that a meaningful multi-disciplinary perspective may be possible to achieve. Whether PBMA may be the vehicle for fostering such collaborative work remains as a possibility for the future.

───────── **FURTHER READING** ─────────

The book by Mooney (1992, 2003) *Economics, Medicine and Health Care*, covers several of the issues raised in this chapter, especially the very different perspectives and world views adopted by economists and doctors. He also asserted that some clinicians continue to hold the opinion that the resources made available for the health services should be unlimited.

The paper by Weinstein (2001) in the *Journal of Medical Ethics*, 'Should physicians be gatekeepers of medical resources?' analyses very carefully the important ethical and policy issue of who should be responsible for resource allocation in health.

There is a lengthy and persuasive discussion of PBMA in the book by Donaldson and Gerard (2005) *Economics of Health Care Financing*, to which reference has been made previously.

Discussion questions

- What are the reasons that the perspectives of medical clinicians and health economists about resource allocation are so different? Do you believe that the perspectives of nursing clinicians on this issue would or would not be different from their medical colleagues?
- Summarise the different interpretations of 'evidence' that exist amongst health services groups including health economists. What is meant by stating that the notion of evidence is a contested domain?
- What are some of the conditions that might be required for doctors to incorporate the findings of health economists in their decision-making processes?
- Evidence has been quoted that the members of the public wish to have their preferences for health resource allocation incorporated in policy-making. Do you perceive that there may be problems in achieving this aspiration?
- It has been emphasised in this chapter that knowledge of managerial structures and organisational incentives is of considerable importance in facilitating inputs by

groups such as health economists to policy-making and related activities. Give examples of why this may be the case.

- Describe the essential features of PBMA. Why is it claimed by its supporters that this method of economic evaluation may have a greater chance of bridging the gaps, and fostering collaboration, between the various actors in the health care system than other methods?

Comparison of the Methods of Organising, Providing and Funding Health Services Internationally

10

Overview of health care systems

In this chapter we review the data regarding many of the aspects of the provision and outcomes of health care systems in the mainly economically affluent countries of the Organisation for Economic Co-operation and Development (OECD). Much of the published international information is based on the experience of developed countries, and these countries are the focus of attention in this chapter. In Chapter 11 we discuss the health systems of developing and transitional countries, especially in regard to whether, and to what extent, they have drawn on the financing models of developed countries.

The OECD data include the very important information that has been generated about aggregate expenditure on health services, the sources of this expenditure, workforce and other inputs to the health services, and measures of the mortality experience of each country.

We also examine how the greatly divergent methods of organising and financing the health services across all developed countries may be summarised into a manageable number of categories. This is a further example of modelling. The purposes of this endeavour are to highlight the differences between each system and country, and to facilitate comparisons between country groups with a view to assisting policy-makers to revise their own systems by drawing on the experience of other countries.

From this perspective we consider in some detail the health care systems of seven countries, the United States, the United Kingdom, Australia, Canada,

Switzerland, the Netherlands and Sweden. Our objective here is to provide an assessment of the performance of each country in relation to measures of efficiency and equity, to the extent that these can be deduced from the available information. In addition, we endeavour to relate these assessments to the categories to which they belong in a model of the funding and organisational characteristics.

The OECD data

With regard to the developed countries we noted in Chapter 6 that a large range of data about the health services is provided by the OECD based in Paris. The OECD membership consists of 30 countries mainly from Europe but also including Turkey, Japan, Korea, Australia and New Zealand in addition to the United States, Canada and Mexico.

All the member countries, with some exceptions, could be described as having developed economies but there is considerable variation in the levels of GDP and income per capita between the countries. See Table 10.1 for the 2002 values.

Of the lower income countries, Mexico, Turkey, Poland, the Czech Republic, the Slovak Republic and Hungary, might be best described as transitional economies. At the other end of the income scale, Luxembourg, the United States and Norway are the richest countries in the world on a per capita basis. Luxembourg's small population of less than 500,000 is concentrated in remunerative service industries, notably banking. The GDP of Norway has been boosted considerably by the discovery of large oil resources. Most of the other OECD countries are clustered between $US 20,000 and $US 30,000.

These values for the most affluent countries in the world are put into perspective by noting that many of the developing nations of the world, where the great majority of the world's population live, have GDP per capita values of less than $US 1000 (WHO, 2006).

Sources and limitations of the data

In the compilation of health-related data the OECD relies primarily on information provided by each member state. However, the OECD personnel have developed a standard method of defining the key terms, and they endeavour to adjust the definitions and methods used by each country to make the data as comparable as possible between the countries.

It needs to be borne in mind in using the data that the source material for each country may be subject to errors of varying magnitude. In general, the finer the classifications and cross classifications used the greater is the scope

Table 10.1 OECD Countries 1990–2002. GDP per capita US Dollars, current prices and PPPs (Actual values divided by 10)

	1990	1991	1992	1993	1994	1995	1996	1997	1998	1999	2000	2001	2002
Australia	1666	1703	1786	1875	1979	2097	2175	2285	2404	2544	2622	2733	2806
Austria	1869	1980	2049	2086	2175	2281	2376	2443	2543	2650	2786	2837	2887
Belgium	1793	1885	1953	1972	2072	2163	2218	2299	2374	2455	2591	2709	2771
Canada	1910	1914	1954	2024	2141	2224	2279	2397	2504	2663	2836	2929	3030
Czech Rep	1108	1020	1039	1064	1109	1202	1288	1293	1297	1313	1366	1486	1510
Denmark	1830	1913	1966	2005	2152	2247	2356	2467	2552	2700	2814	2922	2923
Finland	1799	1735	1700	1711	1807	1903	1982	2168	2324	2366	2535	2639	2649
France	1771	1845	1909	1929	2002	2073	2138	2242	2343	2423	2529	2655	2721
Germany	1762	1904	1979	1990	2073	2148	2216	2266	2340	2402	2485	2545	2591
Greece	1107	1173	1201	1204	1247	1298	1339	1412	1468	1522	1607	1702	1843
Hungary	..	817	813	830	875	902	940	995	1059	1114	1187	1304	1389
Iceland	2004	2053	2009	2055	2166	2205	2349	2478	2628	2713	2794	2903	2839
Ireland	1289	1354	1421	1487	1600	1788	1939	2206	2392	2592	2803	2982	3264
Italy	1736	1824	1879	1900	1977	2076	2151	2210	2324	2376	2468	2537	2556
Japan	1871	1996	2059	2108	2169	2248	2365	2449	2446	2480	2598	2663	2695
Korea	741	831	888	950	1039	1145	1234	1309	1228	1371	1518	1591	1701

Luxembourg	2506	2784	2865	3014	3148	3216	3328	3613	3945	4412	4842	4923	4915
Mexico	628	651	679	696	729	693	727	776	810	835	911	914	921
Netherlands	1780	1874	1934	1979	2066	2164	2254	2368	2479	2557	2698	2871	2900
New Zealand	1398	1394	1438	1529	1633	1701	1750	1823	1827	1937	2041	2123	2178
Norway	1790	1913	2013	2105	2249	2386	2622	2777	2732	3000	3581	3658	3548
Poland	603	580	607	643	689	752	818	881	932	974	1017	1049	1084
Portugal	1080	1172	1202	1205	1239	1315	1368	1449	1542	1636	1715	1788	1843
Slovak Republic	..	..	670	696	752	810	881	930	980	1001	1065	1132	1225
Spain	1301	1380	1424	1440	1502	1575	1644	1718	1823	1947	2031	2134	2240
Sweden	1866	1900	1910	1906	2012	2128	2204	2276	2353	2510	2657	2690	2720
Switzerland	2430	2459	2483	2513	2572	2614	2607	2758	2859	2854	2975	3003	3045
Turkey	452	464	494	537	509	548	591	632	649	613	673	604	640
United Kingdom	1635	1666	1706	1785	1898	1990	2093	2234	2327	2401	2532	2662	2794
United States	2300	2341	2440	2531	2657	2755	2876	3027	3160	3301	3460	3517	3612
EU15	1658	1742	1797	1825	1908	1993	2068	2156	2251	2331	2436	2533	2601
OECD total	1666	1729	1791	1841	1922	1997	2082	2179	2253	2336	2457	2517	2581

Source: OECD Health Data 2005 CDROM, October 05.

for definitional and measurement errors to arise. Thus we may place more reliance on broad aggregates such as health expenditure per capita, than on values such as the sources of funding of individual categories of health expenditure.

A further problem with the health expenditure data is that many of the values of the outputs of the components of the health industry are derived from the cost of the inputs. Health *per se*, as we have noted previously, is not traded in a market, thus the ultimate product does not have a value associated directly with it. This is unlike the case of other components of GDP where the values of most non-government products are established in markets, of varying degrees of 'imperfection'. It is an unfortunate fact of health economic life that improved productivity and technical efficiency of hospitals, for example, in generating better patient outcomes without additional costs will not be reflected in the national health accounts.

Use and interpretation of the data

In drawing conclusions from the international comparisons of health care expenditure it is important to emphasise that the interpretation of the reasons for the differences between countries is the key consideration, especially where policy-relevant issues are being analysed. In Britain, Torgerson and his colleagues have cautioned against the conclusion that the fact that the proportion of GDP devoted to health expenditure in that country is lower than in most other comparable countries establishes the case that health expenditure should be increased (Torgerson et al., 1998).

They pointed out that apart from errors in the data a number of other factors are relevant to the different levels recorded. These include the age distribution of the population, the prevalence of morbidity conditions which may reflect dietary and smoking habits, the relative prices of the components of health expenditure and the efficiency with which health care is delivered.

We must be cautious, however, about assuming that many of these factors are independent of the characteristics of the health care system. Obesity and smoking rates can be influenced considerably by health promotion activities and government legislation regarding advertising. Similarly, the prices of inputs are often a reflection of the degree of control that governments choose or are capable of exercising over providers. We return to a consideration of these factors shorltly, especially in regard to the comparison of the perform-ance of the British and American health care systems.

Components of the health accounts

In recent years the OECD has provided the data on health services charac-teristics on a CD-ROM disk. The OECD Health Data 2005 contains data on more than 1200 indicators for 2002/2003 with some time series showing the values going back to 1960 for a selection of the countries. Summaries of the main tables are also presented in the OECD website (www.OECD.org) and in commentary papers about the health services of individual member countries (OECD, 2005a, b). The main data fields covered are:

- health status
- health care resources
- health care utilisation
- expenditure on health
- health care financing
- demographic characteristics
- general economic indicators

Health status includes life expectancy at birth, infant mortality, mortality rates by age group and in some cases mortality rates by measures of socio-economic status. Health care resources include number of hospital beds classified by type of institution, number of nursing home and long stay institution bed-days and number of medical practitioners by specialty area. Health care utilisation shows the number of bed-days of hospital and other facility utilisation, number of medical service contacts, usually classified by type of practitioner, and number of pharmaceutical prescriptions written by type of drug.

Expenditure on health services is usually classified by the type of expenditure, such as on hospitals and other institutions, medical services, the services of other health professionals including dentists, pharmaceutical products and on public health and community health services. Capital expenditure is usually added to recurrent expenditure in the definition of health expenditure, but this type of expenditure may be shown separately for some purposes.

Health care financing is classified by the source, notably governmental and private along with health insurance where relevant. Demographic characteristics of the population being served concentrate on the age and sex composition values which are incorporated in the health status and util-isation measures. The general economic indicators include the aggregate measures of economic performance, notably GDP, which are used as the denominators of indicators for some purposes.

Problems with money values

For the data and indicators expressed in money terms two problems arise. The first is to make these as comparable as possible between the various countries included in the analysis. For this purpose the OECD has adopted the convention of expressing the money values in US dollar terms based on the exchange rate between the currency of the home country and the United States. However, these market exchange rates are adjusted for purchasing power parity (PPP). The latter adjustment is designed to reflect the fact that the exchange rates may not reflect the ability of each country's currency to purchase goods and services relative to that of other countries. The OECD produces these exchange rate PPP estimates which are published separately.

The second problem with the indicators expressed in money terms is that in analysing time series data for most purposes it is necessary to separate price changes from quantity changes. It is a standard procedure in analysing economic data to convert the money values over time to what are referred to as constant price terms. The latter are designed to reflect the movements in the money values which are independent of price changes.

For this purpose it is necessary to deflate the money values by values which reflect these price movements. This process takes account of general inflationary changes over each time period which influences the original money values. The estimates in constant price terms are sometimes referred to as estimates in real terms since they are designed to reflect the underlying quantity change in the values of the variables.

There are two options in determining the deflator in the procedure of converting to constant price terms. Where a price index is available that is specific to the prices of the goods and services, in this case of all health expenditure items, the division by this index would provide the best basis for the constant price estimates. However, in the absence of a price index of this kind the usual procedure in dealing with national health accounts is to use a generic deflator derived from the aggregate national income data. In comparing the constant price estimates of health expenditure and its components between different countries it is essential to use the same baseline year for each country.

Examples of important OECD health data

Some of the more important data about health care expenditure collected by the OECD are presented in the following tables.

Table 10.2 shows the total health expenditure on a per capita basis for each OECD country, expressed in $US adjusted for purchasing power parity. The latest values included in this table are for 2003 but for some of the countries earlier figures only are available.

Note that for about half the countries data are available back to 1960. However, for all these countries the earliest values are likely to be subject to

Table 10.2 OECD Countries 1960–2003. Total health expenditure per capita, US$ PPP

	1960	1965	1970	1975	1980	1985	1990	1995	2000	2001	2002	2003
Australia	94	136[1]	188[-1]	464	691	1004	1307	1745	2403	2521	2699	2699[-1]
Austria	77	107	191	424	764	919	1338	1973	2161	2163	2236	2302
Belgium	..	..	149	346	637	960	1345	1820	2279	2424	2607	2827
Canada	123	177	294	484	783	1264	1737	2051	2502	2709	2843	3001
Denmark	..	..	395[1]	590	955	1290	1567	1848	2382	2556	2655	2763
Finland	63	107	192	358	592	968	1422	1433	1718	1857	2013	2118
France	70	118	210	397	711	1118	1568	2033	2456	2617	2762	2903
Germany	..	..	270	571	965	1390	1748	2276	2671	2784	2916	2996
Greece	..	..	160	..	487	707[2]	840	1253	1617	1756	1854	2011
Iceland	57	94	165	351	708	1135	1614	1858	2625	2742	2948	3115
Ireland	43	61	117	276 b	518	662	793	1216	1804	2089	2386	2451
Italy	..	..	..	..	..	1195[3]	1391	1535	2049	2154	2248	2258
Japan	30	72	149	298	580	867	1115	1538 b	1971	2092	2139	2139[-1]
Luxembourg	..	..	163	339	643	925	1547	2059	2985	3264	3729	3705
Netherlands	..	..	330[2]	460	757	987	1438	1826	2259	2520	2775	2976
New Zealand	..	..	211	416	506	643	995	1247	1605	1701	1850	1886
Norway	49	78	142	321	667	953	1396	1897	3083	3287	3616	3807
Portugal	..	..	51	168	295	422	670	1079 b	1594	1693	1758	1797
Spain	16	42	96	214	365	498	875	1198	1525	1618	1728	1835
Sweden	..	..	309	526	936	1260	1579	1738	2273	2404	2595	2703
Switzerland	166	199	352	631	1033	1478	2033	2579	3182	3362	3649	3781
United Kingdom	84	110	164	301	482	710	986	1374	1833	2032	2231	2231[-1]
United States	144	203	347	586	1055	1759	2738	3654	4539	4888	5287	5635

Source: OECD Health Data 2005 CDROM, October 05.

Notes:

a) −1, −2, −3, 1, 2, 3 shows that data refers to 1, 2 or 3 previous or following year(s).
b) For Germany, data prior to 1990 refer to West Germany.
c) "b" means there is a break in the series for the given year.

a good deal of inaccuracy, including a lack of comparability between the countries in the definitions used.

If we concentrate on the year 2003 values, it is evident that the United States spends far more on health care than any other country with a per capita expenditure of $US 5635. With the exception of Switzerland the other more affluent countries represented in the table have per capita expenditure of around $US 2000 to slightly more than $US 3000.

The relatively higher US costs as compared with the other countries have been maintained consistently throughout the 40-year period covered by the data. In this table the values have not been deflated to constant price terms and the very large increases shown for the countries from 1960 onwards reflect periods of high inflation over that period. For this reason the representation of the expenditure values as ratios of GDP as shown in Table 10.3 provides a better picture of the movements over time for each country, and their relationships to one another.

From this table it is clear that in all OECD countries substantial increases over time in the proportions of national resources devoted to the health services have occurred. For most countries the ratio of health expenditure to GDP has more than doubled between 1960 and 2003. These changes have reflected both the allocation of greater resources such as workforce inputs and pharmaceuticals, health facilities and equipment provided to the health services, and a tendency for the prices of these inputs to increase relatively to other prices in the economies. The underlying reasons for these changes are complex and have no doubt arisen out of a great variety of political, economic, social and technological changes.

It should also be noted that amongst the developed countries shown in Table 10.3 there has been fairly considerable variation between them in the ratio of health expenditure to GDP. For 2003 these range from 15 per cent for the United States to less than eight per cent for a number of countries, including the large economies of the United Kingdom and Japan.

As we indicate below the factors affecting the health expenditure figures, especially the position of the United States as an outlier value, have been subjected to a good deal of analysis in the health economics literature, including several OECD review papers (OECD, 2002; Docteur et al., 2003, Docteur and Oxley, 2003). It is evident that the level of income as measured by the GDP per capita of each country is a major determinant of total health expenditure. Using the year 2003 values, expenditure per capita and GDP per capita are very highly correlated statistically for the developed OECD countries. Over 90 per cent of the variation in expenditure per head is explained by the GDP variations.

A further perspective on the characteristics of each country is shown in Table 10.4 where the proportion of health expenditure derived from public

Table 10.3 OECD Countries 1960–2003. Total expenditure on health – % of gross domestic product

	1960	1965	1970	1975	1980	1985	1990	1995	2000	2001	2002	2003
Australia	4.1	4.3[1]	4.6[-1]	7.1	7	7.4	7.8	8.3	9	9.1	9.3	9.3[-1]
Austria	4.3	4.6	5.1	6.9	7.4	6.4	7	8.5	7.5	7.4	7.5	7.5
Belgium	..	..	4	5.8	6.4	7.2	7.4	8.4	8.7	8.8	9.1	9.6
Canada	5.4	5.9	7	7.1	7.1	8.2	9	9.2	8.9	9.4	9.6	9.9
Denmark	..	..	8.0[1]	8.9	9.1	8.7	8.5	8.2	8.4	8.6	8.8	9
Finland	3.8	4.8	5.6	6.3	6.4	7.2	7.8	7.5	6.7	6.9	7.2	7.4
France	3.8	4.7	5.4	6.5	7.1	8.2	8.6	9.5	9.3	9.4	9.7	10.1
Germany	..	..	6.2	8.6	8.7	9	8.5	10.6	10.6	10.8	10.9	11.1
Greece	..	..	6.1	..	6.6	7.4[2]	7.4	9.6	9.9	10.2	9.8	9.9
Iceland	3	3.5	4.7	5.7	6.2	7.3	8	8.4	9.3	9.3	10	10.5
Ireland	3.7	4	5.1	7.4 b	8.4	7.6	6.1	6.8	6.3	6.9	7.3	7.4
Italy	..	..	..	..	..	7.7[3]	7.9	7.3	8.1	8.2	8.4	8.4
Japan	3	4.4	4.5	5.6	6.5	6.7	5.9	6.8 b	7.6	7.8	7.9	7.9[-1]
Luxembourg	..	..	3.6	4.9	5.9	5.9	6.1	6.4	6	6.5	7.2	6.9
Netherlands	..	..	6.9[2]	7.1	7.5	7.4	8	8.4	8.3	8.7	9.3	9.8
New Zealand	..	..	5.1	6.6	5.9	5.2	6.9	7.2	7.8	7.9	8.2	8.1
Norway	2.9	3.4	4.4	5.9	7	6.6	7.7	7.9	8.5	8.9	9.9	10.3
Portugal	..	..	2.6	5.4	5.6	6	6.2	8.2 b	9.2	9.4	9.3	9.6
Spain	1.5	2.5	3.6	4.7	5.4	5.5	6.7	7.6	7.4	7.5	7.6	7.7
Sweden	..	..	6.9	7.6	9.1	8.7	8.4	8.1	8.4	8.8	9.2	9.4
Switzerland	4.9	4.6	5.5	7	7.4	7.8	8.3	9.7	10.4	10.9	11.1	11.5
United Kingdom	3.9	4.1	4.5	5.5	5.6	5.9	6	7	7.3	7.5	7.7	7.7[-1]
United States	5	5.5	6.9	7.8	8.7	10	11.9	13.3	13.1	13.8	14.6	15

Source: OECD Health Data 2005 CD-ROM, October 05.

Notes:

a) −1, −2, −3, 1, 2, 3 shows that data refers to 1, 2 or 3 previous or following year(s).

b) For Germany, data prior to 1990 refer to West Germany.

c) "b" means there is a break in the series for the given year.

d) Some OECD countries, with relatively low GDP, have been omitted.

Table 10.4 OECD Countries 1960–2003. Public expenditure on health, % total expenditure on health

	1960	1965	1970	1975	1980	1985	1990	1995	2000	2001	2002	2003
Australia	50.4	50.9[1]	57.2[-1]	73.1	63	71.4	67.1	66.7	68.5	67.8	67.5	67.5[-1]
Austria	69.4	70.3	63	69.6	68.8	76.1	73.5	69.7	68.2	67	67.8	67.6
Belgium	..	..	..	..	..	..	..	..	..	..	..	..
Canada	42.6	51.9	69.9	76.2	75.6	75.5	74.5	71.4	70.3	70.1	69.7	69.9
Denmark	..	..	83.7[1]	85.4	87.8	85.6	82.7	82.5	82.4	82.7	82.9	83
Finland	54.1	66	73.8	78.6	79	78.6	80.9	75.6	75.1	75.9	76.3	76.5
France	62.4	71.2	75.5	78	80.1	78.5	76.6	76.3	75.8	75.9	76.1	76.3
Germany	..	..	72.8	79	78.7	77.4	76.2	80.5	78.6	78.4	78.6	78.2
Greece	..	..	42.6	..	55.6	59.9[2]	53.7	52	52.6 b	54.2	51.6	51.3
Iceland	66.7	63.1	66.2	87.1	88.2	87	86.6	83.9	82.6	82.7	83.2	83.5
Ireland	76	76.2	81.7	79.0 b	81.6	75.7	71.9	71.6	73.3	75.6	75.2	78
Italy	..	..	..	..	..	77.6[3]	79.1	71.9	73.5	75.8	75.4	75.1
Japan	60.4	61.4	69.8	72	71.3	70.7	77.6	83.0 b	81.3	81.7	81.5	81.5[-1]
Luxembourg	..	..	88.9	91.8	92.8	89.2	93.1	92.4	89.3	87.9	90.3	89.9
Netherlands	..	..	60.2[2]	67.9	69.4	70.8	67.1	71	63.1	62.8	62.5	62.4
New Zealand	..	..	80.3	73.7	88	87	82.4	77.2	78	76.4	77.9	78.7
Norway	77.8	80.9	91.6	96.2	85.1	85.8	82.8	84.2	82.5	83.6	83.5	83.7
Portugal	..	..	59	58.9	64.3	54.6	65.5	62.6 b	69.5	70.6	70.5	69.7
Spain	58.7	50.8	65.4	77.4	79.9	81.1	78.7	72.2	71.6	71.2	71.3	71.2
Sweden	..	..	86	90.2	92.5	90.4	89.9	86.6	84.9	84.9	85.1	85.2
Switzerland	..	..	..	..	..	50.3	52.4	53.8	55.6	57.1	57.9	58.5
United Kingdom	85.2	85.8	87	91.1	89.4	85.8	83.6	83.9	80.9	83	83.4	83.4[-1]
United States	23.3	22.4	36.4	41	41.5	39.9	39.6	45.3	44.2	44.8	44.9	44.4

Source: OECD Health Data 2005 CD-ROM, October 05.

Notes:

a) −1, −2, −3, 1, 2, 3 shows that data refers to 1, 2 or 3 previous or following year(s).

b) For Germany, data prior to 1990 refer to West Germany.

c) "b" means there is a break in the series for the given year.

sources is shown for all OECD countries. In this table values going back to 1960 are presented for those countries which compiled the estimates from that year onwards.

It is again evident, as we noted in Chapter 6, that the United States and Switzerland rely heavily on private sources, with private health insurance contributions and out-of-pocket payments by patients as the principal sources of their funding. What we define below as national health service-type systems, notably the United Kingdom, Sweden and Norway, have over 80 per cent of their health expenditure derived from public sources, mainly from income taxes. Countries with mixed systems of health insurance arrangements tend to have ratios of around 70 per cent or less from public sources, including government subsidies of private health insurance.

In assessing the overall effectiveness and efficiency of the health services we have to rely initially on mortality-based measures notably life expectancy, normally at birth, and infant mortality rates. It is well recognised that these are relatively crude measures which are influenced by factors other than the effectiveness of health services provision. Nevertheless, these measures appear to possess a good deal of face validity, that is, they produce rankings and changes over time that are broadly consistent with information and preconceptions based on other criteria. Tables 10.5 and 10.6 show life expectancy and infant mortality data for all available OECD countries.

These tables indicate that in all the OECD countries there have been substantial improvements in both measures of performance over the period covered by each country's data. It is evident that several countries have achieved life expectancy values at birth (effectively a summary of all current death rates) of over 80 years. The Japanese figure of 81.8 years is clearly the highest in the world. Amongst the lowest in the developed countries is the value for the United States of 77.2 years.

The infant mortality data display a similar pattern of substantial improvement since 1960 but with considerable variation between the OECD countries. Most of the developed countries have now achieved rates of fewer than five deaths per thousand live births, with the values for Iceland and Japan of 2.4 and 3, respectively, indicating the potential for further improvement in other countries. Again, the United States' rate of seven per thousand is the highest amongst the developed countries. Two transitional countries, Turkey and Mexico, have rates of over 20 per thousand. (The definitions of transitional and developing countries are discussed later.)

Again it is illuminating, though depressing, to note that the developing countries of the world typically have life expectancies of around 50 years and infant mortality rates of nearly 100. In some individual countries, especially in sub-Saharan Africa, life expectancies may be closer to 40 years and infant mortality rates well over 100 (WHO, 2006).

Table 10.5 OECD Countries 1990, 2000 and 2003. Life expectancy (in years) females, males and total population at birth

	1990			2000			2003		
	Females at birth	Males at birth	Total pop. at birth	Females at birth	Males at birth	Total pop. at birth	Females at birth	Males at birth	Total pop. at birth
Australia	80.1	73.9	77	82	76.6	79.3	82.8	77.8	80.3
Austria	78.8	72.2	75.5	81.1	75.1	78.1	81.6	75.6	78.6
Belgium	79.4	72.7	76.1	80.8	74.6	77.7	81.1[1]	75.1[1]	78.1[1]
Canada	80.8	74.4	77.6	81.9	76.7	79.3	82.1[1]	77.2[1]	79.7[1]
Czech Republic	75.4	67.6	71.5	78.4	71.7	75.1	78.5	72	75.3
Denmark	77.7	72	74.9	79.3	74.5	76.9	79.5	74.9	77.2
Finland	78.9	70.9	74.9	81	74.2	77.6	81.8	75.1	78.5
France	80.9	72.8	76.9	82.7	75.3	79	82.9	75.8	79.4
Germany	78.4	72	75.2	81	75	78	81.3	75.5	78.4
Greece	79.5	74.6	77.1	80.6	75.5	78.1	80.7	75.4	78.1
Hungary	73.7	65.1	69.4	75.9	67.4	71.7	76.5	68.3	72.4
Iceland	80.5	75.4	78	81.4	78	79.7	82.4	79	80.7
Ireland	77.6	72.1	74.9	79.1	73.9	76.5	80.3[1]	75.2[1]	77.8[1]
Italy	80.1	73.6	76.9	82.5	76.6	79.6	82.9	76.9	79.9

Japan	81.9	78.9	84.6	77.7	81.2	85.3	78.4	81.8[-1]
Korea	75.1[-1]	71.0[-1]	79.2[-1]	71.7[-1]	75.5[-1]	80.4[-1]	73.4[-1]	76.9[-1]
Luxembourg	78.5	75.4	81.1	74.8	78	81.5[-1]	74.9[-1]	78.2[-1]
Mexico	74.1	71.2	76.5	71.6	74.1	77.4	72.4	74.9
Netherlands	80.9	77.4	80.5	75.5	78	80.9	76.2	78.6
New Zealand	78.3	75.4	81.1	76.3	78.7	81.1[-1]	76.3[-1]	78.7[-1]
Norway	79.8	76.6	81.4	76	78.7	81.9	77	79.5
Poland	76.3	71.5	77.9	69.7	73.8	78.9	70.5	74.7
Portugal	77.4	73.9	80	73.2	76.6	80.6	74	77.3
Slovak Republic	75.4	71	77.4	69.2	73.3	77.8[-1]	69.9[-1]	73.9[-1]
Spain	80.3	76.8	82.5	75.7	79.1	83.7	77.2	80.5
Sweden	80.4	77.6	82	77.4	79.7	82.4	77.9	80.2
Switzerland	80.7	77.4	82.6	76.9	79.8	83.0[-1]	77.8[-1]	80.4[-1]
Turkey	68.7	66.5	70.4	65.8	68.1	71	66.4	68.7
United Kingdom	78.5	75.7	80.2	75.5	77.9	80.7	76.2	78.5
United States	78.8	75.3	79.5	74.1	76.8	79.9[-1]	74.5[-1]	77.2[-1]

Source: OECD Health Data 2005 CD-ROM, October 05.

Notes:
a) −1, −2, −3, 1, 2, 3 shows that data refers to 1, 2 or 3 previous or following year(s).
b) For the 22 European countries, the Eurostat NewChronos database is the main data source for the data shown.

Table 10.6 OECD Countries 1960–2003. Infant mortality rate, deaths per 1,000 live births

	1960	1965	1970	1975	1980	1985	1990	1995	2000	2001	2002	2003
Australia	20.2	18.5	17.9	14.3	10.7	9.9	8.2	5.7	5.2	5.3	5	4.8
Austria	37.5	28.3	25.9	20.5	14.3	11.2	7.8	5.4	4.8	4.8	4.1	4.5
Belgium	23.9	23.7	21.1	16.1	12.1	9.8	8	6.1	4.8	4.5	4.4	4.3
Canada	27.3	23.6	18.8	14.3	10.4	8	6.8	6	5.3	5.2	5.4	5.4^{-1}
Czech Republic	20	23.7	20.2	19.4	16.9	12.5	10.8	7.7	4.1	4	4.2	3.9
Denmark	21.5	18.7	14.2	10.4	8.4	8	7.5	5.1	5.3	4.9	4.4	4.4
Finland	21	17.6	13.2	9.6	7.6	6.3	5.6	3.9	3.8	3.2	3	3.1
France	27.5	22	18.2	13.8	10	8.3	7.3	4.9	4.4	4.5	4.1	3.9
Germany	35	24.1	22.5	18.9	12.4	9.1	7	5.3	4.4	4.3	4.2	4.2
Greece	40.1	34.3	29.6	24	17.9	14.1	9.7	8.1	5.9	5.1	5.1	4.8
Hungary	47.6	38.8	35.9	32.8	23.2	20.4	14.8	10.7	9.2	8.1	7.2	7.3
Iceland	13	15	13.2	12.5	7.7	5.7	5.9	6.1	3	2.7	2.2	2.4
Ireland	29.3	25.2	19.5	17.5	11.1	8.8	8.2	6.4	6.2	5.7	5	5.1
Italy	43.9	36	29.6	21.2	14.6	10.5	8.2	6.2	4.5	4.7	4.5	4.3
Japan	30.7	18.5	13.1	10	7.5	5.5	4.6	4.3	3.2	3.1	3	3
Korea	..	..	45	..	17.0^{1}	13	12.0^{1}	7.7^{1}	6.2^{-1}	6.2^{-2}	6.2^{-3}	..

Luxembourg	31.5	24	24.9	14.8	11.4	9	7.3	5.6	5.1	5.8	5.1	4.9
Mexico	..	..	79.3	63	50.9	41.1	36.1	27.5	23.3	22.4	21.4	20.1
Netherlands	17.9	14.4	12.7	10.6	8.6	8	7.1	5.5	5.1	5.4	5	4.8
New Zealand	22.6	19.5	16.7	16	13	10.9	8.4	6.7	6.3	5.6	5.6^{-1}	5.6^{-2}
Norway	18.9	16.8	12.7	11.1	8.1	8.5	7	4	3.8	3.9	3.5	3.4
Poland	54.8	43.2	36.7	29	25.5	22	19.3	13.6	8.1	7.7	7.5	7
Portugal	77.5	64.9	55.5	38.9	24.3	17.8	11	7.5	5.5	5	5	4.1
Slovak Republic	28.6	28.5	25.7	23.7	20.9	16.3	12	11	8.6	6.2	7.6	7.9
Spain	43.7	37.8	28.1	18.9	12.3	8.9	7.6	5.5	3.9	4.4	4.1	4.1
Sweden	16.6	13.3	11	8.6	6.9	6.8	6	4.2	3.4	3.7	3.3	3.1
Switzerland	21.1	17.8	15.1	10.7	9.1	6.9	6.8	5	4.9	5	4.5	4.3
Turkey	189.5	163.5	145	132.5	117.5	88	57.6	45.6	41.9	40.6	39.4	29.0 b
United Kingdom	22.5	19.6	18.5	18.9	13.9	11.1	7.9	6.2	5.6	5.5	5.2	5.3
United States	26	24.7	20	16.1	12.6	10.6	9.2	7.6	6.9	6.8	7	7.0^{-1}

Source: OECD Health Data 2005 CD-ROM, October 05.

Notes:

a) −1, −2, −3, 1, 2, 3 shows that data refers to 1, 2 or 3 previous or following year(s).

b) In the US, Canada and some Nordic countries, very premature babies with a low chance of survival are registered as live births which may not be the case in other countries.

c) For the 22 European countries, the Eurostat NewChronos database is the main data source for 1985 onwards.

d) "b" means there is a break in the series for the given year.

The principal inputs to the health care services, as we indicated in Chapter 7, are the number of nurses and doctors. Comparative data on these workforce members are shown in Tables 10.7 and 10.8.

As we suggested in Chapter 7, the nursing figures are subject to a number of definitional problems. Whilst the OECD data are for 'practising' nurses, that is those in full or part-time positions of all qualification levels, the numbers reported for some countries may include only nurses employed in hospitals, or simply full-time equivalent numbers. Other differences are stated in the notes to the table.

It is evident that the stocks of these key health services personnel in relation to population vary considerably from country to country. However, it is also clear that these variations do not seem to bear any close relationship to the health expenditure value for each country. For example, the United States and Japan do not have disproportionate numbers of these personnel in relation to other countries. The very low values for Greece, Belgium and Italy are also surprising.

Again there are some problems in the methods of defining a 'physician'. As the notes to the table indicate some countries base their estimates on full-time equivalents rather than head counts. A few countries report the number of doctors qualified to practice rather than those who are actively practising medicine. The relatively low values in the more affluent countries of Canada, New Zealand, the United Kingdom and the United States are of interest. The high value for Greece, in conjunction with the low figure in that country for nurses, suggests that the possibilities for substituting nursing personnel for medical staff should be explored carefully.

Finally, Table 10.9 provides information about another important input to the health services, namely the ratios of acute hospital beds to population.

The OECD table indicates that the definition of an acute bed may vary somewhat from country to country. The United Kingdom acute hospitals have included many long stay patients in their system and this may also be the case in Germany and Japan. Duration of hospital stays, and hence the required number of beds, is also sensitive to the method of financing hospitals. Cost reimbursement and per diem payments do not provide incentives for reducing long lengths of stay as we indicated in reviewing the reasons for the introduction of casemix funding in a number of countries, which now include Germany and Japan.

It is to be noted that for most countries the availability of acute hospital beds per capita has declined considerably over the periods of time covered by the data. The decreases reflect an international consensus that acute hospital beds were overused, and that the proportion of health expenditure

Table 10.7 OECD Countries 1960–2003. Practising nurses, density per 1 000 population, 1960 to 2003

	1960	1970	1980	1990	2000	2001	2002	2003
Australia	..	6.7	10.3	11.6	10.5	10.4	10.6	10.2
Austria	2.5	3.4	5.4	7.3	9.3	9.3	9.3	9.4
Belgium	..	..	..	..	5.4	5.5	5.6	5.8
Canada	..	6.9	9.6	11.1	10.1	10	9.4	9.8
Czech Republic	..	..	6.8	8.4	8.9	9.2	9.4	9.4
Denmark	..	..	6.9	9.3^{-1}	10	10.2	10.3	10.3^{-1}
Finland	..	..	..	6	8.2	8.6	9	9.3
France	..	3.1^{1}	4.7	5.6	6.7	7	7.2	7.3
Germany	..	..	..	..	9.4	9.5	9.6	9.7
Greece	..	1.4	1.9	3.4	3.9	3.9^{-1}	3.9^{-2}	3.9^{-3}
Hungary	1.7	2.7	3.7	4.5	4.9	4.9	5	5.1
Iceland	1.4	4.2	8.9	12.5	13.3	13.1	13.3	13.7
Ireland	..	..	..	11.3	13.9	14.8	15.3	14.8
Italy	..	..	..	5.0^{3}	5.3	5.4	5.5	5.4
Japan	1.8	2.5	4	5.8	7.6	7.6^{-1}	7.8	7.8^{-1}
Korea	..	..	..	..	1.4	1.5	1.7	1.7
Luxembourg	..	..	..	..	9.9	10.2	10.6	10.6^{-1}
Mexico	..	..	..	1.7	2.2	2.2	2.2	2.1
Netherlands	..	..	..	..	13.4	12.8	12.8^{-1}	12.8^{-2}
New Zealand	..	..	6.1	9.3	9.6	9.6	9.4	9.1
Norway	..	..	..	..	10.3	10.4	10.4^{-1}	10.4^{-2}
Poland	2.1	3	4.4	5.5	4.9	4.9	4.9	4.9
Portugal	..	1.8^{1}	2.3	2.8	3.7	3.8	4	4.2
Slovak Republic	..	..	..	..	7.4	7.3	6.9	6.5
Spain	..	..	..	..	6.4	6.6	7.3	7.5
Sweden	3.1	4.3	7	9.2	9.8	9.9	10.2	10.2^{-1}
Switzerland	..	..	..	..	10.7	10.7^{-1}	10.7^{-2}	10.7^{-3}
Turkey	..	..	1	1.3	1.7	1.7	1.7	1.7
United Kingdom	..	..	..	7.8	8.3	8.6	8.9	9.1
United States	2.9	3.7	5.6	7.2	8	7.9	7.9	7.9^{-1}

Source: OECD Health Data 2005 CD-ROM, October 05.

Notes:
a) −1, −2, −3, 1, 2, 3 shows that data refers to 1, 2 or 3 previous or following year(s).
b) Austria and Italy report only nurses employed in hospitals; they do not include nurses working in other health facilities.
c) In France, nursing assistants are not included.
d) In Germany, Mexico and Norway, data refer to full time equivalent nurses (not headcounts).
e) Spain includes only publicly employed nurses (nurses employed in the National Health Service).

devoted to these hospitals was excessive in relation to other health services activity. It is again clear from these data that the United States is a modest provider of acute hospital beds relative to that of a number of other OECD countries.

Table 10.8 OECD Countries 1960–2003. Practising physicians, density per 1 000 population, 1960 to 2003

	1960	1970	1980	1990	2000	2001	2002	2003
Australia	1.1^1	1.2^1	1.8^1	2.2	2.5	2.5	2.5	2.5^{-1}
Austria	1.2	1.4	1.6	2.2	3.2	3.3	3.3	3.4
Belgium	1.3	1.6^{-1}	2.3	3.3	3.9	3.9	3.9	3.9^{-1}
Canada	1.1^1	1.4	1.8	2.1	2.1	2.1	2.1	2.1
Czech Republic	..	1.8	2.3	2.7	3.4	3.4	3.5	3.5
Denmark	..	..	1.8	2.5	2.8	2.8	2.9	2.9^{-1}
Finland	..	..	..	2	2.6	2.6	2.6	2.6
France	..	1.2	1.9	3.1	3.3	3.3	3.3	3.4
Germany	..	..	..	2.8^1	3.3	3.3	3.3	3.4
Greece	1.3	1.6	2.4	3.4	4.3	4.4	4.4^{-1}	4.4^{-2}
Hungary	1.5	2	2.3	2.8	3.1^{-1}	3.2^1	3.2	3.2
Iceland	1.2	1.4	2.1	2.8	3.4	3.5	3.6	3.6
Ireland	..	..	..	2.0^2	2.2	2.4	2.4	2.6
Italy	..	..	..	3.8^3	4.2	4.4	4.4	4.1
Japan	1	1.1	1.3	1.7	1.9	1.9^{-1}	2	2.0^{-1}
Korea			0.5^1	0.8	1.3	1.4	1.5	1.6
Luxembourg	1	1.1	1.7	2	2.5	2.5	2.6	2.7
Mexico	..	..	..	1	1.6	1.5	1.5	1.5
Netherlands	1.1	1.2	1.9	2.5	3.2	3.3	3.1	3.1
New Zealand	1.1^1	1.1^1	1.6	1.9	2.2	2.2	2.1	2.2
Norway	1.2	1.4	2	2.6^1	2.9	3	3.1 b	3.1
Poland	1	1.4	1.8	2.1	2.2	2.3	2.3	2.5
Portugal	0.8	0.9	2	2.8	3.2	3.2	3.3	3.3
Slovak Republic	..	..	..	..	3.2	3.1	3.1	3.1
Spain	..	..	..	..	3.2	3.1	2.9	3.2
Sweden	1	1.3	2.2	2.9	3.1	3.2	3.3	3.3^{-1}
Switzerland	1.4	1.5	2.5	3	3.5	3.5	3.6	3.6^{-1}
Turkey	0.3	0.4	0.6	0.9	1.3	1.3	1.4	1.4
United Kingdom	0.8	0.9	1.3	1.6	1.9	2	2.1	2.2
United States	1.1	1.2	1.5	1.8	2.2	2.2	2.3	2.3^{-1}

Source: OECD Health Data 2005 CDROM, October 05.

Notes:
a) −1, −2, −3, 1, 2, 3 shows that data refers to 1, 2 or 3 previous or following year(s).
b) Data for Belgium, Denmark, France, Luxembourg and United States includes physicians working in industry, administration and research.
c) The Czech Republic, Mexico and Norway report full time equivalents (FTE) rather than headcounts.
d) Ireland and Netherlands provide the number of physicians entitled to practise rather than only practising physicians.
e) "b" means there is a break in the series for the given year.

Modelling health care systems

The models of the funding and organisational arrangements that have been developed in the literature draw heavily on economic variables especially in regard to health insurance and related matters. Health economists have been

Table 10.9 OECD Countries 1960–2003. Acute care beds, density per 1 000 population, 1960 to 2003

	1960	1970	1980	1990	2000	2001	2002	2003
Australia	6.5	6	6.4	4.8^{-1}	3.8	3.7	3.6	3.6^{-1}
Austria	..	..	..	7.1	6.3	6.1	6.1	6
Belgium	..	4.7	5.5	4.9	4.1	4	4	4.0^{-1}
Canada	..	..	4.6	4	3.2	3.2	3.2	3.2^{-1}
Denmark	..	5.5^{2}	5.3	4.1	3.5	3.4	3.4^{-1}	3.4^{-2}
Finland	3.9	4.8	4.9	4.3	2.4	2.4	2.3	2.3
France	..	..	6.2	5.2	4.1	4	3.9	3.8
Germany	..	..	..	8.3^{1}	6.8	6.7	6.6	6.6
Ireland	..	..	4.3	3.3	3	3	3	3
Italy	..	..	7.9	6.2	4.2	4.1	3.9	3.9^{-1}
Japan	..	..	..	12.3^{3}	9.6	9.3	8.9	8.5
Luxembourg	..	..	7.4	6.8	5.9	5.8	5.7	5.7
Netherlands	5.1	5.5	5.2	4.3	3.5	3.3	3.2	3.2^{-1}
Norway	..	..	5.2	3.8	3.1	3.1	3.1	3.1
Portugal	3.6	4.2	4.2	3.4	3.3	3.2	3.1	3.1
Spain	..	..	3.8	3.6	3.3	3.2	3.1	3.1
Sweden	..	5.5^{3}	5.1	4.1	2.4	2.4^{-1}	2.4^{-2}	2.4^{-3}
Switzerland	8.2	7.1	7.2	6.5	4.1	4	3.9	3.9
United Kingdom	..	..	..	..	3.7	3.7	3.7	3.7
United States	3.5	4.1	4.4	3.7	2.9	2.9	2.9	2.8

Source: OECD Health Data 2005 CDROM, October 05.

Notes:
a) −1, −2, −3, 1, 2, 3 shows that data refers to 1, 2 or 3 previous or following year(s).
b) The definition of "acute care" beds may vary from one country to the other. Cross-country variations should therefore be Interpreted with caution.
c) "b" means there is a break in the series for the given year.

prominent in the creation of these models but contributions have also come from other disciplinary groups notably from sociology and public health.

From a policy-making perspective the most interesting question is whether the differing methods of financing and organising the provision of health services found in the OECD countries and elsewhere have an independent influence on the expenditure on health services, on health outcomes and on the equity of health service provision. In other words do certain financing and related arrangements lead to greater or lesser expenditure on the health services, and more or less effective and equitable outcomes when account is taken of GDP differences between countries?

Where there are concerns about increasing expenditure on health services, a phenomenon which is common to all countries over the last 30 years, it may be possible to draw some conclusions from the data about which arrangements may facilitate or impede cost containment goals. In addition, there have been some recent attempts to use the international data to throw light on the issue of the relative equity of health care systems as we discussed in Chapter 8 (van Doorslaer and Wagstaff, 1999; Wagstaff and van Doorslaer, 1999, 2000).

The policy issue of the relationship between expenditure on health services and the achievement of efficiency and equity goals for each country can only be resolved comprehensively by the use of evaluation procedures, including those described in Chapter 8. Nevertheless, there has been an underlying assumption of policy-makers and governments in recent years that some of their own problems may be reduced by reference to the experience of other countries. Moreover, it is this possibility that has led the OECD to generating the statistical and related information on health expenditure and health outcomes for the member countries.

The special problem of the outlier status of the US health care system as indicated in the international data has generated a large volume of research in that country and elsewhere designed to explore this phenomenon, and closely related issue of cost containment (Reinhardt et al., 2002, 2004; Bodenheimer, 2005a, b, c,).

For the purpose of drawing conclusions about the effects of the varying methods of organising, financing and providing health services it is essential to categorise the methods into a manageable set. The establishment of a useful typology of health service characteristics is not an easy task since a large number of aspects of the health services exist which might form the basis of such a classification. The following is a list of the principal characteristics which can be considered for this purpose and which have been used in classifying countries:

- the sources of funding, private and public
- the ownership and control of health care facilities
- the provision, nature and coverage of health insurance
- the method of paying physicians

For each characteristic it must be emphasised that in every country there is a mixture of each of the characteristics. No country relies solely on one funding method or on one method of paying for medical services. Similarly, a number of different arrangements for the ownership and control of hospitals and other health care facilities exist in each country. Health insurance may be provided by different organisations for the various age and income groups.

However, in each case it is possible to distinguish the predominant modes adopted by each country. It is also important to recognise that the typologies which emerge from a consideration of these characteristics usually encompass combinations of them.

The term national health service is usually applied to those countries where most funding is derived from general taxation revenue and private funding is low, the ownership and control of health care facilities is primarily the responsibility of governments, most medical services are provided by doctors who are salaried or paid for using capitation arrangements, and health insurance is mainly publicly provided with universal coverage of the population. The health services of the United Kingdom, Portugal, Denmark, Ireland, Sweden, Norway, Finland and Italy would usually be included as national health services amongst the OECD countries.

At the other end of the public/private spectrum are those countries which rely heavily on private funding, ownership and control of health facilities. The United States is the obvious example and possibly the only clear-cut case, although Switzerland might be included as having sufficient of the private characteristics to be placed in this category. Unlike the United States, however, Switzerland has complete coverage of the population by health insurance. The detailed features of each of these countries have been reviewed extensively in the health services literature and we discuss the differences between them in our case studies later in this chapter.

All the other OECD countries have what might be described as mixed systems in which public funding and ownership/control predominates but there is a substantial private sector in terms of the ownership of facilities, the provision of health insurance or the status of medical staff. Each has insurance arrangements for health care which cover the whole population. However, the methods of doctor payments and the organisation of health insurance vary considerably amongst these countries.

For example, in comparing Canada and Australia, the former country has almost a complete absence of private hospitals and the use of private health insurance is restricted to a relatively small number of services. In Australia private hospitals and private health insurance are important features of the system. Fee-for-service, and the private status of doctors, is almost universal in Canada, whereas Australia makes quite extensive use of the salaried payment of medical staff in the (free) public hospital system.

As we discuss in more detail shortly, a further distinguishing characteristic of the health care systems of each country is the extent of governmental control and regulation of the health services. These factors are linked with the ownership of health care facilities where in national health services, mainly funded through taxation, governments have a direct financial interest in keeping costs as low as possible.

Even in the mixed systems of public and private ownership, and of health insurance arrangements, the degree of government regulation of private activities may be considerable. Government regulation of private health insurance may set out very detailed requirements for the conditions that must be applied by private insurers such as community rating rather than risk rating of health insurance members. The rates charged may also be the subject of regulations.

It should be noted that the typology of health care systems set out above has similarities and differences from that of Hurst (OECD, 1992; 1994) which was also used in an OECD econometric study of factors affecting health spending (Gerdtham and Jonsson, 2000). What Hurst calls 'public integrated models' correspond to national health services as defined above. However, his 'public reimbursement' countries include France, Belgium, Australia and Japan as falling within this category, together with the United States and Switzerland. As we have noted earlier the United States and Switzerland rely so heavily on private insurance and other private sources of funding that they would seem to differ fundamentally from the other countries included in this category. It is ultimately a matter of judgement and the objectives of the study to determine how many categories should be formed, how they are defined and the countries which should be placed in each.

Country case studies

For a selection of OECD countries where reliable information is available regarding their health services structures and characteristics we present below the essential features of each, including data on their performance and efficiency in achieving outcome and financial objectives. We devote considerable attention to the United States and British systems partly because of the sharp contrast between the two, partly because of the wealth of information (and mis-information!) about each, but most importantly because in some circles in other countries the models represented by these countries have been regarded as ideals to be emulated. In both countries, moreover, reforms have been high on the policy agendas as the problems and limitations of the systems have increasingly become the focus of community, patient and provider dissatisfaction.

In the selection of the other OECD countries for review, we have endeavoured to provide a mix of those with both public and private elements, and those defined as national health services. The selections have been influenced also by the availability of published sources of information about the characteristics of the health services in individual countries.

The United States

It has already been noted that the US health care system differs dramatically from other systems in the developed world. It is also the only developed country where a consensus has emerged about the need for substantial reforms, but with greatly divergent views being present about the preferred structure of the reforms.

Summary of characteristics

- Per capita expenditure and the per cent of GDP associated with health expenditure are higher by a considerable margin than those of any other country.
- The increases in health expenditure over time for most periods have been uniformly greater than those of other countries.
- The proportion of health expenditure funded from private sources, including private health insurance and the out-of-pocket payments of patients, is substantially higher than in any other developed country.
- Unlike other OECD countries where some form of health insurance covers the whole resident population about 15 per cent of Americans lack such coverage.
- The mortality experience of the US population, as measured by life expectancy and infant mortality rates, is mediocre as compared with that of other developed countries (see Tables 10.5 and 10.6).
- The United States has an unusually high ratio of specialist medical staff to general practitioners. Patients may seek care directly from a medical specialist; general practitioners do not act as gatekeepers to the system as in many other OECD countries.

Why is the United States an 'outlier'?

The reasons for these differences in the characteristics of the US health care system have been the subject of a number of research studies by policy analysts, mainly based in the United States. The studies which have focused on comparisons with other countries have proliferated in recent years and have sought to explain the reasons for the differences (Reinhardt et al., 2002; Anderson et al., 2003, 2005; Bodenheimer, 2005a, b, c).

The papers by Reinhardt et al. and of Anderson et al. effectively debunked the explanations for high expenditure often put forward by many US commentators, which focus on such factors as the practice of defensive medicine and the threat of malpractice litigation, the more extensive use of high technology procedures and the existence of supply constraints in other countries which lead to waiting lists for services. The studies put together an impressive array of data from the OECD and other sources that demonstrated the differences between the United States and other OECD countries in regard to these factors, which can only explain a very small proportion of the differences in expenditure.

In their 2005 study Anderson and his colleagues conducted a review of malpractice claims and payments in the United States, Australia, Canada and the United Kingdom. They found that in 2001 the number of claims per capita in the United States was somewhat higher than in the other countries, 0.18 as compared with 0.12, 0.04, and 0.12, respectively. However, in none of the countries did the payments made as a result of successful malpractice claims exceed 0.5 per cent of total health expenditure.

They acknowledged that it is impossible on the basis of the available evidence to estimate the extra costs that might be incurred as a result of physicians practising more defensively in the United States because of the fear of being sued. However, they stated that a study by the US Congressional Budget Office concluded that savings resulting from tort law reform would be 'small'. They also argued that some defensive medicine is likely to be practised in other OECD countries.

Anderson and his colleagues also cited the international evidence that measures of the availability of resources for providing health services are no greater than in other OECD countries. From Table 10.9 we note that the stock of acute hospital beds in the United States was 2.8 per thousand of population in 2003 as compared with a median value of approximately 3.7 for all OECD countries (OECD, 2005b). The number of physicians per thousand of population in the United States was 2.3 in 2002 as compared with the median value for all OECD countries of about 3.1 per thousand of population (Table 10.8). When the poorer OECD countries are excluded similar results are cited by the OECD for the number of MRI units and CT scanners per thousand of population, but the comparability of these values between countries is more doubtful (OECD, 2005b).

Higher prices of US inputs

The high ratio of health expenditure to GDP in the United States seems to be the product of a number of factors of which the most influential is the prices of the goods and services rather than the volumes of these (Reinhardt et al., 2002; Anderson et al., 2003, 2005). In other words the fees, wages and salaries and other prices of the items making up health expenditure are greater in the United States as compared with other countries. Why this is the case is not known with any degree of certainty. However, it is evident that some of the free market approaches that actually exist in the United States favour a lack of controls over medical fees and the prices of pharmaceutical products. Moreover, whilst there may be a lesser degree of the rationing of some health services in the United States as compared with other countries for those comprehensively insured, some rationing is based on prices and the large pool of uninsured members of the population, of the order of 45 million people.

The evidence for the role of prices as the major factor leading to the much higher proportion of GDP devoted to health services in the United States is compelling. Combining the much higher expenditure per head data for the United States with the much more modest measures of health services utilisation in that country inevitably leads to the conclusion that higher prices per unit of resource input are present (Anderson et al., 2003).

Moreover, every available direct indicator of price differentials between the United States and other countries displays a remarkable divergence. Thus the average cost per acute hospital bed-day in the United States was 2.8 times higher than the median value in other comparable OECD countries in 1999 (Reinhardt et al., 2002). The average income of doctors in the United States was 2.7 times as much as in other OECD countries. For pharmaceutical products the differentials obtained from various sources vary greatly depending on the methods used, whether account is taken of subsidies and rebates, and whether wholesale or retail prices are compared (Danzon and Furukawa, 2003). However, there can be little doubt that the cost to governments, health insurance organisations and consumers of pharmaceutical products is higher than in most other countries. The cost of capital intensive and expensive health technologies such as CAT and MRI is also much higher in the United States than elsewhere.

Part of the reason for the much higher cost per acute hospital bed-day in the United States is the tendency for a greater proportion of higher cost procedures, notably coronary artery by-pass procedures, being performed in US hospitals than in other countries. However, the somewhat more complex casemix of US hospitals is unlikely to explain more than a small proportion of the large cost differential.

The reasons for the higher prices of health care inputs in the United States are complex, but their analysis is illuminating in relation to the issue of how the methods of organising and paying for health services in different countries affect the efficiency of health care provision. They also throw light on how some approaches to the application of health economics may have greater explanatory power than others.

Less government regulation

The American political system with its ethos of minimum government intervention and the ability of well-organised and funded lobby groups to influence Congressional decision-making cannot be discounted as a factor in the favourable conditions created for health service providers. It should also be borne in mind that in spite of the growth of prospective payment systems there remains a large amount of cost reimbursement of hospitals by health insurers. As we noted in Chapter 6, cost reimbursement places fewer constraints on hospital budgeting to achieve greater efficiency in staff payments and their deployment.

We have indicated previously that countries may differ considerably in the extent to which governments exercise regulatory controls over all aspects of their health care systems, including those of the private provision and insurance sectors. These variations may reflect underlying political and ideological factors, and the way in which the health services are organised and funded.

The role of ideology and politics

In the United States it is probably an accurate summary of the impact of these ideological and political factors that governmental influence via institutional regulations is smaller than in all or most other developed countries. We leave to the political scientists and sociologists the explication of the detailed reasons for the lesser ability of governments in the Unted States to exercise control and influence over institutions and services than their counterparts in other countries. However, an aversion to big government and regulatory interference seems to be characteristic of the American 'psyche' and possibly carefully cultivated by those provider interests that stand to gain from the absence of government involvement (Evans, 1997).

One recent account stresses the role of pressure groups, including the medical profession, private health insurance providers and pharmaceutical manufacturers, with a strong interest in maintaining the status quo as the principal political obstacles to reforms in the United States (Quadagno, 2005).

The interaction between providers and purchasers

The health services of the United States are characterised by a multiplicity of subsystems or markets in which providers and suppliers interact with payers and purchasers. Providers and suppliers include doctors and other health services personnel, hospitals, nursing homes and other organisations, together with the manufacturers of medical equipments and pharmaceuticals. Payers and purchasers include governments, health insurance organisations, employers and private individuals. The nature of the interaction is one of conflict since the providers and suppliers wish to maximise their incomes and the other groups wish to minimise their outgoings (Bodenheimer, 2005a).

These conflicts are present in all health care systems but what is crucial is the respective market power of the various actors in the different systems. In the United States there is clear evidence that the market power of providers and suppliers is much greater than in other countries (Bodenheimer, 2005c). The dominance of providers historically can be traced back to the emergence of health insurance where the Blue Cross and Blue Shield health insurance organisations were established by hospital and physician groups. This led to a major barrier to health insurers serving the interests of their subscribers and patients in the way that their counterparts in most other countries have done.

However, the absence of a strong role for governments in the US health care system to act as a countervailing power to the influence of providers has possibly been the principal factor leading to the higher prices of health care inputs in the United States as compared with other developed countries. It has been well documented, moreover, that the multiplicity of private health insurers, together with the detailed patient charging methods necessarily adopted by hospitals because of the way that hospitals are funded by a large number of payers, generate much higher administrative costs than in other countries (Reinhardt et al., 2002). Reinhardt and his colleagues remark that US policy-makers should perhaps fund more research on 'evidence-based administration', along with evidence-based medicine!

Positive and negative results of the US system

When the health expenditure data are reviewed in conjunction with the data on the measures of health services outcomes, notably life expectancy and infant mortality previously quoted, it is difficult to avoid the conclusion that the allocative efficiency of the US health care system is relatively low. However, mention must be made of the very positive contributions of the United States in a number of health-related areas.

There is no doubt that the United States leads the world in medical research as evidenced by such indicators as the number of Nobel prize winners the country has produced, and the huge number of research publications emanating from that country. The US record in health services research is also highly impressive. Amongst the many contributions that researchers from a variety of backgrounds have made in this area, the development of the diagnosis-related group (DRG) casemix system by Fetter and Thompson which is revolutionising the funding of hospitals in a large number of OECD countries, as we discussed in Chapter 6, is deserving of special mention.

It might also be noted that the work of Fetter and Thompson was inspired in part by the distinguished Harvard economist Martin Feldstein's pioneering study on the British NHS where he demonstrated using econometric methods that the casemix of hospitals had a considerable influence on hospital costs (Feldstein, 1967).

It is pleasing to note that cogent criticisms of the US health care system, rather than defensive stances, are now emanating from prominent US health economists and physicians as we have indicated in this chapter.

The United Kingdom

The United Kingdom consists of England, Scotland, Wales and Northern Ireland. There are some differences between these countries in the way that the health services are organised and managed, following on the devolution in 1997 granting a measure of autonomy to Scotland and Wales. However, the British government based in London exerts the ultimate financial responsibility. For our present purposes we shall treat the National Health Service (NHS) as a single entity in discussing its salient features.

Two chapters in the recent book dealing with the public-private mix for health in a number of countries (Maynard, 2005), present up-to-date information about the UK NHS (Klein, 2005; Maynard, 2005a).

Summary of characteristics

- The service is funded by the central government out of general taxation revenue.
- Most services, including hospital and medical services, are free to patients. The whole population is covered by the NHS.
- General practitioners act as gatekeepers for the medical care system; referrals to hospitals and specialist practitioners are made via the general practitioners.
- Hospital-based specialists are paid for on a salaried basis. However, there has been a recent proposal for fee-for-service (FFS) remuneration for surgeons. The payments to general practitioners are based on capitation, but with some FFS payments to encourage the provision of services such as preventive measures.
- There is a small but growing private sector including the provision of hospital services and private health insurance. Private payments, including out-of-pocket expenses for dentistry and other services, represent only about 16 per cent of all health expenditure.
- Total health expenditure per capita and the proportion of GDP per capita represented by health expenditure are lower than that of most comparable OECD countries. The per capita value of health expenditure in purchasing power parity (PPP) $US is approximately one half that of the United States.
- The mortality experience of the United Kingdom as measured by life expectancy and infant mortality are close to the OECD average and slightly better than the US values (see Tables 10.5 and 10.6).

High allocative efficiency?

As judged by these indicators of expenditure and mortality experience, the NHS must be judged as more efficient relative to the United States and a number of other developed countries. The reasons for the lower per capita expenditure again may be traced to the lower prices of inputs, notably of medical and other clinical staff, of pharmaceuticals and of medical devices. As Tables 10.7–10.9 have indicated, the provision of health services inputs is similar to that in other OECD countries. However, an important exception is the lower availability of high technology medical devices, notably MRI units and CT scanners (OECD, 2005b).

Low input prices and administrative costs

The lower prices in the NHS as compared with the United States reflect the fact that payments for these services are predominantly controlled by the central government. As the sole purchaser of the services the government through its administrative agencies is in the position of a monopsonist (one buyer) in its dealing with providers and is therefore better placed to secure lower prices than purchasers of health services in the United States and other countries. Overall, in NHS type systems, where most revenue for health services is government controlled, the total funding of health services can be capped by the central authority.

Practice/quality variations

Despite the evidence of the overall relative allocative efficiency of the British NHS, in recent years there have been sustained attempts to increase the technical efficiency of service delivery. There was concern in policy circles that the variations between health regions in such measures as hospital length of stay, and referral rates to specialist treatment between general practitioners and regions, indicated that there was scope for efficiency gains.

In Chapter 6 we discussed the measures designed to increase efficiency, initiated by the Thatcher conservative government in the early 1990s, which were based on introducing competition between providers of health services, derived from the work of Enthoven. We also noted in that chapter that the success of the measures was very limited. As we indicated previously, evaluations of the technical efficiency of NHS hospitals and other health services have been very few, as compared with other countries.

There has also been growing concern in the NHS that more needed to be done to improve the quality of clinical services. This followed on the avoidable deaths of many children at Bristol hospital in 1995 following on cardiac surgery and the revelation that the safeguards in the system to avoid such fiascos were weak. As we noted in Chapter 6, the first initiative has been to strengthen 'clinical governance', which has meant the achievement of greater monitoring and managerial control over clinical activities. It is probably the case that in the NHS in the past there have been fewer formal mechanisms to assure the quality of medical care delivered in hospitals than exist in the US system.

The second initiative has been to promote the establishment of more guidelines about clinical practice, including the use of technology, following on the revelation of considerable variations in practice between regions. As we indicated in regard to work of this kind in the United States, the existence of these variations points to there being considerable scope for the achievement of greater quality and cost reductions in service provision. In principle, an NHS funding and organisational arrangement should provide a greater capacity, given the political will, to confront these problems than in the United States and elsewhere.

Waiting lists and rationing

The other major problem in the NHS, and politically the most daunting, is the existence of lengthy waiting lists for elective surgery and other discretionary hospital admissions. In our view, as we indicated in discussing the reasons for the higher health expenditure in the United States as compared with Britain and other OECD countries, the presence of waiting lists in the latter countries is likely to make only a modest contribution to the expenditure differentials.

Nevertheless, the publicity given to the waiting lists and other signs of service rationing cannot be ignored by governments. According to an OECD report the waiting lists in the United Kingdom are worse than in any other OECD country (Koen, 2000).Whether the British government's decision in 2000 to spend more on the NHS in relation to GDP is likely to alleviate the problem remains to be seen (Klein, 2001, 2006).

The waiting list problem is one aspect of the rationing issue in government-funded health care systems. In Britain in the past what has been described as implicit rationing seems to prevail (Mechanic, 1976, 1997). This means that a good deal of discretion is afforded to specialist medical staff to decide on which types of patients should be treated, especially where the treatment costs are high. Thus older patients whose condition might be improved by renal dialysis or cardiac surgical interventions may not be offered these options, if rightly or wrongly, the senior medical personnel regard it as preferable to use the limited resources, capped in aggregate by the government, for the treatment of other patients.

Implicit rationing of health services has the advantage of transferring the responsibility for crucial resource allocation decisions to the medical staff and possibly avoiding the opprobrium that would otherwise fall on the government if these rationing decisions could be attributed directly to it. Implicit rationing may also service the interests of the medical profession in preserving its much valued clinical autonomy.

However, implicit rationing is likely to have the consequence of contributing to undesirable variations between regions and individual hospitals in medical practice. In turn this may mean that similar age and disease groups may be treated less equitably depending on their geographical location. Left in the hands of individual groups of clinicians, moreover, the rationing process is unlikely to be influenced by relative cost-effectiveness considerations, as we noted in the previous chapter. This is no doubt an important reason for the proliferation of government-funded cost-effectiveness and cost utility studies in Britain, as we indicated in Chapter 8.

The recent attempts in the NHS to create more guidelines for clinical practice via the use of evidence-based medicine, clinical trials evaluations and technology assessment may be perceived as a move in the direction of a more explicit rationing process based in part on economic inputs.

Equity and the NHS

Despite the potential for inequities in the NHS there can be little doubt that the overall funding characteristics produce a greater degree of equity in the workings of the system than in the United States and in other more privatised funding and organisational arrangements. The evidence for this conclusion is based on the work of van Doorslaer and Wagstaff and their colleagues quoted in Chapter 8 who reviewed the equity outcomes of the funding policies adopted in a number of European countries and the United States (van Doorslaer and Wagstaff, 1999).

An index of progressivity was developed by Kakwani (1977) for the purpose of measuring how progressive is the incidence of a taxation system, that is, how much redistribution of income from higher income groups to lower income groups it produces. van Doorslaer and Wagstaff adapted the Kakwani index to measure the achievement of horizontal and vertical equity by the health care system financing methods. These versions of the equity principle were also defined in Chapter 8.

For the United States and the United Kingdom, Wagstaff and van Doorslaer (1997) have calculated the Kakwani indexes for total health care funding. For the United States the value was −1.3 and for the United Kingdom it was 0.5. Negative values of the Kakwani index represent a regressive impact of the financing methods and positive values indicate a progressive impact. A value of zero indicates no redistributive impact of the funding arrangements.

Australia

The health care system in Australia is characterised by a mix of public and private financing, the predominance of publicly funded health insurance and of publicly owned and controlled acute hospitals but with a quite substantial private insurance and private hospital sector. It is therefore part of the mixed systems which characterise many of the European OECD countries.

A federal system of government operates in which the federal (Australian) government finances the health insurance system and the states and territories are responsible for the public hospitals which provide free medical, medication and accommodation care with Australian government subsidies.

Summary of characteristics

- The percentages that health expenditure represents of GDP and health expenditure per capita are similar to the OECD median values as Tables 10.2 and 10.3 indicate.
- The proportion of health expenditure derived from private sources is somewhat higher than the median for OECD countries, but much lower than the US value.
- Private health insurance covers about 40 per cent of the population, and is mainly designed to cover private hospital costs. Additional services such as dentistry and allied health may also be covered by private health insurance, but not the difference between the Medicare rebate and the actual payment for a medical service.
- Private hospitals are responsible for about 30 per cent of acute hospital bed-days.
- The public health insurance program (Medicare) covers the entire population and meets a high proportion of patient costs for services provided by doctors, optometrists and most recently clinical psychologists.
- Under an agreement between the state and territory governments and the Australian government, free public hospital services, including the associated medical and pharmaceutical services, are available to all Medicare beneficiaries. There are no co-payments.
- Most services provided by general practitioners are remunerated on an FFS basis. Hospital-based specialists in public hospitals are paid for using a part-time salaried method, supplemented by FFS in smaller hospitals.

- The use of medical specialists outside hospitals requires a referral from a general practitioner.
- Infant mortality rates and life expectancy are better than in most OECD countries including the United States and the United Kingdom (see Tables 10.5 and 10.6).

Politically induced changes in health insurance

Australia is one of the few countries which have moved from voluntary health insurance to one in which health insurance covered the entire population, reverted to a modified version of the voluntary system and then changed back to the current Medicare scheme. These changes have been driven by politics and ideology. After World War II, the labor (democratic socialist) government had taken some tentative steps towards the establishment of an NHS-type system. These were vigorously resisted by the medical profession and on the basis of a High Court decision it appeared likely that further measures would be declared unconstitutional.

With the election of a conservative government in 1949 a voluntary health insurance scheme was introduced in which private health insurance was subsidised by the Australian government. Private health funds were established which followed closely the patterns of their American Blue Cross and Blue Shield counterparts. It also shared the US characteristic of leaving a significant proportion of the population uninsured.

With the election of a labor government in 1972, a universal health insurance program (Medibank) was introduced in 1975. The then opposition parties, the medical profession and the private health funds bitterly opposed the changes. In some respects Medibank was modelled on the recently introduced Canadian program of medical and hospital insurance. The design of the program was largely the responsibility of two prominent Australian health economists, Drs Richard Scotton and John Deeble.

Following on the return to government of the conservative coalition parties in 1975 most of the Medibank system was dismantled culminating in a return to what was largely the previous voluntary health insurance program. However, when the labor party was elected again in 1983 high priority was given to the return to what was essentially the Medibank program, under the name of Medicare.

Despite the defeat of the labor party in 1996 the coalition parties to date have retained most of the features of Medicare, largely because of its popularity with the electorate. However, the present Federal government has taken steps to encourage private health insurance by a generous set of subsidies and tax incentives especially for more affluent Australians to acquire private health insurance (Hall and Savage, 2005). The coverage of the population by private health insurance had dropped from the mid-80s levels of over 60 per cent to just over 30 per cent by the late 1990s; the subsequent subsidies and other measures led to an increase to slightly more than 40 per cent in the last few years.

Perhaps to a greater extent than in other comparable countries the health insurance system in Australia has been the subject of bitter political conflict for the last 60 years. The debate has reflected a deep-seated division between the major political parties and their supporters in regard to the values that prevail in most European countries favouring equity principles based on ability to pay, and those that seem dominant in the United States (Duckett, 2000b; Palmer and Short, 2000). The role of the private hospital and insurance sectors has enabled the more affluent members of the community to avoid the problems created by waiting lists for elective procedures in public hospitals. As in the case of the United Kingdom long waiting lists for certain types of surgery have created continuing problems, especially for state and territory governments.

A weakness of the public health insurance system is that there is no direct control over the fees charged by doctors. Fees for general practitioner and specialist services are established by the federal government for health insurance purposes, but there is no legal or other obligation for doctors to adhere to these schedules (unlike the Canadian situation discussed next).

However, a direct billing option is available to doctors whereby they can claim a high proportion of the schedule fee by submitting a direct claim for each patient to Medicare. In this case there is no charge to the patient. Competitive pressures and the simplicity of the billing procedure have led to this option being fairly popular with general practitioners and about 70 per cent of medical bills have been paid for in this way. Most specialists, except pathologists, do not undertake direct billing and the out-of-pocket payments for these services may be very high for certain specialty groups.

Good performance overall?

The overall allocative efficiency of the Australian health care system, in the light of the expenditure per capita and mortality data would seem to be relatively high. However several problems are present.

Aboriginal health remains deplorable

The health and mortality experience of the indigenous population is very poor and is similar to that of a third world (developing) country (Australian Institute of Health and Welfare, 2005). Some improvements have taken place in recent years following on large increases in expenditure on Aboriginal health but much remains to be done. It has become well recognised recently that problems of overcrowded and inadequate housing, along with those associated with alcohol abuse and poor diets make greater contributions to the poor health status of the indigenous than do any problems of access to health services.

Equity concerns

There are question marks about the equity of the financing and provision methods. Very recently van Doorslaer has included Australia in a study of the equity of the utilisation of health services for a number of countries (van Doorslaer and Masserid, 2004). The results were somewhat equivocal because of the absence of some key data for Australia. However, it is likely that Australia in a comprehensive review of the equity of the system using the van Doorslaer and Wagstaff methods would not fare well in comparison with many OECD countries. As we noted earlier, the relatively large role of private health insurance and the fairly high out-of-pocket payments by patients lead to an above average proportion of funding from private sources.

In respect of the ability to pay principle and the fact that many persons in lower income groups contribute to private health insurance and use private hospitals, these results raise doubts about the degree of vertical equity generated by the Australian system. At the same time, with the funding of public hospitals and of the public insurance system being mainly from general taxation revenue based on a reasonably progressive scale (subject to an increasing reliance on regressive indirect taxes recently), this leads to a greater tendency to meet the ability to pay principle.

The equity of the Australian funding methods remains in doubt until more empirical work based on the recent European studies is undertaken. However, the questionable degree of equity currently achieved does point to the implications of further attempts to apply user pay principles, and the further transfer of health funding and other activities to the private sector.

Federal system problems

A further problem for the Australian health care system is the division of responsibilities between the federal and state governments. We noted above that public health insurance is funded and administered by the federal government which also subsidises and regulates private health insurance. However, the state and territory governments own and manage most public hospitals and also exercise oversight of private hospitals. This situation has led to some administrative waste from the overlapping responsibilities, the attempt of each level of government to blame the other for funding and other shortfalls, and to the implementation of policies the main 'benefits' of which are the transfer of expenditure from one level to the other.

The state governments, bearing most of the direct funding responsibility for public hospitals, have had a strong financial incentive to transfer eligible patients quickly to nursing homes, where the financial costs are borne mainly by the federal government and private contributions. Similarly, the rapid process of 'de-institutionalisation' of psychiatric patients implemented in all states in the 1980s was driven in part by the objective of transferring the responsibility for these patients from the state psychiatric hospitals to federally subsidised nursing homes, boarding houses and social security payments. The promised financial support by the states for additional community mental health services has been slow to materialise. In both these examples the implications for the quality of life of the patients involved has been questionable.

Canada

The Canadian health care system due to its geographical proximity to the United States has often been the subject of comparisons with its southern neighbour, leading to a good deal of information being generated about the costs of administration in the two countries, and the strengths and weaknesses of each system.

Canada is usually regarded as having a mixed health care system but it differs from the others in this category in that private health insurance is limited to a relatively few items, notably pharmaceuticals and long-term care. However, it does not fit into the national health service group in that the hospitals are not owned and controlled by governments, the proportion of private health expenditure is relatively high and FFS remuneration of doctors is almost universal for inpatient and out of hospital medical treatment. A detailed account of the Canadian health care system and its problems is provided by Evans (2000).

Summary of characteristics

- The Canadian system of government is a federal one but with more autonomy residing with the provinces than in other federal systems.
- The eight Canadian provinces and three territories fund and administer the health insurance program. Medicare, under Federal government guidelines and funding transfers.
- Income tax is the main source of funding for the Canadian Medicare program.
- All members of the Canadian population are covered by the public insurance system.

- The percentage of GDP devoted to health care and expenditure per capita on health services are somewhat higher than the OECD median values but much lower than the US values.
- All hospital services and other medical services are free to patients.
- The fees payable to doctors are negotiated between the medical profession and the Canadian government. Extra billing, that is the charging above the schedule of fees by doctors, is illegal under Canadian government legislation.
- Despite the free hospital and medical services the proportion of private funding of health services is relatively high largely because other health services are not funded under the Medicare program.
- Total expenditure on pharmaceuticals and the proportion of this expenditure derived from private sources are fairly substantial with separate benefit plans operating in each province with high co-payments, and with support for aspects of this expenditure being provided by private health insurance.

Good performance overall?

With above average mortality performance and expenditure per capita only modestly greater than the OECD median value the Canadian system emerges as relatively efficient on the basis of these somewhat crude indicators. The low administrative costs as compared with the United States are no doubt a product of the single government health insurer in each province and the fact that no charges are levied for hospital services.

A 2004 survey by the Commonwealth Fund indicated that the satisfaction of the Canadian population with their health care system was quite high with only 14 per cent of the population indicating that the system should be rebuilt as compared with 33 per cent in the United States, 22 per cent in Australia and 13 per cent in the United Kingdom.

Equity goals achieved?

The funding of medical and hospital services from taxation revenue provides a presumption that the ability to pay principle is well imbedded in the Canadian health services with the usual implications for the presence of an equitably financed service. Again, however, there has been no study in Canada of which we are aware that confirms this conclusion.

Problems of growing resource use

The foregoing account of health care in Canada should not be interpreted as indicating that there is an absence of problems and pressures to reform or modify aspects of the current economic and other policies. In common with other countries with similar financing methods for the health services there is constant pressure for the expenditure to increase and a reluctance of government and voters to fund via taxation the additional expenditure. Attacks on the public health insurance program, with claims that the system is 'unsustainable', have been analysed recently by Evans and Vujicic (2005). They argue that these attacks, supported by the media, have a strong political motivation, being based on a pro-rich bias.

Jurisdictional complexity

Canada is possibly unique in the jurisdictional complexity of health care funding and provision. As compared with other federal systems such as Australia with similar health insurance funding and payment methods, the more limited role of the Canadian federal government in health insurance and the provision of pharmaceutical benefits supports this conclusion.

The issue of the additional administrative and other costs associated with the decentralisation of health insurance to the individual jurisdictions does not seem to have been pursued in the studies of the Canadian system, possibly because this method of operation is unlikely ever to change given the political constraints. These include the strength of the separatist movement in Quebec.

Concentration of government support on medical and hospital charges

Canadian policy-makers and others have tended to regard the health care system as consisting only of hospitals and doctors, as the summary of its characteristics by Evans and Vujicic (2005) suggests. This perspective has no doubt contributed to the Canadian system of health insurance, as instituted by the federal government, having concentrated on generous subsidy and free treatment for the services provided by these two groups. As we have already noted, the subsidy arrangements for pharmaceuticals and long-term care are less generous, leading to the surprisingly high percentage of total health expenditure derived from private sources.

Critiques; medical savings accounts

A recent paper by Byrne and Rathwell (2005) also indicated that almost since its inception there have been numerous critiques of the Canadian health insurance program and many proposals for changing the system. Many of these seem to have arisen from an appraisal of US health funding characteristics, leading to proposed reforms for Canada including an increased use of patient contributions in reducing demand and the need for government funding. The most recent example explored in detail by Byrne and Rathwell is the proposed use of the US policy initiative of creating medical savings accounts (MSAs).

The MSAs are designed to operate as a bank account in which consumers contribute funds with the outgoings needing to be earmarked for health expenditure. Their underlying purpose is to make patients more price sensitive and hence to use demand side measures to control costs. Byrne and Rathwell subject the theoretical and empirical evidence regarding MSAs to a thorough critical review and express considerable reservations about the requirements for them to work effectively in the Canadian context.

As we have emphasised in previous chapters all proposals to have greater consumer cost sharing and influence are based on a simplistic reliance on neoclassical free market economics and ignore the effects on equity, and the influence of providers on decision-making and health services utilisation.

Switzerland

The Swiss health care system operates within a federal system of government in which the cantons play an important role. The system, overall, does not fit very well into either of the two categories of a privately dominated or a mixed public and private system. In other words it shares some of the characteristics of the US funding and organisational arrangements, but there are also features which are common to the other mixed systems of Europe.

Expenditure per capita on health services is higher than in any other country except the United States, and the proportion of expenditure derived from private sources is also exceeded only by the United States amongst the OECD countries (Tables 10.2 and 10.4). Gross Domestic Product per head in Switzerland is also higher than in other OECD countries, again with the exception of the United States and Luxembourg (Table 10.1).

Summary of characteristics

- All Swiss residents are covered by a fairly extensive package of health insurance which is provided by about 90 separate organisations.
- Following the passage of federal legislation in 1994, the terms and conditions under which the private health funds operate are tightly controlled by the federal government.
- The control of private health insurance leads to the requirement of community rating of health insurance premiums with a few exceptions, and the offering of a range of choices of deductibles and of co-insurance by each organisation. No claim bonus rebates are also available.

- Unlike other private health insurance schemes the Swiss health insurance premiums are based on per capita payments. Large families pay proportionately more than small families for the same policy coverage.
- Government subsidy of private health insurance is confined to the premiums paid by people in the lower income groups.
- Payments to doctors are on an FFS basis with the fee schedules being derived after negotiations between the health insurance funds and the medical profession.
- The charges made by hospitals are also based on payment rates negotiated between hospital groups and the insurers.

Reliance on private health insurance and inequities

The funding methods of the Swiss health system, notably the heavy reliance on private health insurance and the consequent high proportion of funding emanating from private sources, have led van Doorslaer and Wagstaff to conclude that Switzerland has the most regressive method of funding of any European country (van Doorslaer and Wagstaff, 2000). This conclusion was derived by applying the methods described in Chapter 8 and the present chapter as part of the ECuity project to measure the redistributive effects of health funding in twelve European countries.

The extensive use of private health insurance where ability to pay does not form one of the criteria applied to the payment for coverage, except for some subsidy of persons on low incomes, is the source of the principal inequities in the Swiss system. It is understood that further reforms are being designed to address the regressive nature of the funding methods (Reinhardt, 2004).

Consumer choice or government regulation?

The Swiss health care system has been the focus of two recent papers in the *Journal of the American Medical Association*. The article by Herzlinger and Parsa-Parsi (2004), after a detailed examination of the Swiss funding methods, concluded that the system is more cost-effective and equitable than that found in the United States. They attributed the Swiss superiority to the much larger role for consumer choice in that country. Reinhardt (2004) in his commentary on the Herzlinger and Parsa-Parsi paper agreed with their conclusion about the superior characteristics of the Swiss system.

However, Reinhardt disagreed with their attribution of this superiority to the large range of choice regarding the type of health insurance which they elect to purchase, that is the mix of deductibles and co-insurance that are available. He pointed to evidence that most of the Swiss population do not avail themselves of changing health insurance options and only a very small number take out managed care type policies. It is therefore difficult to see how the range of consumer choices is likely to promote the efficiency and equity characteristics of the Swiss system.

Reinhardt argued that it is the tight federal government regulation of private health insurance that provides the key to the understanding of the greater efficiency and equity of the Swiss health care system as compared with that of the United States. This regulation leads to cartels of insurers being able to negotiate with provider groups about fees and charges on the basis of a parity of bargaining strengths. This, in turn, leads to much lower prices per unit of input than in the United States. The premium rates charged by the health funds are also subject to federal government regulation.

A model for the United States?

Reinhardt claims that Switzerland may act as a model for possible reforms of the United States funding arrangements, including the provision of health coverage for the entire population, if there is continued resistance to the idea of comprehensive social health insurance in that country.

The Netherlands

The Dutch health care system is representative of a number of European countries with systems of health insurance and provision which consist of both private and public sources of funding. These characteristics are shared with Germany and France but the relatively recent reforms in the Netherlands have produced several features which are unique to that country. These have been promoted under the rubric of 'managed care' and have been designed to place greater competitive pressures on the main health services organisations by increasing the role of consumer choice.

Summary of characteristics

- All Dutch residents are covered by a system of health insurance which is provided by a number of private, not for profit, sickness funds and by other private health insurance organisations.
- Social insurance is the main source of funding for health care with taxation playing only a minor role.
- Social insurance does not cover higher income earners and civil servants who are required to take out private health insurance. Contributions to these health funds are not income related. The contributions to social

health insurance are income related and shared between the employee and his/her employer. Those insured by social insurance make up about 60 per cent of the Dutch population (Wagstaff and van Doorslaer, 1997).

- Reform of the health insurance system has been high on the policy agendas of successive governments since the Dekker Commission report of 1987 and its advocacy of a managed care model.
- Expenditure on health services in the Netherlands, currently at about 9 per cent of GDP, is close to the OECD median value.

Recent reforms to achieve increased efficiency

The reforms that have taken place, or that have been foreshadowed, in recent times in Dutch health insurance have been designed to secure greater efficiency in the health care system. They have followed a similar pattern to those introduced in other European countries, including the United Kingdom, that have sought to place more competitive pressures on providers and funders. The approach has been labelled as 'managed care' but the processes involved in the Netherlands have been markedly different from those used in either the United States or the United Kingdom.

An outline of the way in which greater technical efficiency of the health care system might be achieved in the Netherlands, by increased competition, was provided in the Dekker Commission report. Many of the recommendations have been implemented, though slowly and cautiously as the changes set out below indicate.

The introduction of a more competitive relationship between the health insurance organisations was based on allowing the population to move between health funds. Previously the holders of social health insurance policies were required to use a health fund in their own region. In addition, the funds were required to offer a number of different policies to their members so that they might be able to trade off, for example, a higher deductible against a greater range of health service coverage. Contracting between the sickness funds and health care professionals was permitted, and the sickness funds and private insurers were allowed to offer subscription rates below those officially established.

These measures were designed to provide incentives to the insurance agencies to take a more active role in promoting the interests of their insured members with hospitals, doctors and other provider groups. Prior to the reforms, the insurance agencies had not been active participants in inducing the more efficient operation of providers. As with other health insurance systems in Europe providing social health insurance, the control of the system, including cost containment methods, was based on extensive regulation of providers including the hospitals.

As van Doorslaer and Schut (2000) pointed out, centralised supply side governmental control in the Netherlands was subject to a number of limitations and criticisms. First, from an economics perspective it may fail to achieve technical efficiency amongst hospitals that might be based on input substitution and exploiting economies of scale and scope. Second, by restricting the choices of consumers it was claimed that this was a further obstacle to the achievement of allocative efficiency.

Compatibility of managed competition with equity goals

The unwillingness of governments in the Netherlands and elsewhere to pursue the objectives of managed care vigorously has been described as arising out of a reluctance to move quickly from the proven ability of extensive provider and health fund regulation to contain costs and ensure universal coverage to the uncertainties associated with a more competitive set of relationships.

These uncertainties include the ability and willingness of the principal actors to respond to the incentives of a managed competition environment, including the willingness of consumers to exercise the new range of choices offered to them. It will be recalled that the Swiss system's reliance on consumer choice was designed to ensure quality and promote greater efficiency, but the evidence suggested that allowing greater choice did not necessarily translate into wide ranging actions to change their existing insurers or the type of policy which covered them.

A further and more fundamental uncertainty which van Doorslaer and Schut emphasise is the compatibility of the methods of managed competition with the objectives of equitable and universal social health insurance coverage that underlie the social insurance systems of many OECD countries. For example, a truly competitive health insurance system would see premiums being related to the risk profiles and the expected costliness of consumers to the funds rather than being based on the community rating system that underlies most social health insurance. Risk rating would obviously lead to a major departure from the ability to pay principle and hence undermine the achievement of horizontal and vertical equity.

Later reforms

Following on the reforms introduced in 1995 the Dutch health care financing arrangements have been segmented into three separate systems (van Doorslaer and Schut, 2000). The first compartment covers mental health and long-term care where the ability of consumers to exercise choices about health insurance coverage is recognised as being limited. Thus there is no basis for competition between insurers in this compartment.

The second compartment consists of the acute care sector including hospital care, general practitioner and specialist medical services, together with most prescribed pharmaceuticals. Measures to promote competition amongst insurers, including the bearing of greater financial risks by them, have been concentrated in this compartment.

The third compartment deals with what has been described as amenity care and other services that are easily affordable. Insurance for these items is not included in the scope of social insurance but can be covered by supplementary private health insurance. The terms of this coverage are not subject to governmental controls.

Pro-rich redistributive bias

When the ECuity methods are applied to the Dutch health funding and taxation systems the conclusion reached is that, overall, these systems have a pro-rich redistributive bias (Wagstaff and van Doorslaer, 1997). They stated that most of the redistribution is due to the income-related payments of the lower income group, and that those on higher incomes taking out private health insurance do not have income-related health insurance contributions.

Again, in the Netherlands, the breakdown of the ability to pay criterion as the basis of health funding leads to the generation of vertical inequity. It is part of the reason for undertaking the ECuity project that policy-makers in reforming their health care systems are aware of the equity implications of the choices they are making.

Sweden

The Swedish health care system represents a further example of a national health service and is fairly typical of other Scandinavian countries that have chosen this method of organising and funding health services. However, there are a number of distinctive characteristics of the Swedish model which differentiate it from the UK NHS. Of these the most important is the responsibility of the local counties for the funding of health services from taxes and for the provision of hospital and other health care services.

Summary of characteristics

- All residents of Sweden are covered for medical, hospital, dental and pharmaceutical costs.
- All medical and other health services are subject to modest co-payments by patients. However, the proportion of health expenditure derived from

private sources is amongst the lowest in the OECD. There is negligible private health insurance.

- There are no limitations on the choice of doctor or hospital by patients following recent reforms.
- To date, most medically qualified persons are specialists with general practitioners making up only a small proportion of the medical workforce.
- Sweden was the first country to develop an extensive system of multi-disciplinary health centres staffed by salaried doctors and other health service personnel.
- Patients may seek treatment from specialist medical staff and hospitals directly without a GP referral.
- Sweden has one of the best health outcomes in terms of infant mortality and life expectancy of any country in the world.
- Despite the high proportion of older persons in the Swedish population, the percentage of GDP devoted to health services is somewhat below the OECD median value.

High standard of health status; low rates of obesity, and of alcohol and tobacco consumption

A striking feature of the Swedish system is the high performance on the mortality measures. The extent to which the very favourable life expectancy values are a product of the health care system or of the low rates of obesity, and of alcohol and tobacco consumption, is an open question.

It is important to note that there has been a long standing government policy of discouraging the use of alcohol and tobacco by means of high excise taxes. The degree to which greater equality is fostered in Sweden by long standing government policies may also be a relevant factor in influencing the mortality experience of the population.

Managed care and changes in primary care

Two recent developments in Sweden have been the attempt to place more competitive pressures on providers by separating the roles of purchasers and providers of services, and the introduction of private medical practitioners under contract arrangements with the counties to bolster primary medical care (Saltman and Bergman, 2005).

In the past, hospitals have provided a considerable amount of primary care via their outpatients' departments. A shift in emphasis to the more readily accessible out-of-hospital medical and other services was seen as being consistent with a new policy emphasis on meeting the needs of consumers as patients.

The role of the counties

As we have noted above the funding and provision responsibilities of the Swedish health care system have been assigned to the counties into which the country is divided for governance purposes. Most importantly the counties are able to levy local income taxes to fund the health services. However, these health specific taxes are not progressive but are a fixed proportion of income.

In the regionalised Swedish system each county is responsible for a local hospital whilst the whole country has been divided into nine regions with at least one major teaching and referral hospital being present in each. These regional hospitals are the responsibility of the county council in which they are located. Co-ordination of county policies about health services are undertaken by the Federation of County Councils.

The central government provides the basic legislation that determines the characteristics of the health care funding, payment arrangements and provision responsibilities. A recent important health legislation of the Swedish government was one which restricted the right of councils to contract out the management of hospitals to other organisations. The legislation, which took effect from the beginning of 2006, mandates that each council must continue to be fully responsible for at least one hospital, and that the organisations contracted to run the county hospitals must be non-profit ones. The councils were also prohibited from devolving their responsibilities for the regional hospitals.

The Swedish government legislation reflects concerns about the enthusiasm of some councils to use contracts with non-government organisations for the provision of hospital services. The government's policy position was that profit-making organisations were incompatible with the underlying rationale of social solidarity for the Swedish hospital system.

Differences from the British NHS

Sweden shares all the characteristics of a national health service including the fact that most of the funding is from income taxation, and the control and ownership of the health service agencies is a government responsibility. It differs from the UK NHS in that proportionate taxes raised by the counties, rather than national progressive taxes, are the main source of funding. Until recently all general practitioners were salaried employees but there is now provision for private doctors to provide these services on a contract basis with presumably their having a similar relation to government as GPs in the British NHS.

Less equitable than expected

The ECuity method of determining the progressivity of health care financing systems has been applied to Sweden by Wagstaff and van Doorslaer (1999). When they calculated the Kakwani index for all the sources of finance a small negative value was obtained, indicating that the financing arrangements were slightly regressive. The main source of this somewhat unexpected result for a national health service was the heavy reliance on county-based income tax and its proportionate rather than progressive nature.

Cost containment and high quality care

In common with other National Health Service type arrangements Sweden has managed to contain total health expenditure, whilst maintaining what appears to be a high quality health care system with good outcomes. The fact that the proportion of older people in the population, about 18 per cent, is higher than in other OECD countries with values of 12 to 16 per cent should make policy-makers less inclined to accept uncritically what has become the conventional wisdom that an ageing population in their countries will generate considerable pressures on health services expenditure.

As in the United Kingdom case, difficulties in securing non-emergency hospital care, as reflected in waiting times for elective surgery, have led to a search for reforms that will generate greater technical efficiency. The nature of these and other reforms was described by Saltman and Bergman (2005) who note that they do not impinge on the core characteristics of the Swedish system. It is too early to judge whether the reforms in hospital funding, greater reliance on contracts with GPs and the expansion of primary medical care will produce the expected benefits.

Summary and conclusions

The development of extensive funding and demographic data for OECD countries has facilitated an interest in comparisons of the health care systems of the member countries. As we have noted, these data have promoted a number of studies by US health economists of the differences between their insurance and funding methods and that of a range of other countries.

This is a desirable change since there was a tendency in the past for the United States to ignore other countries or to confine their comments to the UK NHS. These comments were often designed to exaggerate the problems of the NHS and to point to the superiority of the US system. Amongst the more conservative Americans there has been a continuing mind set that characterises all developed non-US countries as having 'socialised medicine' – a pejorative and politically loaded term that by no feat of mental gymnastics can be taken as representative of the actual situation in all or most OECD countries.

We have suggested that there is scope for all countries to learn from the experience of others in their consideration of health reform options, a process that seems to be high on the policy agendas of most countries. In addition there is scope for using the international data to draw conclusions about the efficiency and equity of each country's funding and provision of health services. It is clear that the largely private systems of the United States and Switzerland have high health services expenditure combined with inequitable funding methods. There is no evidence that the additional expenditure in these countries is warranted by overall better quality of care or the more efficient use of resources.

At the other extreme, the UK model of a national health service has been able to set limits on total health care expenditure so that the proportion of GDP devoted to health and expenditure per capita are both low as compared with OECD countries. In assessing the performance of the NHS the accessibility of health services and the quality of care provided raise some problems about the level of efficiency of the health services. There is also the possibility that in the past the medical profession in Britain has been able to exercise too much influence over policies and decision-making. Evidence about poor clinical governance and the considerable variations in the performance of procedures between different regions has led to the recent proliferation of activities to correct these deficiencies.

Since current health policies in almost all countries have emphasised the need to reduce government expenditure, thereby requiring greater contributions from individuals, the UK NHS model is unlikely to be adopted by more countries, despite the proselytising zeal of some of its active supporters within Britain and elsewhere. However, the evidence that national health type funding and ownership arrangements are able to combine cost containment and equity principles better than the other models is considerable. The US system, despite all its inadequacies, is still promoted actively by some international organisations and American-based management consultants who are faithfully devoted to the neoclassical economic models that provide some of the rationale for the US model and proposed reforms.

We have noted that the majority of OECD countries have opted for mixed systems of public and private funding and provision. These have emerged as being highly variable between different countries but all have common features of being based on some notion of solidarity, that part of the requirements for a unified country is the implementation of measures that ensure that all population members are protected from the financial consequences of disease. Thus the willingness of individuals to pay for services does not overshadow the ability to pay principle from which the equity basis of the health services in these countries is derived.

In the non-European OECD countries, notably Australia and Canada, the solidarity argument has been given less emphasis as one of the rationales for their forms of social health insurance. In Australia the inadequacies and inequities of the previous 'voluntary' health insurance programs may have given the labor governments sufficient grounds for health reform so that the solidarity case was not needed. In both countries the pressures to achieve social solidarity are possibly less acute than in European countries with their long histories of internal and external conflicts.

However, in each of the OECD countries that have adopted the mixed social health insurance model there has been historically a reluctance to embrace the national health service type model, arising out of opposition from providers to the amount of government control implied, and some support from the community for this position.

In our case studies of individual countries, including recent reform measures, it became clear that many of the countries were driven by a perceived need to contain increases in health expenditure and to reduce the burden of government funding on the tax system by extracting greater contributions from the users of the services. At the same time, governments are under increasing pressure to ensure the quality of services is high and that technological and pharmaceutical developments are widely available. The different forms of social health insurance offered in each country represent attempts to reconcile these conflicts in the context of the existing institutions, cultural traditions and political circumstances.

What is a cause for concern, however, is that the pressures to reform may lead to measures being implemented that detract from the equity of the funding arrangements and possibly serve only the interests of providers. Reforms in the Netherlands based on a cautious application of the managed care model have led to an appreciation of the problems and contradictions arising from the principles of managed care being applied in social health insurance. These include the possibility of introducing inequities into the funding methods when greater emphasis is placed on patient contributions or, as in the Swedish case, the reliance on non-progressive income tax arrangements.

The economic and health services performance of Sweden with its high proportion of older persons casts some doubt on the gloom and doom prophecies in other countries that the rising numbers of the aged will inevitably place great burdens on the financing arrangements. The analyses of Reinhardt (2003) and of Zweifel and his colleagues (Zweifel et al., 2004) also support the maintenance of a sceptical stance on this issue. There is probably a much greater risk of financing problems of this kind arising out of high and increasing obesity rates in countries such as the United States and Australia, with their implications for diabetes and other chronic diseases, unless policies to reverse these trends are implemented comprehensively and quickly.

FURTHER READING

The extensive range of OECD publications provides a very great volume of information and analysis about many of their member countries. Details of the methods of generating the data that we have drawn upon in this chapter, and their limitations, are also set out in these sources, especially OECD (2005) *OECD Health Data*. We indicated above that some of this material is made available at the OECD website, www.OECD.org and the relevant links. The whole OECD health database is available on a CD-ROM.

The paper by Reinhardt and his colleagues in *Health Affairs* (2002) 'Cross national comparisons of health systems using OECD data, 1999' provides possibly the best available account of the value and limitations of international comparisons.

Discussion questions

- Summarise the main characteristics of the OECD data on health expenditure. In what ways can comparisons over time (time series) and between countries for the same period, illuminate health policy issues?
- In our discussion of the characteristics of a number of OECD countries we have classified the countries into three groups. Describe the distinguishing features of each group and indicate the possible applications of the classification.
- From the tables presented above produce a graph for the latest year available of GDP per capita and expenditure on health per capita for each OECD country. What conclusions can you derive from the graph? Students with some knowledge of statistics might calculate the correlation coefficient measuring the strength of the relationship between the two variables, and comment on its value.
- From the tables presented above construct a graph for the latest year available of per capita expenditure on health and the infant mortality rate for each OECD country. What conclusions, if any, can you draw from this analysis?
- For the countries described in our case studies produce a graph of the values from 1980 to 2003 of both health expenditure per capita and the percentage this value represents of GDP. Produce a table that shows the percentage increase in each of

these variables for each country from 1980 to 2003. What conclusions about health policies in each country can you draw from this information?

- In our applications of the OECD data we have attempted to draw (tentative) conclusions about the overall efficiency of the countries' health care systems by comparing expenditure on health care with their life expectancy and infant mortality experience. How valid is this approach?

Health Economics and Developing Countries

11

Introduction

This chapter begins with an overview of the particular features characterising health economics as applied to developing countries. The stage is thereby set for the ensuing discussion of a select group of key features which distinguish developing nations from developed countries. These features and their evolution lead to a more general outline of a strategy for applying health economics in relation to the organisation, provision and funding of health services in developing and transitional countries. We have noted previously that there is no clear distinction between the last two groups, but the developing countries are generally those with the lowest incomes per capita, and the transitional countries are of higher incomes and are well on the path to becoming 'developed'.

Unlike our approach to the developed countries, we have not attempted to develop case studies of individual countries in the developing world. Our reasons for this are several. First, detailed information about individual countries is of questionable accuracy, as compared with the OECD data for developed countries. The World Health Organisation (WHO) has recently published what purport to be health expenditure estimates for all 192 member counties (WHO, 2006). However, in the light of all the definitional and other problems noted in the previous chapter with the comparable OECD data for countries with well-developed statistical systems, this exercise of WHO can only be regarded as heroic!

Second, the limited number of detailed studies of specific developing countries are often produced by personnel from developed countries. As we indicate later in the chapter, they frequently rely on a free market framework of analysis, and an ideological point to make such as the superiority of private sector initiatives. Third, the great diversity of service and financing arrangements, along with the sheer number of developing countries, make any generalisations from such studies much more doubtful than for the affluent countries of the globe.

In the following sections we have concentrated, with a few exceptions, on a general set of issues about these countries, based on the work of scholars who display a considerable degree of knowledge, skill and sympathy in their writing about the developing world and their health services problems.

Evolution of international health economics

Background

The application of the theories, concepts and techniques of health economics to low and middle income countries is a relatively recent phenomenon. Mills (1997) traced the evolution of health economics as an applied discipline in developing countries during the 1970s, 1980s and 1990s, adapting to the changing concerns of planners, bureaucrats and managers. The initiative to apply it came initially almost entirely from economists in developed countries (Abel-Smith, 1989). The following section briefly summarises the history of health economics in developing countries as presented by Mills and Abel-Smith.

The early work on economics in developing countries in the 1960s (Abel-Smith, 1963, 1967) found that expenditure on health services as a proportion of GDP increased on average as countries grew richer, with wide variations between countries at a similar per capita income level in respect of the proportion of GDP devoted to health. These studies reported that generally the private sector was larger than the public sector, and that the greatest share of public sector expenditure was spent on hospitals. The earliest contributions of health economics in developing countries dealt with the economic impact of preventing tropical disease with benefit defined largely in terms of gains in production.

Efficiency and equity in the public sector

In the 1970s, health economics applications in developing countries were primarily focused on improving efficiency and equity performance in government health services. At this stage in the United Kingdom and United States, there was an increasing involvement of economists in government who were working on issues of resource allocation and the use of techniques such as cost-benefit analysis (CBA). The rapid expansion of cost-effectiveness studies extended to developing countries, largely in the area of immunisation.

During this period, economic studies in the health sector were conducted usually at the instigation of outside agencies with local support.

Economists began to work with Ministries of Health in developing countries to improve the planning and management of public sector health services in three main areas of work: first, improving resource allocation from the national level to districts, second, feeding in cost implications to planning decisions and third, improving information on sources of funds and expenditure (Mach and Abel-Smith, 1983). These initiatives laid the groundwork for establishing economic ideas and techniques as a legitimate component of health sector decision-making in these countries (Mills, 1997).

Healthcare financing and market mechanisms

The 1980s were characterised by an emphasis on health care financing in developing countries and elsewhere, with an increase in studies of demand analysis for health services and the desirability of using prices to influence consumer behaviour. The call for more efficient use of available resources was mooted by de Ferranti (1985) who proposed categories of user charges. The key World Bank publication *Financing Health Services in Developing Countries: An Agenda for Reform* (World Bank, 1987) argued for the introduction of a modest user charge for curative services in order to reallocate funds to preventive programs and health services for the poor.

These recommendations were based on studies in Malaysia and the Philippines which suggested that the aggregate demand for outpatient and inpatient use was highly price-inelastic but consumers were sensitive to the relative prices of alternative sources of care. This perspective was challenged by a number of economists (Gilson, 1988) who pointed out that market-driven allocation of resources neglected equity concerns, and that there were considerable difficulties in implementing a fee system that benefited the poor. These included the problems people have in distinguishing between necessary and unnecessary services, finding money to pay the fees, and the problems that providers face in devising effective systems to exempt the poor from fees.

These concerns were supported by studies which showed that user fees reduced access to care proportionally more for the poor than the rich in Peru (Gertler et al., 1987). Waddington and Enyimayew (1989) demonstrated a shift in utilisation in favour of the 15–45 year age group at the expense of the elderly after fees were substantially increased for government health services in Ghana, and identified a change in culture which encourages activities which brought in revenue and discouraged those which did not.

In the 1990s, an increased sophistication of economic techniques was achieved and the number of empirical studies on developing countries expanded considerably. Health economics spanned a greater range of topics, including public sector priorities, resource allocation, private sector behaviour and organisational issues. Mills (1995) identified markets and competition as clear themes for the 1990s, with the recognition of the value of employing some market mechanisms in the public sector context. The World Development Report 1993 (World Bank, 1993) proposed the disability adjusted life year (DALY) as an indicator of effectiveness for priority setting and comparing different programs and interventions. The DALY has a similar role to the quality adjusted life year (QALY) discussed in Chapter 8, except as the title indicates, disability is used as a measure instead of quality of life.

Globalisation and developing countries in the 2000s

Key themes

In the 2000s, what are the key themes arising in the application of health economics in low- and middle-income countries?

The first key theme is globalisation and its impact on health. International health conventionally refers to health matters which involve two or more countries and, in development assistance, applies to developing countries. Thus, an example of international health is the control by country authorities of the spread of infectious diseases due to increased international trade. Increasingly, the capacity to deal with health matters transcends territorial boundaries and requires a more global approach.

Global health has been defined as 'processes that are changing the nature of human interaction across a wide range of spheres including the socio-cultural, political, economic, technological and ecological' (Lee, 2001). Lee and Goodman (2002) noted that the need to gain insight into the effects of current neoclassical, market driven forms of globalisation on public and social policy had initially focused on economic and financial sectors (Stiglitz, 1999; World Bank, 2000), but these had gradually spread to health as a prime example of the undersupply of global public goods. These are defined as exhibiting characteristics which are 'non-excludable, [and produce] non-rival benefits that cut across borders, generations and populations' (Kaul et al., 1999).

Global health, rather than international health, applies to various arenas including the impact on health of worldwide economic crises which diminish public sector expenditure on health programs; the production, financing, distribution and regulation of pharmaceuticals within world trade agreements; control of illicit drug trafficking; environmental degradation and its health effects; and the migration of skilled health workforce members globally.

The impact of globalisation on lower and middle income countries (LMIC) in regard to income inequity and health has been extensively described by Labonte et al. (2005), who argued vigorously for a fundamental shift by the G8 group of developed countries in the priorities and values guiding economic and political decision-making on overseas development assistance, debt cancellation and fairer trade.

The questions that arise regarding the consequences of globalisation on health are summarised in Box 11.1.

Box 11.1   Globalisation – questions for health

Globalisation and disease
How has globalisation affected the epidemiology of disease within and across countries? Which diseases are most affected? What populations are most affected? What are the implications for strategies for prevention, control and treatment of disease? What are the implications for international health regulations?

Global migration and mobility of people
How is the spread and control of infectious disease affected by increased movement of people across national boundaries? What are the health needs of globally migrant labour, (un)documented migrants, displaced people?

Global financing of health care
How will national governments pay for health care within a globalised economy of mobile labour and capital? Can a global tax base exist? How has the globalisation of finance influenced health financing? What global trends exist in health-sector aid?

Global trade and production
How should global trade and production be regulated to protect human health against infectious diseases, industrial hazards, product risks, export of hazardous wastes, and so on? Can occupational health and safety standards be adopted globally? What are the implications for health care of free trade agreements?

Global information and telecommunications
What impact are global communications having on the provision of health services? What implications are raised by global inequities of access to telecommunications? Are health needs represented in technological development? How can global communications be used more effectively to address health needs?

Global civil society and governance
Who are the key agents and are they changing (eg., non-government organisations (NGOs) and the private sector)? To what extent is pluralism emerging in global health policy? Are existing international health organizations, notably the World Health Organisation, adequate to represent the complexity of emerging interests? How can global power and global responsibility be balanced? What institutional mechanisms are needed to facilitate the global policy process?

Global health law and legal system
Do international health regulations need to have more teeth to deal with global health issues? How can accreditation of health care facilities and licensing and certification of health professionals be maintained in a globalised context? What issues of intellectual property rights (eg., pharmaceuticals, medical technology and knowledge) need to be addressed?

Source: Lee, K. (1998) 'Shaping the future of global health co-operation: where can we go from here?', *The Lancet* 351: 899–902.

Effect of globalisation on health care

The effect of globalisation on health can be analysed by considering the policy context, policy actors, policy content and policy process (Buse et al., 2002). The policy context is crucial since the costs and benefits of globalisation will be experienced differently by different individuals, communities, countries, genders and socioeconomic classes. Indeed, as Buse pointed out, globalisation is occurring in an environment of widening income disparities (UNDP, 2005; World Bank 2005). The United Nations Development Programme (UNDP) has estimated that the ratio of the income of the richest 20 per cent of the world's most affluent people to the poorest 20 per cent has increased from 30 to 1 in 1960 to 78 to 1 in 1994. More significantly, inequality *within* countries has substantially increased (Chen and Wang, 2001, Cornia, Addison and Kiiski, 2004). It is argued that it is not so much the maldistribution of income that is important, but that of opportunity that matters. Why is this so?

Various factors in the global economy have contributed to this outcome (Rowson, 2000). International Monetary Fund (IMF) stabilisation programs introduced in developing countries over the past two decades have been associated with recession and worsening income inequality. World Bank Structural Adjustment Programs have had a regressive impact particularly in the agricultural sectors of LMICs with benefits flowing disproportionately to skilled labour at the expense of unskilled and unprotected workforce members. According to Rowson, these regressive equity reducing effects are compounded by financial liberalisation and privatisation, transferring capital to the financial elite. Increased wage flexibility in this global scenario has stripped the poor in developing countries of the protection afforded by the minimum wage.

Pressures arising from globalisation have constrained the ability of states to respond effectively to changing health needs. There is an increasing blurring between public and private sectors in health and a move towards 'privatisation' of state activities. The erosion of state control over areas such as maintaining peace and security spills over to other public sector responsibilities such as the health services. Increasingly, health in the globalising world is centrally placed as a structural determinant of economic development and thus a key focus for global economic policy. Buse et al. (2002) pointed out that for the first time, health and its impact on world trade, peace and security, has found its way into the UN Security Council agendas (United Nations, 2000) and the US National Security Strategy (White House, 1999).

Buse et al. (2002) noted that whilst medical professionals once dominated health policy in ministries of health and WHO, today they are joined by other professionals: economists, social scientists and other specialists working across other ministries, foreign aid agencies, industry and academic institutions.

There appears to be evidence of a diffusion of power and pluralism arising from the increased policy actors in health (Frenk, 1995; Walt, 1994).

Sharing and collaboration in the global environment has led to a convergence on global concerns driving health policy, such as the focus on reproductive health, injury prevention and violence against women. The question that arises is whether global health policy is sufficiently adapted or sensitive to local conditions or whether, as Makinda (2000) suggests, globalisation requires that the 'values, institutions, interests and norms of some peoples and societies have to be sacrificed' and it is power that determines whose standards become 'global'.

The role of financial institutions

The second key theme is the increasing role of financial institutions and the ascendance of health economists. The growing role of economics in health services development is apparent in the increasing visibility of the World Bank health sector reviews, the United States Agency for International Development (USAID), the IMF, the Asian Development Bank and the African Development Bank in the area of health care financing and health policy. Rowson (2000) highlighted the promotion of privatisation and deregulation in health care reform by developed countries, the role of key international financial institutions such as the World Bank and IMF in encouraging trade liberalisation in developing countries through loan conditions, and the influence of the World Trade Organisation (WTO) set up in the 1990s to oversee the freeing up of trade internationally.

The World Bank and the IMF have important roles to play in the coordination of short- and long-term policies across the world, but they have often imposed flawed policies on developing countries through their sometimes insensitive agendas, overly grand designs and lack of engagement with the way the poor see their own problems (Easterly, 2006; Sen, 2006). Easterly, a former World Bank economist, has argued in somewhat vitriolic terms that the developed countries have done more harm than good by their ill-conceived policies regarding aid to developing countries. The title of his book is: *The White Man's Burden: Why the West's Efforts to Aid the Rest Have Done So Much Ill and So Little Good.*

Following on the push in the 1990s to introduce and extend user fees to government health services in developing countries, economists began paying more attention, not only to mechanisms to raise finances for health, but also to how these funds were being spent (Lee, 2002). Thus, by the 2000s, the debate and work had shifted from the public versus private health care financing issue to differences in financial arrangements and prioritisation – numerous insurance schemes, incentive packages, and public and private combinations.

The World Bank played a leading role in the development and support of key measures such as the DALY and the global burden of disease. In contrast, WHO was relegated to a subsidiary role compared with the other international agencies, due mainly to smaller financial resources and limited health economic expertise (Lee and Goodman, 2002). Since the World Bank has few health economists in-house, WHO and the Pan American Health Organisation (PAHO) rely on a number of other organisations for health economic expertise.

The influence of health economists and the private sector

There is an increasing influence of health economists in health policy, as noted by Lee and Goodman (2002), and Kumaranayake and Walker (2002), coupled with the trend to greater involvement of the private (for profit) sector in health. These health economists, as we have noted above, almost invariably adopt the neoclassical approach to the problems of the developing countries with their emphasis on user charges, the role of the private sector and the deregulation of health matters.

The influence of private sector interests is typified by the concentration of power and control over production and distribution of pharmaceuticals arising from the acquisition and mergers in the biopharmaceutical industry of the 'Big Pharmas' (Tarabusi and Vickery, 1998; Mytelka and Delapierre, 1999). Such private for profit sector involvement has played a key role in influencing the agendas for bilateral and multilateral world trade agreements, including those involving developing countries, for national governments and key organisations such as the WHO and the World Bank.

Reliance on expertise of developed countries

The third key theme is the continuing reliance of developing countries on developed country expertise. Donors and powerful Western governments wield immense power and influence over health policy directions and strategies – this inequality in relationship between donors and recipients poses considerable challenges to the oft-quoted advantages of global liberalisation. While capacity building in developing countries is a key objective, evidence points to the continuing empowerment of global elitists who possess specialised technical expertise in health economics. The dominant representation of the global elite from Western countries in multilateral negotiations in organisations, such as the WTO, skews the discourse and direction of health policy in favour of corporate interests in high income countries.

There are major problems in applying developed country solutions to developing countries (Abel-Smith, 1989). Health care policy reforms are introduced into the specific contexts of poor countries which lack the institutions and structures that facilitate the operation of markets in more developed settings. The reforms take for granted trained managers, sophisticated information systems, accepted standards of behaviour, and functioning of civil and political institutions. Developing countries vary considerably in their capacity to articulate health policies and implement programs (World Bank, 1997).

Ministries of Health are suspicious of World Bank policies. In the health sector, understanding of key organisations such as the WTO, let alone the capacity to engage on an equal footing, is woefully inadequate in LMICs (Ranson et al., 2002). The LMICs usually play passive roles as targets in health policy reform. When, for example, public health concerns have attempted to protect the interests of 'cheap' labour in LMICs, such measures have been over-ridden by global economic imperatives from WTO agreements (Fustican et al., 2002).

At the country level, one of the key underlying problems in many developing countries is that management at central, provincial and district levels is placed in the hands of doctors who have not been given any training in management. Developing countries lack local expertise in health economics and management. There are few academic courses available in health economics in developing countries. Health economics is excluded from the curricula in many schools of public health in these countries.

The problem of dependence on external consultants, recognised by consultants themselves, continues. Ministries of Health may be forced to accept help from external consultants they have not chosen, when a large loan sought for another purpose contains a clause that a small part will be used for work on financing. Short-term consultants often provide highly theoretical advice and fail to come to grips with the administrative and political realities of the country or present solutions wholly based on developed country experience. Some countries clearly have suffered from consultant fatigue (Abel-Smith, 1989).

There is no clear career structure for health economists involved in developing country work. A typical career path was described by Lee and Goodman (2002) as a 'revolving door': PhD training in economics followed by an academic position, project work funded by donor agencies such as the World Bank or government aid agencies and subsequent employment by the agencies as a consultant. Thus health economists prominent in international health often play multiple roles as academics, consultants and government advisers.

2010 and beyond for developing countries

Problems of poverty

What role can economics play in responding to the plight of the poor in developing countries without neglecting to insist that help comes in useful and productive forms?

The solutions offered in *The World Development Report 2006* (WHO, 2006) support the role of public action in levelling the global market playing field by investing in human capacities, expanding access to justice, land and infrastructure, and promoting fairness in markets. Policies promoting greater equity in terms of access to markets, resource flow and governance are advocated. It is disappointing that such approaches still focus on the enterprise of supplying what is in demand and thus links to people's ability to pay, rather than to the business of supplying goods and services to people whose incomes do not allow their needs to be translated into a demand in the market (Sen, 2006). For example, the *Report* maintained that, in order to decrease inequity and minimise market distortions in health care provision, demand side subsidies should be provided, for example, for maternal and child health, and that public provisioning and regulations should be encouraged to provide risk pooling for all.

The failure of many grand development and poverty-alleviation schemes results from their disregard for the complexity of institutions and incentives systems and their neglect of individual initiative, which must be societally encouraged rather than bureaucratically stifled (Easterly, 2006). These deficiencies call for better economic reasoning and a louder voice for the poor in the governance of such organisations as the World Bank and the IMF.

Information and initiatives can and do come from the poor themselves. An example of this enlightened approach is the Voices of the Poor, a World Bank project which received direct support from the then President James Wolfensohn. Muhammad Yunnus of Bangladesh pioneered the micro-credit movement through his Grameen Foundations while fellow activist Fazle Hasan Abed launched a huge cooperative through the Bangladesh Rural Advancement Committee (Sen, 2006). The People's Health Movement, convened in the early 2000s through the auspices of medical academics in developing countries, enables participation in global health governance by disadvantaged or excluded population groups. Representation of health interests at all levels of policy-making on trade is one of the fundamental objectives of the movement.

Governance and corruption

Perhaps the most far-reaching innovation in Wolfensohn's often tumultuous 10-year stint as World Bank President was his explicit recognition of politics as a key consideration. The Bank's articles of agreement that is its founding charter, enjoins its officers to be rigorously apolitical. This changed in the late 1990s: at the World Bank's 1996 meeting, Wolfensohn stated that the Bank needed to deal with the cancer of corruption (*The Economist*, 2005). The *World Development Report 1997* was the first World Bank publication to adequately address and re-examine the role of the state and political institutions in development. Empirical work by the World Bank (Dani Kaufmann) and the National Bureau of Economic Research offer more insight into potential measures or indicators of good and poor governance, the extent of the rule of law and public sector competence. Much work remains to be done in terms of understanding:

- Internal organisation of providers and how different financing, ownership and management arrangements affect behaviour.
- Incentives inherent in different ways of paying for health care.
- Regulatory mechanisms which are more likely to work when governments are relatively weak (Kumaranayake, 1997).

Between 2000 and 2004 fiscal years, lending by the World Bank for economic reforms fell by 14 per cent per year whereas lending to improve governance rose by 11 per cent. Australian contributions to overseas development and aid (ODA) have been increasing over the past five years, a step in the right direction. Budget allocation has risen from 0.25 per cent of GDP in 2001–02 to 0.28 per cent GDP in 2005–06. A significant and worrying trend is the increasing focus on governance which attracts 36 per cent of ODA. Only 12 per cent of ODA in 2005–06 is devoted to health, substantially below countries like the United Kingdom (22 per cent) (Zwi, Grove and Ho, 2005).

Summary and conclusions

To date the application of health economics to developing countries has probably done more harm than good since the emphasis on the use of co-payments and market mechanisms, based on neoclassical economics, has the potential to have an even more devastating set of consequences for the poor in these countries than elsewhere. It has unfortunately been the case that the international agencies, principally the World Bank and the IMF, that channel most of the assistance from affluent countries to developing countries, in the past have been dominated by economists whose thinking has reflected the neoclassical paradigms we have criticised in earlier chapters.

We have argued previously that this approach to the economics of health is fatally flawed when applied uncritically to the health services of developed countries. In the case of developing countries the almost total neglect of equity issues makes policies about health based on market mechanisms extremely detrimental to the welfare of the very poor in these countries. As we have seen, criticisms of the role of the international agencies in providing aid to developing countries have proliferated recently, and there are some indications in the work of existing and former World Bank staff that these criticisms may be addressed in the future.

This chapter also serves to highlight once again the theme that economists working in the health field need a good appreciation of the structures of policy-making and governance of the arena in which they are endeavouring to apply their skills and knowledge. An awareness of the lack of a sophisticated infrastructure of management and public administration, coupled with the presence of endemic corruption, should be the most important knowledge that staff, including health economists from the developed world, need to acquire if they are to provide useful and meaningful health economics and policy advice to developing countries.

FURTHER READING

The book by Easterly (2006), *The White Man's Burden*, should be essential reading for everyone concerned with the plight of low-income countries. It is not primarily concerned with health and economics, but its message has a great deal of relevance for this area. The review of the book by Sen (2006) in the journal *Foreign Affairs* is somewhat critical of what he regards as the author's more exaggerated claims, but he agrees with the general thrust of many of his arguments. The review, along with Easterly's response, is available at www.foreignaffairs.org.

The recent WHO (2006) report, *Guide to Producing National Health Accounts*, is designed with special reference to low-income and middle-income countries. It has been prepared in a collaborative exercise with OECD staff. The Report provides very detailed advice on the desirable structure of the accounts, the sources of financing and expenditure data and the surveys that may be required to support a national health accounting venture.

The book by Lee and colleagues (2002), *Health Policy in a Globalising World*, gives a comprehensive description and analysis of many aspects of health and financial issues as they affect developing countries.

Discussion questions

- What are the main differences between the notion of international health and the recently invented phrase of global health? In what ways is the role of health economics for developing countries different as between the two perspectives?

- Summarise the impact of the international agencies, especially the IMF and the World Bank, on the health economies of the developing countries.
- What may have been the principal failings of health economists from developed countries when they apply their knowledge and skills to the problems of developing countries?
- Why is it of importance for health economists and other advisers from affluent countries to be alert to the different institutions, infrastructure and customs of the low-income and middle-income countries? If possible provide concrete examples of the consequences of ignorance of these characteristics.
- Assess the reasons why health economists working in developing countries should incorporate considerations of horizontal and vertical equity into their analyses and advice to these countries.
- If your role was that of a senior manager or clinician dealing with a developing country what arguments might you deploy if the advice you received from a health economist was that user charges for health services should be increased substantially to reduce moral hazard?

Summary, Conclusions and Advice

12

Introduction

Here we summarise the principal conclusions and lessons which may be derived from the foregoing chapters. Based on this material we explore the implications for the research priorities of health economists. We argue that there has been, in our view an undue concentration of the intellectual effort of many health economists on the applications of those aspects of economics which emphasise the role of free market solutions. This has partly been a product of US health economists seeking solutions to the manifold problems of their own health insurance arrangements.

With respect to the pre-occupation of many British health economists with evaluation, we suggest that at this time it is difficult to come to a clear-cut conclusion about the value of this work and the quality adjusted life year (QALY) enterprise. However, it is clear from the criticisms made by prominent health economists that in focusing on the benefits, effectiveness and utility of health interventions there has been a notable absence of attention to the cost element in all these endeavours.

We argue that a more balanced approach to the research priorities of health economics should be given serious consideration. In our scenario health economists might focus more of their efforts on the individual services, organisations and providers that constitute the health services.

The history of economic thought

Greatly divergent views and many 'schools'

Our brief review of the history of economic thought, and recent critiques of the discipline, have highlighted the fact that since its early development economists have held widely divergent views about a number of key issues. These included the determinants of prices and values, the relative import- ance of free markets and their underlying assumptions in the framing of eco- nomic policy, and the priority to be given to micro-economic theory and conventional welfare economics as compared with alternative approaches to the explanation of economic phenomena.

The foundations of neoclassical economics have been challenged by many competent economists

The currently common perception amongst some economists and others including clinicians that 'economic rationalism', broadly identified with a heavy reliance on free market economics and utility maximisation, is the only approach that economists do or should take is therefore highly misleading. On the demand side the relevance of marginal utility theory, one of the foun- dations of conventional microeconomics, and its emphasis on a satisfaction- maximising individual has been the subject of trenchant criticism. On the supply side the text book theory of the firm is based on the profit maximisa- tion principle and assumptions about the relationship between costs and volume of output which are of dubious relevance even for private sector enterprises.

The relevance of neoclassical economics to health services issues

Special characteristics of relationships and behaviour

In the application of economics to health and the health services the well-documented limitations of conventional micro-economic theory are exacerbated by a number of special characteristics of the institutions and relationships within these services.

On the consumer demand side, the ability of doctors and other health providers to influence the utilisation of their services is of paramount importance since it violates the basic principle of the complete independ- ence of demand and supply factors which underlies conventional price theory.

Since most of the supplier entities, including hospitals and other institu- tions, are non-profit ones in all countries, determinants of their behaviour other than profit maximisation are required for policy-making and related purposes.

The domination of health economics by the United States and the United Kingdom

Despite the important contributions from other countries, notably Canada, Australia, Switzerland and the Netherlands, the literature of health economics has been dominated by contributions from the United States and Britain. We have also noted that the institutional frameworks including the underlying values of the health care systems in these two nations are very different from each other. They also differ from the majority of other developed countries with more mixed systems of ownership, management, funding and provision.

Differences in research priorities

These differences in how the health services are organised, along with how health expenditure is primarily funded from private or public sources, have generated widely divergent research priorities amongst health economists and others in the United States and Britain. In the former country the two main problems have been the very high level of overall expenditure on the health services coupled with the less than impressive record on health performance, and the failure to cover with any form of health insurance a substantial portion of the population.

In the United Kingdom it is now generally appreciated by the government and others that the tight national controls exercised over total expenditure have created problems of long waiting lists for hospital admissions and possibly inadequate or delayed access to high technology medical services such as cardiac surgery and renal dialysis.

The implications for other countries

We have emphasised here that this domination of the interests of American and British health economists may have had some unfortunate consequences for the development of the discipline and its applications in other countries. The issues about health insurance in the United States are not reflected in other countries where the predominant role of either public provision of services or of publicly funded or heavily subsidised health insurance are almost universally accepted by populations and governments.

Many health economists in the United States have devoted much of their research and scholarly endeavours to advocating the greater use of market-based reforms in promoting more efficient systems of health insurance. Their approach has been based on the use of welfare economics, with its neoclassical underpinnings, to highlight alleged departures from maximum efficiency in current and proposed health insurance methods.

Their work has often given scant attention to the well-documented limitations of welfare economics as a guide to health policies, and of the advantages of comprehensive health insurance in ensuring a fairer distribution of health care resources across population members. A devastating critique of the application of welfare economics to the health services and the implications of ignoring distribution issues have been provided by Evans (1998) and Reinhardt (1998) whose work we featured in Chapter 3.

In the United Kingdom with a national health service and no charges for most health services at the point of delivery, health economists in recent years have concentrated on the development of techniques for the evaluation of health service projects and programs. Cost utility analysis (CUA) and the use of QALYs have loomed large in these endeavours. Quality adjusted life years have been the subject of considerable controversy amongst health economists as we have documented in Chapter 8, and it is still unclear how successful CUA may prove to be in the long run. The focus on health gain and the extra-welfarist approach adopted by Culyer and others in Britain is undoubtedly an improvement on the pure welfare theoretical approach favoured by many US and other health economists.

Nevertheless, it has led to some strange conclusions such as the need to base hospital funding on the contributions that each makes to health gains of their populations. In the light of all the other factors that contribute to the health of populations as well documented by Evans, Fuchs and others, this method may be judged to be counterproductive when it is perceived to preclude other more feasible and effective methods of hospital funding, notably casemix-based allocations.

The study of specific types of institutions and their technical efficiency has not been an important aspect of the interests of most UK health economists. The official approach in the United Kingdom, in association with the other reforms we have discussed in previous chapters, has been to emphasise the use of a number of indicators of hospital performance to draw indirect conclusions about their relative efficiency in treating patients and providing access to care. The economic rationale for these indicators does not seem to have been the subject of much research. We consider technical efficiency issues in our review of priorities. Similarly we regard economic inputs to workforce planning, in which health economists have an important role to play, as a relatively neglected area in the United Kingdom and elsewhere.

Problems and issues in other countries

Other developed countries, often with mixed systems of public and private provision and funding of the health services, have been faced with the problem of reconciling the pressures to increase the utilisation of inputs to health service provision, and the consequent escalation of health expenditure in relation to GDP, with the retention of universal coverage of the population and modest outlays from private individuals.

The principles of solidarity, communitarianism and equity which are widely accepted in most developed European countries have not to date been subverted substantially by these pressures. The work of van Doorslaer, Wagstaff and their colleagues has provided a great deal of evidence about the relative equity of the systems of funding and utilisation in a number of OECD countries.

In Australia and Canada where it is likely that the principles of solidarity and equity may be less well developed than in economically comparable European countries there have been continuing threats to the underlying principles of the health system financing arrangements. We have noted that the Australian health care system has been the subject of protracted political conflict between the major political parties for much of the post-World War II period. Australia has been the only country that has moved twice with changes of government between a 'voluntary' health insurance scheme and universal coverage. The present conservative government to date has retained the main elements of comprehensive insurance but has introduced very large and inequitable subsidies of private health insurance and hence of private hospitals (Hall and Savage, 2005).

In Canada the main threat to the current health insurance arrangements with their emphasis on free hospitalisation and medical care seems to come from conservative think tanks and those economists who derive their analytical and policy emphases from their southern neighbour. The greater resort to the private sector, the market and the use of co-payments are featured in these proposed reforms (Evans and Vujicic, 2005).

In all developed countries, including the United States and the United Kingdom there are similar concerns about a range of common problems. These include the considerable variation in the utilisation of specific medical and surgical interventions between areas, the associated issue of variations in the quality of the care delivered and the widespread belief that the overall efficiency of the health services is less than optimal. In addition, shortages of doctors, nurses and other health professionals have surfaced recently as a major cause for concern.

International comparisons of health care systems

In our view one of the most promising developments in recent times has been the assembly of a rich database of information by the OECD about its member countries. We have made extensive use of these data in comparing the characteristics of a number of OECD countries with a view to drawing some tentative conclusions about the ability of each type of system to achieve efficiency, equity and other goals. It is also encouraging to note that these data have also been used by American health economists, notably Reinhardt, Anderson and their colleagues, to dispel some of the myths in common currency in that country about the relative performance of their own and other OECD countries with 'socialised medicine'.

Our possibly biased interpretation of this evidence suggests that, in terms of overall performance, those countries with more tightly regulated health care systems have been better placed to achieve equity and efficiency goals. They are also able to protect the interests of all patients than those countries that rely on so-called market forces and incentives, and afford a lesser role to government intervention.

We have also noted the mounting evidence that the health status of populations is influenced by a number of factors other than the performance of the health services and their modes of organisation and funding. It seems likely that those countries which share greater concerns about the welfare of their inhabitants, and strive to promote greater equality and self-confidence amongst all members of their societies are also able to achieve better health outcomes, possibly independently of the direct impact of these values on the health services *per se*.

The relationship between health economists and the medical profession has undoubtedly been fraught with conflict in the United Kingdom and elsewhere. As many writers have demonstrated the ethical position of physicians emphasises their responsibility to individual patients whilst economists take a much wider view of societal issues and the impact of individual medical decision-making on the resources available in alternatives uses. We have stressed the importance, if the conclusions of health economists are to be implemented, of their giving much more attention to the structures and institutions of the health care system, including the roles and attitudes of the medical profession.

We have emphasised strongly the nature of the advice provided by the consultants and international organisations from developed countries to the developing nations of the world. We have argued that the conclusions derived in these studies, especially those from health economists, have often been based on free market solutions, including the application of user charges and an enhanced role for private sector initiatives. Equity concerns and analyses have been largely absent from their recommendations. We quote the extensive evidence that this advice has been counterproductive, especially in alleviating the deplorable health standards of the poor in these countries.

Perspectives on priorities of health economics

The evaluation of technical efficiency

In view of the large amount of expenditure on hospitals, nursing homes and other institutions it is surprising to us that this issue has not been the subject of much research and development activity by economists. We cannot envisage a satisfactory response to our argument that for those working within the free market, welfare economics paradigm, they can avoid the conclusion that a *necessary condition* for maximum Paretian efficiency is the achievement of the optimum technical efficiency by all the services contributing to the satisfaction of consumers.

For those British and other economists adhering to the extra-welfarist perception of health issues it is perhaps more understandable that in concentrating on health as the final outcome many should ignore the efficiency of the inputs to the production of health to which the health services may make only a modest contribution. However, to ignore the inputs of institutions which absorb such a high proportion of total health expenditure appears to us to be misguided given the overall aim of maximising health outputs for a relatively constant set of resources.

It has been a source of irritation for us that economists generally have been sceptical about the use of DRGs for hospital funding despite the mounting evidence of its applications and achievements for this purpose in many major developed countries. Our own interest in casemix has been in part stimulated by our perception of the opportunities it afforded for benchmarking exercises and the ability to assess the relative technical efficiency of individual hospitals. Studies of this kind are now undertaken frequently by policy-makers and managers in Australia using the national hospital dataset of the Australian Department of Health.

Workforce planning

An area of potentially considerable interest to health economists and clinicians has been that of workforce planning and analysis. We noted the important points made by Robert Evans that policies about the workforce are treated by economists as an aspect of the development of human capital, which in turn represents an input into a production process. He emphasised, moreover, that in the health field the development of private human capital is heavily subsidised by governments as they allocate substantial funds to educational and training activities.

The planning of the health workforce in the sense of ensuring that the future stock of personnel matches that of the requirements of the population becomes an inevitable aspect of government policy even in health systems with a preference for market solutions. However, the conceptual and statistical problems of determining whether the existing population ratios represent a surplus or a deficit, and of forecasting the future values, are daunting. Evidence from Australia, Canada and the United States indicates that workforce planning for the medical and nursing workforces in the past has produced very dubious results with rapid shifts in perceptions of a surplus to one of a deficit and *vice versa*.

The production function approach of economists stresses that this process should not simply be a numbers game of population projections matched against the likely number of outputs of personnel from educational programs and attrition from each occupational group. Due attention should be paid to the possibility of substituting alternative forms of labour for one another where there is evidence that overall costs would be reduced without prejudicing the quality of care. Moreover, in the context of technological change, the substitution of capital for labour raises further possibilities for achieving greater efficiency.

Empirical studies of the kind required to apply a cost-benefit or cost-effectiveness/utility approach to these issues are still lacking. The political problems, including opposition of the medical profession to date, have mainly thwarted attempts, for example, to substitute nurse practitioners for doctors in areas where the evidence is clear cut that a shortage of the latter group exists.

Recent workforce planning studies have concentrated on the perceptions and signs of shortages of key medical and nursing personnel in a number of countries. These studies have normally focused on assuming optimum ratios of the workforce numbers in the given category to population, often the existing ratio, and then using demographic projections of varying degrees of sophistication to assess the likely ratio at future dates.

Our belief is that work of this kind would benefit greatly from collaboration with health economists who understand the role of supply-induced demand, flat of the curve medicine and the production function-based potential for substituting more cost-effective personnel for other members of the health workforce.

In some areas of shortage, such as nursing, the role of traditional economic incentives, notably salary increases, should be investigated further in certain countries. We again wish to emphasise the need for multi-disciplinary studies in this highly complex area where specialised statistical, demographic and epidemiological skills are also essential together with detailed knowledge of the local employing and educational institutions, other services and the regulatory environment.

Costing studies

On the one hand, as Reinhardt and others have suggested, economists have a better conceptual framework to draw upon in the costing field than other disciplinary groups. They are well drilled in the distinctions between fixed and variable costs, and between marginal and average costs. They also have been immersed in the important notion of opportunity cost.

Nevertheless, when we review the critiques of studies conducted using cost-effectiveness and cost-utility analysis the queries about the accuracy and validity of the cost estimates seem to arise persistently (Stone et al., 2000; Drummond and Sculpher, 2005). This observation is consistent with our own impression that the theoretical background about costs that all competent economists acquire may act as an obstacle to progress when health economists are faced with the task of generating cost estimates from imperfect and fragmentary cost data. There seems to be an attitude of mind that this is merely *accounting* cost data and hence a matter deserving of contempt amongst economists with their superior knowledge of the underlying concepts.

The reality is that the accounting data is often the only available source of estimates about the costs of treating specific disease categories and for other health services purposes. The alternative of detailed time and motion studies of the costs of individual inputs to the treatment process has repeatedly proved to be too expensive to undertake or fraught with other problems. In these circumstances it is not surprising that by default it has been left to operations researchers and mathematicians to devise modelling techniques to make the most of the available accounting data.

A notable example is the creation of the Yale Cost Model (YCM) by the Yale University group of casemix researchers whose work has been referred to previously in connection with the development of DRGs (Fetter et al., 1976). The YCM has been used extensively in Australia and other countries to generate costs by DRG for casemix funding purposes.

It is of considerable interest, moreover, that what is often regarded as the most important development in industrial cost accounting, activity–based costing (ABC), was the work of the distinguished Harvard professor Robert Kaplan whose background was also in operations research (Kaplan and Anderson, 2007). The ABC has been applied extensively to the costing of hospital activities (Finkler and Ward, 1999). We are not aware of any costing studies by health economists that have drawn on the principles of ABC.

It would be pleasing if we could assume that more health economists might develop an interest in bridging the gap between their knowledge of cost theory, and the practical application of cost-related data to the cost side of CBA and CUA applications, and to funding issues, in the clinical and related fields.

Concluding homilies

An important outcome of studying and assimilating the contents of this book should be the ability to adopt a more critical approach to the nostrums for health care reform put forward by management consultants, including some economists, often US-based, and international agencies, notably the World Bank. They typically have a very limited understanding of the inappropriateness of applying simple economic models as the centre-piece of their proposals, and the complexities of health care systems (sometimes including their own). Some examples were provided of how policy advice of this kind has been influential in developing and transitional countries of the world.

A further conclusion to be drawn is that health economics, especially where coupled with sound empirical work which often health economists are well equipped to undertake, has much to contribute to an improved under-standing of health-related phenomena. It has been emphasised in the work of Evans, Fuchs and others that this is especially the case where the work is of a multi-disciplinary nature, for example, involving collaboration with clinicians and epidemiologists. But as the distinguished Cambridge econo-mist Professor Joan Robinson has affirmed, *an important reason for studying economics is to safeguard against being misled by economists*, especially in the health services context when they attempt to draw policy conclusions from normative and dubious assumptions!

Glossary of Terms*

Activity based costing (ABC). An important method of cost accounting that distinguishes causal factors in production (cost drivers) that influence aspects of the processes. It has been used in the costing of hospital processes and outcomes.

Adverse selection. The situation where certain groups of patients with a high risk of incurring large medical costs may be excluded by the health insurance organisation.

Agency. In health economics an agency relationship may be assumed to exist between a doctor and a patient in which the patient's treatment is designed to reflect his/her preferences. However, the relationship may be an imperfect one in that the doctor's preferences for income and leisure may affect the treatment choices. Moreover, the doctor may be unaware of the patient's preferences.

Aggregate consumption. In **Keynesian economics** total expenditure in an economy is conceptualised as being the sum of spending by consumers on goods and services together with expenditure on investment.

Allocative efficiency. For most economists allocative efficiency means the same as economic efficiency. However, in the health field the term may also be applied, in an **extra-welfarist** framework, to the achievement of an allocation of scarce resources to health services which generates the maximum benefit in terms of health status improvement.

Austrian school. A group of economists based in Vienna who in the latter part of the nineteenth century made important contributions to the development of price theory. The principal members of the school included Menger, von Wieser and Bohm-Bawerk. The tradition with its emphasis on individualism in economic affairs was carried on in the United States by a number of economists of whom von Hayek was the most influential.

Average cost curve. A diagrammatic representation of a postulated relationship between the average costs incurred by a firm and the number of units of production. The curve is typically shown as having a U shape,

---

* More detailed descriptions of these terms are provided in A.J. Culyer, *The Dictionary of Health Economics* (Edward Elgar Publishing, 2005).

with average costs declining as fixed costs are spread over larger quantities of output. However, the curve is depicted as rising beyond higher levels of output as the variable cost component is assumed to increase.

Average costs. The total cost of production of a firm divided by the number of units of output. Total cost is the sum of **fixed costs** and **variable costs**.

Benchmarking. The process of establishing a standard of **efficiency** for services or institutions and then comparing the standard with what is achieved by an individual or group of services or institutions.

Big ticket. In the health field a big ticket item of technology is one of high cost per unit, such as an **MRI** device.

Capital good. A durable item such as equipment, the purpose of which is to create other goods and services in the present and future periods.

Capitalist mode of production. A term used by Marxist economists to describe the functioning of economies where the ownership of the means of production lies in the hands of a class of private individuals.

Capitation. The method of remunerating doctors where their income is related to the number of patients for whom they are responsible rather than the number of services they provide.

Cardinal concept of utility. The notion of **utility** as a level of satisfaction which can be added across individuals. This implies that the satisfaction achieved by the **consumption** of a commodity is the same for each individual.

Casemix. The distribution of types of patients, usually within a hospital, based on a classification of patients such as the **DRG system**.

Ceteris paribus. The assumption that other factors remain equal or unchanged when statements are made about the influence of one factor on another. This assumption underlies the price-quantity relationship of a demand schedule where income, for example, is assumed to remain equal at every point on the curve.

Computerised axial tomography (CAT). A device for X-ray imaging of the body.

Classical economics. The body of theory about the functioning of economies originally developed by Adam Smith and David Ricardo which focused attention on the determinants of market prices, the invisible hand of the market, and the specialisation of labour in the process of production.

Clinical care. The services to individual patients provided by health care practitioners notably doctors, nurses and allied health professionals.

Clinical directorates. An organisational arrangement for providing services to patients in hospitals in which the individual directorates are based on the type of medical specialty responsible for the treatment.

Clinical governance. A relatively new term which is mainly used to describe the process of monitoring the activities of clinical staff so as to ensure the safety and quality of the care delivered to patients.

Clinical management. The term has several meanings including the method of managing all the activities associated with **clinical care**, and the management of the needs of individual patients.

Clinical meaningfulness ('coherence'). A criterion for the development of a casemix classification which refers to the need for medical and other clinicians to be able to comprehend the nature of the types of patients included in each category of the classification.

Clinical trial. A study designed to establish the effectiveness of a therapeutic intervention, often of a pharmaceutical product.

Cochrane Effective Practice and Organisation of Care (EPOC). This is one of the review groups established under the Cochrane collaboration designed to promote evidence-based clinical practice and policy-making. The EPOC group is based at the University of Ottawa and undertakes systematic reviews of educational, behavioural and organisational contributions to improved professional practice.

Co-insurance. The term refers to an insurance contract where part of the cost is met by the patient and part by the insurance organisation.

Communitarianism. The term is used to describe the notion that satisfactions are generated by the fact of individuals participating within a community. It is this proposition that has led to many European countries emphasising the principle of solidarity as the basis of their **social health insurance** policies. The communitarian ethos is an example of an **externality** in which the utility of all citizens benefits from the knowledge that persons of low income or with chronic illnesses are protected by the health insurance arrangements.

Community rating. The principle embodied in most health insurance schemes, often mandated by governments, that individuals pay the same insurance premiums irrespective of their age, income and their other characteristics including their current health status.

Constant price terms. The expression of money values, derived from observations over time, in a manner which eliminates the influence of price changes. The original money values are deflated by a measure of the price movements from period to period, in order to reflect the underlying changes in volume.

Consumer goods. Physical items (and services) purchased by final consumers including those that are used in the current period, and those which are used over longer periods of time (consumer durables).

Consumer sovereignty. The principle underlying neoclassical economics that the demands, wants and needs of consumers should be afforded high priority in the functioning of economic systems to achieve the maximum of **economic efficiency**.

Consumer surplus. The difference between how much a consumer would be willing to pay for a commodity and the amount actually paid in the market by the consumer. The concept reflects, in neoclassical theory, the assumption that the value of decreasing marginal utility with quantity of consumption exceeds the price until the equality of the two is achieved.

Co-payment. The percentage of the cost of the service met by the patient with the remainder being paid by the insurer.

Coronary artery bypass grafting (CABG). A surgical procedure designed to clear blocked coronary arteries of the heart. Because of its frequent use and high cost the procedure has been investigated extensively using **cost-effectiveness analysis (CEA)**.

Cost-benefit analysis (CBA). The method of economic evaluation in which the attempt is made to compare in comparable money terms all the costs and benefits associated with a specific program, project or other intervention. Discounting of future costs and benefits to present values using an appropriate rate of interest is an essential part of CBA. In the health field the method implies the contentious view that the benefit of saving a life can be measured in money terms.

Cost-effectiveness analysis (CEA). In this method of economic evaluation a measure of the effectiveness of a program, project or other intervention is obtained such as the number of patients treated successfully. This measure is compared with the cost of achieving the intervention. However, effectiveness is not measured in money terms, but the basis is provided for comparing the cost-effectiveness ratio relative to other interventions measured in the same terms.

Cost function. A postulated relationship expressed in mathematical form between the cost of producing a given product or other outcome and the one or more factors which influence the cost.

Cost of production theory. The perspective advanced by the early classical economists that the price of a product was directly related to the costs, especially labour costs, incurred in the production process.

Cost reimbursement. A funding mechanism whereby the payments made to producers are derived directly from their production costs. This funding arrangement is still frequently used in the United States by **third party payers** to reimburse hospitals.

Cost-utility analysis. A variant of cost-effectiveness analysis applied to the health services in which a measure of health status, normally **QALYs**, is used to measure **utility**.

Cottage industry. In the health services' context the **primary care** segment has been likened to other industries where low technology and a hands-on approach of individual providers prevails.

Cream skimming. In private health insurance programs the opportunity may be available for the insuring agency to concentrate on securing enrolments from low risk population groups and not covering those with higher risk profiles.

Deadweight loss of health insurance. For those health economists applying the welfare economics framework there is a loss of utility associated with the provision of health insurance since the use of health services will be greater than that which would be achieved in a free market where each consumer met the **marginal cost** of the service.

Deductible. The amount of a charge which must be met by the insured person before any cost is re-imbursed by the insurance agency.

Deductive reasoning. The method whereby conclusions are derived from a set of assumptions or axioms by logical reasoning. Economic theory and applications have relied heavily on deduction, partly because of the difficulties associated with empirical verification in **economic relationships**.

Demand schedule. A hypothetical relationship between the quantity of a commodity which would be purchased by consumers for each possible price of the commodity. It is assumed for the purpose of constructing the usual curve in two dimensions that all other factors such as the income of consumers which might influence the relationship are held constant.

Developing countries. Those nations with relatively low incomes per head, and where the available economic resources and institutions cannot as yet support standards of living, including health services, comparable with the more affluent developed countries. The great majority of the countries of the world are placed in this category.

Diagnosis-related groups (DRGs). A method of describing the casemix of hospitals in which the categories of the classification are designed to be relatively homogeneous in respect of resource use and **clinically meaningful**. The DRGs were originally developed and applied in the United States but are now used extensively in a number of countries as a method of funding hospital services by governments and other third party payers.

Disability Adjusted Life Year (DALY). This is the same type of measure for health services evaluation purposes as the **QALY**, except that a measure of the disability of a health condition is used rather than the quality of life.

Disease and service exclusions. Some health insurance contracts, especially in the United States, may contain provision for the exclusion of certain types of illness, notably those of a psychiatric kind, from coverage.

Doctor-to-population ratios. Measures of the available stock of doctors are generated by relating the numbers to the populations for which they are responsible. The ratios are expressed normally per thousand of population.

Econometric models. These models are designed to present mathematical representations of a set of relationships defined by **economic theory**, which purport to depict the functioning of the whole economy or of a subset of the economy. Many econometric models are derived from **Keynesian economics** and are designed to be quantified by reference to empirical data and statistical methods.

Economic analysis. The approach to economic phenomena which operates by reducing the relationships to their component parts for the purpose of understanding and interpreting the causes and effects present in these relationships.

Economic efficiency. For neoclassical economists efficiency in the welfare economics tradition is defined by the Pareto principle that no one can be made better off in terms of satisfactions derived without others becoming worse off.

Economic growth. For the whole economy growth is usually measured by increases in **gross domestic product** adjusted for price changes. These estimates are referred to as GDP in constant price terms.

Economic rationalism. This phrase is often applied by non-economists to those whose perspective on economics is based on the alleged benefits and virtues of free markets, and the relative absence of government intervention in the operation of these markets.

Economic relationships. The activities associated with the production of goods and services and their distribution via markets and other means for **consumption** and **investment** purposes. Flows of financial funds are usually associated with these relationships.

Economic theory. The body of statements about economic relationships used to describe and explain these relationships based on a set of principles and assumptions regarding human behaviour.

Economies of scale and scope. Economies of scale are said to exist when the same proportionate increase in all the factors of production for a firm or industry leads to a decrease in the average cost of production. If it is less costly to produce two or more outputs together than it is to produce each separately, economies of scope are present.

ECuity project. A European Union-financed study designed to establish the equity of the health financing arrangements found in a number of EU and other countries.

Effectiveness. In epidemiology and clinical trials this term denotes the ability of an intervention, such as a drug therapy, to yield a desired outcome for a group of individuals.

Efficacy. This term is often used to distinguish between **effectiveness** for a defined population of patients, and the impact of an intervention on individual patients under an ideal clinical situation.

Efficiency. See **allocative efficiency, economic efficiency** and **technical efficiency**.

Elasticity of demand. The price elasticity of demand is measured by the proportionate change in the quantity demanded as a result of a proportionate change in price. The elasticity concept may also be applied to a supply schedule, and to the effect of other variables such as income changes on the quantity demanded.

Endogenous factor. This term is applied to those causal influences which are an inherent aspect of the economic system under investigation.

Epistemology. The branch of philosophy that is concerned with the nature, methods and limits of human knowledge.

Equilibrium. The situation in which the economic forces affecting a given outcome are in balance so that there is no basis for a change in the factor under consideration. According to economic theory the equilibrium price of a commodity is that price where supply and demand are equal.

Equity. Horizontal equity is the principle, or **value judgement**, that those persons of similar income should be treated equally by the financial arrangements, for example, those contained in the health insurance system. For vertical equity to be achieved, persons of higher income should pay correspondingly more for their health insurance coverage.

Evidence-based medicine. The movement that is based on the principle that the practice of medicine should rely on treatment practices which have been validated by reference to evidence bearing on their **effectiveness**.

Evolutionary economics. An approach to economic relationships modelled on biology which emphasises complex interdependencies in organisations, along with competitive forces, growth and innovation.

Exogenous factor. A causal influence on an economic system which is regarded as lying outside the functioning and control of that system.

Experience rating. According to this criterion charges for health insurance are designed to reflect the factors that may influence the risk of making claims, notably the age and morbidity experience of the persons being covered.

Explicit rationing. As applied to the health services, the arrangement whereby a government sets out clear guidelines about which types of patients are to be refused treatment in the context of resource scarcity.

Externalities. Those factors where benefits or costs accrue to persons or firms for which a money payment is not made. External economies are said to occur where utility for the whole community is generated by actions such as improvements in road safety or an immunisation program. External diseconomies are associated with activities such as those generated by firms causing climate change where the negative impact will fall on whole communities.

Extra-billing. The process whereby health providers charge more that the fee set for health insurance purposes. The practice is generally banned in the Canadian health care system for medical fees.

Extra-welfarist approach. This alternative approach to conventional welfare economics, as applied to the health sector, stresses the use of **health status** as a measure of the benefit of **health policy** initiatives.

Factor of production. A resource required to yield a commodity or service. **Classical economics** classified the factors into land, labour and capital.

Face validity. A measure is said to possess face validity if it is assessed as being consistent with expectations arising out of well-established theoretical principles.

Fee-for-service(FFS). The method of health service practitioner remuneration in which each item of service is associated with a specific charge.

Fee schedules. A scale of fees for individual medical procedures and activities forming the basis of payments to doctors and other practitioners in a FFS remuneration system.

Firm, the. The term applied in economics to all organisations that supply goods and services. In modelling the behaviour of firms it is customary to regard them as profit maximising entities in transforming inputs into outputs.

Fixed costs. In the conventional theory of the firm, fixed costs are those that do not change with levels of output in the short-term.

Flat of the curve medicine. A graphical representation of the claim that beyond a certain point additional units of medical inputs may not lead to any increase in health status in the population.

Full service coverage. In this type of health insurance all the costs of medical and other care are met by the insuring agency. No **co-payments** or **deductibles** are present.

Functional relationship. A causal relationship between variables that can be expressed in a specific mathematical form, usually based in the physical sciences on a theoretical framework which has been verified empirically. The relationships postulated in economic theory cannot be conceptualised as being of this kind.

Gatekeeper. This is the role played in many health care systems by general medical practitioners where a referral to a specialist practitioner is required for health insurance and related purposes.

Global Burden of Disease. A method developed by the World Bank for establishing priorities for health care interventions based on the prevalence of diseases and their effects on the mortality and morbidity of populations.

Globalisation. The process describing the growing interdependence of countries worldwide derived from increased international trade, free trade agreements, reduced controls of international capital movements and the widespread diffusion of technologies.

Gross domestic product (GDP). The money value of all goods and services produced in an economy. Where comparisons over time are required the values of GDP may be converted to constant price terms using an appropriate price index as a deflator.

Health care expenditure. The sum of all types of expenditure on the health services covering such items as expenditure on **hospitals**, nursing homes, medical services, dental and allied health services, and pharmaceutical products. Health care expenditure may be expressed as including or excluding capital expenditure.

Health care quality. In the extensive literature on the subject, quality is often defined in terms of the absence of errors in treatment, especially of the kind which might lead to death or additional morbidity. In a more positive sense quality may also be defined as patient treatment which conforms to best practice based on evidence.

Health gain. The improvement in **health status** associated with the functioning of the health care system.

Health insurance. The system of spreading the risks of the financial costs of health care across a population which may take a variety of forms. In a private health insurance arrangement, individuals or their employers are responsible for the payment of insurance premiums to a private insurer agency. In public health insurance, government agencies provide insurance to cover health care costs which is financed wholly or in part by taxation revenue.

Health policy. The phrase embraces the set of activities, usually associated with governments, designed to determine the characteristics of the health care system. These may include the methods of financing and providing health services, and influencing the **equity, effectiveness** and **efficiency** with which the system operates.

Health promotion. The fostering of activities such as preventive services and healthy life styles which are largely independent of the delivery of health services by health professionals and institutions.

Healthcare Resource Groups (HRGs). The system of casemix classification developed and used in Britain for hospital funding and planning purposes. It is similar to the DRG system but gives more emphasis to surgical procedures in defining the classification.

Health Maintenance Organisation (HMO). A health service arrangement developed in the United States whereby the organisation and its medical staff are placed at risk for expenditures incurred by its client members. Subscribers to an HMO are guaranteed a specified set of health services. HMOs represent an important component of **managed care** in the United States.

Health status. The overall state of physical and mental well-being of the population normally measured by indicators such as mortality and morbidity experience. Improvements in health status are defined as **health gains** and the system of **QALYs** has been used increasingly to measure health status as part of the evaluation of the outcomes of **health policy** initiatives.

Hospital cost containment. Attempts, usually implemented by governments, to slow down the rate of growth in hospital expenditure. Reductions in the number of hospital beds, and changes in financing methods to provide incentives for the achievement of greater efficiency in the provision of hospital services are amongst the methods that have been used for this purpose.

Hospitals. Institutions for the treatment of diseases, accidents and other emergencies where most of the patients receive care of short-term duration. In developed countries hospitals are the most expensive single component of the health services, but as a result of **cost containment** policies the percentage of health care expenditure for which hospitals are responsible has been reduced substantially in most countries.

Iatrogenic. An adverse effect on a person's health generated by a doctor or other health professional.

Ideology. The set of beliefs and values bearing on human affairs held by individuals and groups which may impact on the characteristics of health care systems such as the type of health insurance system implemented. The term is often used in a pejorative sense to characterise the views of those with whom one disagrees.

Imperfect competition. Departures from the assumptions of **perfect competition** where some firms are sufficiently large to influence the prices of outputs and inputs in the market where they operate. Empirically it is evident that most markets experience imperfect competition but in neoclassical economics this inconvenient fact is often ignored.

Implicit rationing. In predominantly government-funded health care systems this phrase describes the situation in which some needs cannot be met within the existing resource constraints. The required rationing process is delegated to medical staff who are obliged to make decisions about which types of patients shall receive treatments and from whom the services are withheld. For example, expensive kidney dialysis or transplant services may not be made available to persons after a certain age has been reached.

Income distribution. The description of the variations in income of individuals or households in a given country or region.

Income elasticity of demand. The proportionate change in demand resulting from a proportionate change in income, with price and other variables held constant.

Incremental cost-utility ratios. In the application of **QALYs** as measures of utility the ratio of the cost of a health project or intervention to the resultant QALY provides an indication of the efficiency of the undertaking. When comparing projects where the ratios vary according to the size of the project, it is the marginal increase in the ratio which provides the appropriate comparative measure.

Indifference curve. A two-dimensional graph of the quantities consumed of two commodities where each point purports to represent the combination of the commodities which yields the same level of satisfaction (utility) for a consumer. The shape of the curve, convex to the origin, reflects the assumption of diminishing marginal utility; at a high level of consumption of one commodity, a small level of consumption of the other commodity produces the same amount of satisfaction.

Indifference map. A graph showing a set of **indifference curves** for a consumer where the curves further to the right indicate higher levels of satisfaction.

Infant mortality rate. The number of deaths of children under one year per 1000 of live births. The rate varies considerably from country to country, and is often used as an important indicator of the overall performance of the health care system.

Information asymmetry. In medical interactions the term reflects the fact that the information possessed by doctors about clinical conditions is much greater than that of their patients.

Interpersonal comparisons of utility. Comparisons between individuals of the total satisfaction gained by the consumption of the same set of commodities. It implies a **cardinal concept of utility**, that the satisfactions of each person can be added in a meaningful way.

Investment. A term in economics which is used in several senses. It may refer to increases in the stock of physical capital, the financial money flow which supports the increase in capital or financial flows of other kinds designed to produce income flows in the future.

Isoquant. A graph which purports to represent the combinations of factor inputs that will yield the same level of output where two factors of production are assumed. The shape of the curve, convex to the origin, reflects the assumption of diminishing marginal productivity of each factor.

Job burnout. The notion that certain stressful occupations, notably nursing in the health field, are associated over time with a lowering of morale and productivity.

Kakwani index. A measure originally designed to assess the degree of progressivity or regressivity of income tax scales internationally, it has recently been applied to the health care financing systems of a number of European and other countries. A positive value for the index indicates progressivity and a negative value indicates the presence of a regressive system.

Ken Bassett's problem. The problem identified by a Canadian physician of why certain clinical procedures continued to be used by doctors when they had been proven to be ineffective. The Canadian economist Robert Evans has applied the term to the use by health economists of concepts such as those incorporated in the application of welfare economics which had been demonstrated to be incorrect or misleading.

Keynesian economics. The body of theory developed by J.M. Keynes in the 1930s largely to explain the phenomenon of the Great Depression. He demonstrated that, contrary to **Say's law** held by classical economists, there was no automatic tendency for a capitalist economy to achieve a full employment state of equilibrium. He proposed government intervention especially to support additional levels of aggregate expenditure to overcome unemployment.

Labour theory of value. The proposition that the only or main determinant of the value of commodities is the amount of labour incorporated in their production. This proposition was held by the classical economists but was given great prominence by Karl Marx.

Law of diminishing returns. The proposition that when additional inputs of a factor of production are applied in a production process, with other inputs held constant, a point will be reached where the additional output decreases.

Life expectancy. The average number of years of life a person of a specified age can expect to live based on current death rates at each age. The most commonly used life expectation is for age zero. Life expectancy at birth provides a useful summary measure for comparative purposes of the mortality experience of each country.

Long-term. In Marshallian economics the long-term is the period when all factors of production, including capital, are capable of being varied.

Macroeconomics. The perspective on economics which focuses on aggregates of consumption, investment and savings and their relationships, especially as set out in Keynesian economics. The origins of the macro approach can also be traced to **Walrasian economics** which conceptualised the whole economy as a set of simultaneous equations.

Managed care. A phrase used in the United States to describe the provision of health insurance in which incentives and constraints are placed on providers to limit the services received by patients.

Managed competition. The essential idea here is that measures can be used to stimulate competition between providers in the circumstances prevailing in each country where it is not feasible to introduce a fully competitive market, also involving price signals for consumers. Reforms introduced into the British NHS in the early 1990s were based on this principle which stressed the separation of the roles of purchasers and providers of health services.

Marginal cost curve. In the formal neoclassical theory of the firm the curve is designed to represent the relationship between the level of output and the extra cost (marginal cost) incurred by each additional unit of output. The U shape of the curve is intended to reflect the assumption that initially marginal costs decrease but they may rise beyond a certain level of output.

Marginalist. That aspect of neoclassical economics which stresses the role of small increments of consumption and production in arriving at decisions about maximising outcomes. For example, the theory that equating of **marginal cost** and **marginal revenue** will maximise the profit of a firm.

Marginal revenue. The extra revenue generated by an additional unit of output. Marginal revenue plays a key role, according to the theory of the firm under perfect competition, in establishing the equilibrium price of the output where **marginal cost** equals marginal revenue and **profits** are maximised.

Marginal social benefit. In an extension of the theory of the firm to the whole economy the phrase indicates the additional benefit to society of an additional unit of output of the product or service in question.

Marginal social cost. The increase in the cost to society of an additional unit of the product or service. According to the theory, marginal social cost should equal marginal social benefit for social welfare to be maximised.

Marginal utility. The additional satisfaction received by a consumer as a result of the consumption of an additional unit of a commodity. In neoclassical theory marginal utility is assumed to decrease with additional units of consumption.

Market failure. In neoclassical economics any departure from the market of perfect competition is regarded as a 'failure'. **Imperfect competition** and **externalities** are the most important examples.

Markets. In economics a market consists of the buyers and sellers who trade in commodities and services, and generate prices. The analysis of the characteristics of these markets forms a major part of economic theory and applications. These include the idealised outcomes of 'perfect' markets and the consequences of departures from perfection-market failure.

Maximising behaviour. The principle that consumers endeavour to achieve the highest level of satisfaction given their budget constraints and that firms endeavour to maximise their profits.

Medicare. The term applies to three government-funded health insurance programs: the universal health insurance systems of Australia and Canada, and the program for people aged 65 and over in the United States, along with the disabled, in the United States.

Medico-Technical model. The belief about health care systems that the medical needs of individuals can be met by the appropriate application of technology irrespective of resource constraints.

Merit good. An item of consumption that is perceived by some people as having properties that warrant its use being encouraged over and above the level that would occur if this were determined by the functioning of a market. It may be argued that government subsidies of education and health services arise out of the attribution of the characteristic to these areas.

Meta-analysis. A method of drawing conclusions about phenomena such as clinical interventions by analysing the results of a number of previously conducted studies (analyses) of the phenomena.

Methodological individualism. The principle favoured by some economists that economic methods should concentrate on individuals as the basic unit of analysis rather than on communities and other social aggregations.

Microeconomics. The body of economic theory that focuses on the behaviour of individual firms and consumers.

Models in economic theory. The construction of representations of reality which concentrate on what are believed to be the most important factors influencing economic behaviour. To manage the underlying complexity of the real world, other factors which may be relevant to the phenomena under investigation are assumed to be held constant or ignored. Models in economics may also represent 'idealisations' or fictions.

Models of health care systems. For purposes of comparing the attributes of the health care systems of different countries it may be useful as a preliminary exercise to group together countries with similar funding and organisational characteristics. For example, national health services may be construed as comprising those countries where the main organisations, notably hospitals, are owned and controlled by governments, the funding for the service is derived from taxation and most services are free at the point of delivery.

Monetarist. A school of economics which emphasises the role of the supply of money in affecting the state of the economy, especially in regard to inflationary movements.

Monopoly. The extreme case of imperfect competition where one supplier dominates a market and hence is able to establish a price which exceeds that which would arise in perfect competition.

Monopsonist. The market situation in which one buyer dominates the market. In a national health service the government normally enjoys this role in respect of the purchasing of many inputs to the health services.

Moral hazard. The term applied where insurance against risk may lead to a greater rate of the occurrence of the events against which the insurance applies. Health economists (mainly from the United States) who use the term argue that the demand for health services will be increased by the existence of health insurance and hence generate a loss of welfare for the community as compared with a free market. Their analysis implicitly ignores the beneficial effects of health insurance in providing access to health services.

Magnetic Resonance Imaging (MRI). A method of body imaging which permits clearer pictures of internal organs than **CAT** scanning.

Medical-Technical model. The common belief amongst medical personnel that needs can be defined comprehensively, and that technology can be applied to satisfy the needs. Resource constraints are not considered.

Multi-disciplinary clinical pathways (MDCP). The integration of clinical information with managerial inputs to establish an ideal sequence of events or end points in clinical management. Observed departures from the ideal can then be reviewed by the multi-disciplinary team to achieve improved performance.

Multi-disciplinary health centres. The method of providing primary care in which a range of health professional personnel are brought together in one organisation and site. The establishment of these centres was pioneered in Sweden but the arrangement has spread to many other countries.

Naïve Economic model. The belief that health services are subject to the same 'laws' of supply and demand that affect other commodities. Economists who hold this view implicitly ignore the role of **supplier-induced demand** in the health services, and the other distinctive characteristics of health. The phrase was introduced by Robert Evans.

National accounting data. All developed countries generate information on the main aggregates, notably **Gross Domestic Product** and its components, which reflect the functioning of the economy and provide a guide to economic policy. National health accounting data are designed to play a similar role as an input to health policy-making.

National Institute for Clinical Excellence (NICE). The organisation set up in the United Kingdom to promote cost-effectiveness studies of technology, quality improvements and other inputs to the NHS.

Need for health services. Health professionals and epidemiologists emphasise that the provision of health services should be designed to meet the needs of populations arising out of the presence of diseases and other potentially life threatening circumstances. Health economists, however, stress that it is impossible to meet all needs thus defined in view of the limitations imposed by resource scarcity.

Neoclassical economics. The approach to the understanding of economic phenomena which stresses group and individual choice, **utility** and **profit maximising** behaviour, and the role of markets in achieving desirable outcomes for societies. The marginalist method of establishing the consequences of economic behaviour is of fundamental importance for this school of economics.

Non-profit health organisations. Most institutions in the health services of developed countries, including hospitals, are managed traditionally by organisations that do not have a private, profit-making motive. To understand their behaviour it is necessary, therefore, to create models which are based on alternatives to the economic theory of the firm based on profit maximisation.

Normative economics. The application of economic theory to derive principles about what measures ought to be undertaken to achieve social and other objectives.

Nurse practitioners. Qualified nurses who have been trained to undertake activities that would usually be performed by medical staff, especially in areas where there are shortages of doctors.

Nursing homes. Institutions of a longer stay kind which are designed to care for the aged and others with chronic disabilities.

Nursing staff. Personnel who perform nursing duties in hospitals, nursing homes and within the community. Distinctions are usually made between registered nurses who are qualified, often by the possession of a University degree, to perform the more complex nursing tasks, and those with lesser qualifications who may have a variety of designations varying from country to country.

Ontology. The philosophy of existence and the classification system it embodies for each individual.

Opportunity costs. The conception of costs emphasised by economists which is based on the definition of a cost as the opportunity foregone by the expenditure undertaken.

Ordinal concept of utility. Since the **cardinal concept of utility** became difficult to defend, economists devised the approach incorporated in the use of the indifference curve that individuals only needed to be able to compare the utilities of different commodities to generate downward sloping demand curves.

Organisation for Economic Cooperation and Development (OECD). The international organisation based in Paris which consists mainly of developed countries. The main function of the organisation is to provide advice to member countries and others bearing on their economic and social policies. The OECD maintains a strong health presence and provides detailed statistics about the health services and outcomes of each country.

Paradigm. The term is used in a number of different ways in the literature of the philosophy of science. However, the most common meaning refers to the approach to the subject matter of a discipline which reflects the dominant views of the period. What is being emphasised is that a different approach, a paradigm change, may take place in the future.

Public goods. Those goods and services for which it is not possible to set a fee in a market but which provide utility to a population. In these cases it is usually a government that has to supply the service. The classical example is the lighthouse. Aspects of public health, notably health promotion activities such as anti-smoking campaigns, may be regarded as public goods.

Orthodox economics. The phrase used to describe the theory and tenets of neoclassical economics especially by those economists and others who subscribe to different views about the understanding of economic phenomena.

Outlier. An observation which differs substantially from those of other members of the population. It can be applied to the performance of a health care system where values such as total expenditure as a proportion of **GDP** are much greater or less than expected on the basis of the GDP per capita of the country.

Out-of-pocket payment. The amount of money that an individual must pay as the contribution to the total cost of a service covered by health insurance. It arises out of the combination of a **deductible, coinsurance** and **any disease or service exclusion** applying to the policy.

Pareto principle. The basis of neoclassical welfare economics derived from the principle that a change is desirable if it makes some people better off without disadvantaging anyone else.

Peer review. In the health services context, the process whereby medical staff review the care provided by their colleagues to ensure the quality of the services they provide. The perceived inadequacies of peer review have led in many countries to the development of more detailed surveillance methods of the **clinical governance** kind.

Perfect competition. The hypothetical state of an economy characterised by a large number of providers none of which is sufficiently large enough to influence the prices of the products or of the inputs to the production system. Also implied are freedom of entry of providers and the homogeneity of the products. With the possible exception of some agricultural markets these conditions are unlikely to exist in any actual systems of production, distribution and exchange.

Population projections. The outcomes of using existing mortality and fertility rates to forecast the population of countries or regions at future dates. Population projections form a vital part of **workforce planning** exercises.

Positive economics. In contrast to **normative economics**, positive economics is concerned with the analysis of the information about the behaviour of economies and their components without the making of value judgements.

Premium. The price paid per period to secure insurance.

Primary care groups (PCGs). Associations of general practitioners, established recently in the UK, who are placed at risk for the use of specialist services in hospitals and elsewhere.

Primary care. Treatments and other services of a non-specialist kind provided mainly by general or family practitioners.

Principal diagnosis. The diagnosis of patients which provides the main reason for admission to hospital. The principal diagnosis forms the basis of the DRG casemix system.

Principal-agency. See **Agency**.

Private health insurance. Insurance arrangements provided by private non-government organisations which may be conducted on a profit or non-profit basis. The role of private health insurance varies greatly from country to country.

Process utility. The **utility** derived from the activities associated with the provision of health services, other than the direct health outcomes. Thus the mere existence of hospitals can be said to generate satisfactions for the populations they serve as a result of the knowledge that their services will be available when needed.

Production function. A relationship, often formulated in a specific mathematical form, which purports to indicate how the production of commodities or services is dependent on a set of inputs to the production process. It is useful in setting out characteristics such as the possibility of substituting one input factor for another, for example, in the context of **workforce planning**.

Profit maximisation. The basic assumption underlying the neoclassical theory of the firm that entrepreneurs act to maximise their profits by equating **marginal costs** with **marginal revenue**.

Profits. For a firm these are defined as the excess of revenue over costs.

Program budgeting and marginal analysis (PBMA). The setting of priorities for resource allocation in health systems by considering costs and benefits, and the shifting of resources to those yielding the highest marginal gains per money value expended. It differs from **cost-benefit analysis** in incorporating the procedure in a prescribed management process.

Public health. The aspect of the health services that deals with the delivery of services to whole populations rather than individuals. Activities such as preventive measures, including the fostering of healthy life styles, and the eradication of physical threats from the environment represent the essence of public health. However, the phrase is also used to distinguish health-related initiatives of governments from those of the private sector.

Purchasing power parity (PPP). When money values are expressed in the currencies of different countries for comparative purposes they need to be expressed in a common unit, usually the US dollar. The initial step is to undertake the conversion using the existing exchange rates between the United States and the other currencies. Then a further adjustment is made to reflect the differences between the purchasing powers of the individual currencies, and thus ensure that all the money values are as comparable as possible.

Quality adjusted life years (QALYs). A measure used in the evaluation of health services based on determining the additional **life expectancy** generated by the intervention, adjusted for the estimated quality of the years of life. Many health economists have been involved in the development of QALYs but the approach has been criticised trenchantly by others.

Quality of life. In general terms this concept recognises that the lives of individuals may experience a range of degrees of satisfaction or comfort. A number of different indicators have been developed or proposed to measure this somewhat elusive but important notion. Of these the most important for health economists is the scale used in the construction of **QALYs** where death is assigned a value of zero and one represents the highest achievable quality of existence. Intermediate states of health may range from minor illnesses and disabilities to very painful disease states or losses of major functions such as mobility or eyesight.

Rate of depreciation. The relative size of the decline in value of the capital stock associated with wear and tear or obsolescence. Net investment may be defined as the increase in the capital stock less depreciation.

Rate of time discount. Based on the notion that individuals value future satisfactions (incomes or other benefits) less highly than those received immediately, it becomes possible to devise a method of determining the current value of all future satisfactions expressed in money terms. The estimated rate of the time discount (or interest rate) permits the establishment of the present values of the future income streams or other benefits. Time discounting is an essential feature of **cost-benefit analysis** and other evaluation methods.

Reductionist approach. The fallacy of making comprehensive statements about complex phenomena based on the analysis of their individual components. The *ceteris paribus* assumption of neoclassical economics may be criticised on these grounds in some contexts.

Refined DRGs. Those **DRGs** where further classes, as compared with the original, are defined based on greater use of diagnostic information. The objective is to give increased weight to variations in the severity of illnesses.

Resource Allocation Working Party (RAWP). The group established in England in the mid-1970s to devise a formula to allocate the resources of the NHS more equitably to regions based on measures of mortality and other indicators for each geographical area.

Resource-based relative value scale (RBRVS). A measure of the relative complexity and resource intensity of medical treatments and procedures developed in the United States to establish fees for medical payments.

Risk aversion. The concept that some individuals have a greater preference for avoiding risk than others. As a consequence they are likely to be willing to pay more for insurance than the average value.

Risk sharing. The notion that underlies the rationale for insurance that the costs associated with the risks being insured against are spread over the whole group of people covered.

Salaried service. In the health context the arrangement whereby medical services are provided by staff who are remunerated by the payment of a salary.

Satisficing behaviour. The notion that many individuals participating in economic relationships do not seek to maximise their incomes or other satisfactions but are content to achieve lesser returns because they do not believe that the extra effort of maximisation is worthwhile for them.

Savings. That part of income that households or countries do not spend on current consumption. Savings are therefore available for **investment** purposes.

Say's law. The belief of classical economists that supply creates its own demand. The rejection of Say's law forms an important aspect of Keynesian economics and the reason for unemployment occurring.

Schools of economic thought. Historically a number of different approaches to the analysis and interpretation of economic phenomena have arisen, including the classical, neoclassical and Keynesian. The existence of these schools, each of which was regarded as the accepted wisdom of the time, suggests that existing approaches to economics, such as the current domination of the **neoclassical** school, may not always be with us.

Short-term. The period of time during which some factors of production, notably the capital stock, are not capable of being changed.

Shroud waving. The phenomenon whereby health professionals seek to secure additional resources by pointing to the likelihood of deaths increasing if their demands are not met.

Social indifference curve. Based on the indifference curve of an individual, it is postulated that a society via its government should determine what combinations of social projects are likely to generate the same level of satisfaction for the whole society.

Social health insurance. In many European and other countries health insurance may be mandated and regulated by governments to secure social objectives notably the facilitation of access to health services at low cost to households.

Social policy. The set of government programs and financing procedures which are implemented to achieve goals such as the payment of benefits to the aged, the unemployed and the disadvantaged. Policies regarding health insurance and the provision of health services by governments are also included.

Social welfare function. The ranking rule required to establish priorities for social outcomes. A social welfare function must incorporate a set of **value judgements** derived from outside economics.

Standard gamble (SG). In the health services quality evaluation context this method is based on establishing the certainty equivalent of an uncertain health state, such as the result of a surgical treatment, to which a probability can be assigned. This method of estimating **cardinal** utility was devised by von Neumann and Morgenstern, and is based on determining the expected value of utility.

Supplier-induced demand. Departures from the perfect **agency relationship** between patients and providers where the latter act to influence the use of services beyond the preferences of their clients or their best interests. The notion of a **demand curve** for clinical services becomes implausible in these circumstances.

Supply schedule. The hypothetical relationship between the price of a commodity and the quantity of the commodity that a firm would be willing to supply at each price.

Technical efficiency. The ratio of the value of the outputs of specific institutions and other health services to the cost of providing the services. Ideally the value of the outputs should be measured in terms of their contribution to health status. As yet the health status gains of populations attributable to institutions such as hospitals are exceedingly difficult to measure and less satisfactory measures of outputs must be used.

Third party payers. In the health insurance context health insurance organisations and governments form the third parties along with the providers and recipients of health services where payments are made.

Time trade-off (TTO). This method of determining the value of a **QALY** is based on each person surveyed estimating how long in a specified state of health would be equivalent to a different period in an alternative state of health.

Total cost curve. The sum of **fixed** and **variable costs** of a firm that changes according to the quantity of output.

Type 1 error. Occurs where a correct hypothesis is rejected by the test procedure.

Type 2 error. Occurs where an incorrect hypothesis is accepted by the test procedure.

User charge. That part of the cost of a health service that is met by the recipient of the service.

Utilitarianism. The philosophical approach which asserts that the prime motivating force for individuals is to maximise their own happiness and minimise their pains.

Utility. The satisfaction that an individual receives as a result of the consumption of a commodity.

Value judgements. Assessments of the priorities that should be afforded to social and political objectives based on individuals' ethical, religious or other beliefs. These judgements constitute an important aspect of **normative economics**.

Variable costs. Those costs of a firm that vary with the level of output in the short-term. Labour and materials costs are the most important examples.

Variance analysis. Analysis of variance refers to a statistical method for determining whether the variation between groups is due to chance or reflects a real difference in the groups. The phrase is also used in accounting and elsewhere to represent the differences between expected and observed outcomes of systems and procedures.

Walrasian approach. The representation of an economic system as a set of simultaneous equations the solution of which provides in principle the equilibrium values of prices and quantities for the economy.

Welfare burden. The basis of the claim that the provision of health insurance leads to a loss of welfare as compared with a free market situation.

Welfare economics. That aspect of normative economics which endeavours to establish rules and policies about how the satisfaction of communities will be maximised. These include the **Pareto principle** that a change is desirable if at least one individual gains without anyone being made worse off.

Willingness to pay (WTP). A measure based on the valuation by a person of a treatment or other intervention which is used frequently in **CBA**. It may reflect the ability to pay.

Workforce planning. The activities that are designed to establish the desirable stock of members of the health workforce to meet the future needs of the population for health services.

World Bank. The organisation that has been established to provide loans, other resources and technical advice to **developing** and **transitional countries**. Education and health are major focuses of its activities.

World Health Organisation (WHO). An agency of the United Nations which is responsible for monitoring the health status of countries and assisting in disease eradication programs.

Bibliography

Abel-Smith, B. (1963) *Paying for Health Services: A Study of the Costs and Sources of Finance in Six Countries*, Geneva: WHO.

—— (1966) 'The economics of population', *Proceedings of the Royal Society of Medicine* 59 (7): 644–6.

——. (1967) 'An international study of health expenditure and its relevance for health planning', *Public Health Papers* 32: 1–127.

——. (1989) 'Health economics in developing countries', *Journal of Tropical Medicine and Hygiene* 92: 229–41.

Access Economics (2004) *Employment Demand in Nursing Occupations. Report to the Department of Health and Ageing*, Canberra: Access Economics.

Agency for Health Care Policy and Research (1992) *Annotated Bibliography: Information Dissemination to Health Care Practitioners and Policymakers*, Rockville, MD: US Department of Health and Human Services.

Aiken, L. (2003) 'Achieving an interdisciplinary workforce in health care', *New England Journal of Medicine* 348 (2): 164–6.

Aiken, L., Clarke S., Sloane, D.M. et al. (2001) 'Nurses' reports on hospital care in five countries', *Health Affairs* 20 (3): 43–53.

Andersen, T.F. and Mooney, G. (eds) (1990) *The Challenge of Medical Practice Variations*, London: Macmillan.

Anderson, G.F., Reinhardt, U., Hussey, P. et al. (2003) 'It's the prices, stupid: why the United States is so different from other countries', *Health Affairs* 22 (3): 89–105.

Anderson, G.F., Hussey, P.S., Frogner, B. et al. (2005) 'Health spending in the United States and the rest of the industrialized world', *Health Affairs* 24 (4): 903–14.

Andrews, G., Issakides, C., Sanderson, K. et al. (2004) 'Utilising survey data to inform public policy: comparison of the cost-effectiveness of treatment of ten mental disorders', *British Journal of Psychiatry* 184: 526–33.

Arestis, P., Palma, G. and Sawyer, M. (eds) (1997) *Markets, Unemployment and Economic Policy: Essays in Honour of Geoff Harcourt*, London: Routledge.

Arnesen, T.M. and Norheim, O.F. (2003) 'Quantifying quality of life for economic analysis: time out for time trade off', *Journal of Medical Ethics* 29 (2): 81–8.

Arrow, K.J. (1963) 'Uncertainty and the welfare economics of medical care', *American Economic Review* 53 (5): 940–73.

Association of American Medical Colleges (2002a) *The Physician Workforce: Position Statement – June 2002*, Washington, DC: Association of American Medical Colleges.

——.(2002b) *Policy on the Physician Workforce*, Washington, DC: Association of American Medical Colleges.

Australian Health Technology Advisory Committee (1996) *Guidelines for Technology Assessment*, Canberra: AGPS.

Australian Health Workforce Advisory Committee (2004a) *The Australian Nursing Workforce – An Overview Of Workforce Planning*, AHWAC Report 2004. 2, Sydney: AHWAC.

—— (2004b) *Annual Report 2003–4, Report 2004.3*, Canberra: AHWAC.

—— (2004c) *Nursing Workforce Planning in Australia. A Guide to the Process and Methods used by the Australian Health Workforce Advisory Committee*, Report 2004:1, Sydney: AHWAC.

Australian Institute of Health and Welfare (2003) *Nursing Labour Force 2002, National Health Labour Force Series 29*, Canberra: AIHW.

—— (2004) *Medical Labour Force 2002, National Health Labour Force Series 30*, Canberra: AIHW.

—— (2005) *Annual Report*, Canberra: AIHW.

Australian Medical Workforce Advisory Committee (1996) *Annual Report 1995–96*, Sydney: AMWAC.

—— (2003) *Annual Report 2002–03*, Sydney: AMWAC.

Australian Medical Workforce Advisory Committee and the National Health Workforce Secretariat (2003) *Specialist Medical Workforce Planning in Australia*, Canberra: AGPS.

Averill, R. (1991) 'Development', in R. Fetter (ed.), *DRGs: Their Design and Development*, Ann Arbor: Health Administration Press.

Baker, R. and Robinson, A. (2004) 'Responses to standard gambles: are preferences "well-constructed"?' *Health Economics* 13: 37–48.

Bannock, G., Baxter, R.E. and Davis, E. (2003) *The Penguin Dictionary of Economics* (7th edn), London: Penguin Books.

Barbien, M. and Drummond, M. (2005) 'Variability of cost-effectiveness estimates for pharmaceuticals in Western Europe: lessons for inferring generalizability', *Value in Health* 8 (1): 10–23.

Barer, M. (2002) 'New opportunities for old mistakes', *Health Affairs* 21: 169–71.

Barer, M.L. and Stoddart, G.L. (1991) *Towards Integrated Medical Resource Policies for Canada, Report Prepared for Deputy Ministers of Health of Federal/Provincial/Territorial Conference*.

Barer, M.L., Evans, R.G., Hertzman, C. et al. (1998) 'Lies, damned lies and health care zombies: discredited ideas that will not die', *HPI*

Discussion Paper 10, Houston: University of Texas – Houston Health Policy Institute.

Barer, M.L., Getzen, T.E. and Stoddart, G.L. (eds) (1998) *Health, Health Care and Health Economics. Perspectives on Distribution*, Chichester: John Wiley and Sons Ltd.

Bator, F.M. (1957) 'The simple analytics of welfare maximization', *American Economic Review* 47: 22–59.

——. (1958) 'The anatomy of market failure', *Quarterly Journal of Economics* 72: 351–79.

Baumol, W.J. (1995) *Health Care as a Handicraft Industry*, London: Office of Health Economics.

Bell, D. (1981) 'Models and reality in economic discourse', in D. Bell and I. Kristol (eds), *The Crisis in Economic Theory*, New York: Basic Books, 46–80.

Bell, D. and Kristol, I. (eds) (1981) *The Crisis in Economic Theory*, New York: Basic Books, Inc.

Black, M. and Mooney, G. (2002) 'Equity in health care from a communitarian standpoint', *Health Care Analysis* 10 (2): 193–208.

Blacker, F., Kennedy, A. and Reed, M. (1999) 'Organising for incompatible priorities', in A.L. Mark and S. Dopson (eds), *Organisational Behaviour and Health Care*, London: Macmillan.

Blaug, M. (1998a) 'Disturbing currents in modern economics', *Challenge* 41 (3): 11–34.

——. (1998b) 'Where are we now in British health economics?' *Health Economics* 7, S63–S78.

Blendon, R.J., Leitman, R., Morrison, K. et al. (1990) 'Satisfaction with health systems in ten nations', *Health Affairs* 9 (2): 185–92.

Blendon, R.J., Benson, J., Leitman, R.C. et al. (1995) 'Who has the best health care system? A second look', *Health Affairs* 14 (4): 220–30.

Bloor, K. and Maynard, A. (1998) 'Rewarding health care teams: a way of aligning pay to performance and outcomes', *British Medical Journal* 316 (7131): 569.

——. (2002) 'Consultants: managing them means measuring them', *Health Services Journal* 112: 10–11.

——. (2003) '*Planning Human Resources in Health Care: Towards the Economic Approach. An International Comparative Review*', Toronto: Canadian Health Services Research Foundation.

Bloor, K., Maynard, A., Hall, J. et al. (2003) '*Planning Human Resources in Health Care: Towards the Economic Approach. An International Comparative Review*', Toronto: Canadian Health Services Research Foundation.

Blumenthal, D. (2004) 'New steam from an old cauldron – the physician-supply debate', *New England Journal of Medicine* 350: 1780–7.

Bodenheimer, T. (2005a) 'High and rising health care costs. Part 1: seeking an explanation', *Annals of Internal Medicine* 142: 847–54.

——. (2005b) 'High and rising health care costs. Part 2: technological innovation', *Annals of Internal Medicine* 142: 932–7.

——. (2005c) 'High and rising health care costs. Part 3: The role of health care providers', *Annals of Internal Medicine* 142: 996–1002.

Bodenheimer, T. and Fernandez, A. (2005) 'High and rising health care costs. Part 4: Can costs be controlled while preserving quality?' *Annals of Internal Medicine* 143: 26–31.

Bosanquet, N. (2001) 'A "fair innings" for efficiency in health services?' *Journal of Medical Ethics* 27: 228–33.

Bowling, A. (1997) *Measuring Health. A Review of Quality of Life Measurement Scales*, 2nd edn, Philadelphia: Open University Press.

Briggs, A.H. (2001) 'Handling uncertainty in economic evaluation and presenting the results', in M. Drummond and A. McGuire (eds), *Economic Evaluation in Health Care. Merging Theory with Practice*, Oxford: Oxford University Press, 172–214.

Brown, G.C., Brown, M.M. and Sharma, S. (2004) 'Health care economic analyses', *Journal of Retinal and Vitreous Diseases* 24 (1): 139–46.

Buchan, J. (2000) 'Planning for change: developing a policy framework for nursing labour markets', *International Nursing Review* 47: 199–206.

Buchan, J. (2002) 'Global nursing shortages are often a symptom of wider health system or societal ailments', *British Medical Journal* 324: 751–2.

Buchan, J., Seccombe, I. and Smith, G. (1998) *Nurses' Work: Analysis of the UK Nursing Labour Market*, Aldershot: Ashgate Press.

Buchan, J., Ball, J. and O'May, F. (2000) 'If skill mix is the answer, what is the question?' *Journal of Health Services Research Policy* 16: 233–8.

Buchan, J. and Caiman, L. (2004) *The Global Shortage of Nurses. An Overview of Issues and Actions*, Geneva: International Council of Nurses.

Buerhaus, P. (2005) Six-part series on the state of the RN workforce in the United States, *Nursing Economics* 23 (2): 58–60.

Buerhaus, P.I., Staiger, D.O. and Auerbach, D. (2000) 'Implications of an aging registered nurse workforce', *Journal of the American Medical Association* 283 (22): 2948–54.

Buerhaus, P., Staiger, D. and Auerbach, D. (2003) 'Is the current shortage of nurses ending?' *Health Affairs* 22 (6): 191–8.

Buse, K., Drager, N., Fustukian, S. and Lee, K. (2002) 'Globalisation and health policy: trends and opportunities', in K. Lee, K. Buse and S. Fustukian (eds), *Health Policy in a Globalising World*, Cambridge: Cambridge University Press.

Butler, J.R. (1990) 'Welfare economics and cost-utility analysis', in P. Zweifel and H.E. Frech III, (eds), *Health Economics Worldwide*, Boston: Kluwer Academic Publishers.

Butler, J.R. (1995) *Hospital Cost Analysis*, Boston: Kluwer Academic Publishers.

Butler, J.R. and Doessel, D.P. (eds) (1989) *Health Economics: Australian Readings*, Sydney: Australian Professional Publications.

Buxton, M.J. and Klein, R.E. (1978) *Allocating Health Resources: A Commentary on the Report of the Resource Allocation Working Party*, London: Her Majesty's Stationery Office.

Byrne, J.M. and Rathwell, T. (2005) 'Medical savings accounts and the Canada health act: complementary or contradictory', *Health Policy* 72 (3): 361–79.

Canadian Coordinating Office for Health Technology Assessment (1997) *Guidelines for Economic Evaluation of Drugs and Clinical Effectiveness of Pharmaceuticals*, 2nd edn, Quebec: CCOHTA.

Carr, W.J. and Feldstein, P.J. (1967) 'The relationship of cost to hospital size', *Inquiry* 4: 45–65.

Carr-Hill, R.A. (1989) 'Assumptions of the QALY procedure', *Social Science and Medicine* 29(3): 469–77.

Cassel, G. (1932) *The Theory of Social Economy*, New York: Harcourt Brace.

Charleton, B. (1997) 'Restoring the balance: evidence-based medicine put in its place', *Journal of Evaluation in Clinical Practice* 3(2): 87–9.

Chen, S. and Wang, Y. (2001) *China's Growth and Poverty Reduction: Recent Trends between 1990 and 1999*, Washington DC: World Bank.

Chipman, J.S. (1974) 'Homothetic preferences and aggregation', *Journal of Economic Theory* 8: 26–38.

Coast, J. (2004) 'Is economic evaluation in touch with society's health values?' *British Medical Journal* 329: 1233–6.

Collège des Économistes de la Santé (2004) *French Guidelines for the Economic Evaluation of Health Technology*, Paris: Collège des Économistes de la Santé.

Colombo, F. and Tapay, N. (2003) *Private Health Insurance in Australia. A Case Study*, Paris: WHO.

Commission on the Future of Health Care in Canada (Romanov Report) (2002) *Building on Values: The Future of Health Care in Canada*, Ottawa: Commission on the Future of Health Care in Canada.

Cooper, M.H. and Culyer, A.J. (eds) (1973) *Health Economics*, Middlesex: Penguin Books.

Cooper, R.A. (1995) 'Perspectives on the physician workforce to the year 2020', *Journal of the American Medical Association* 274: 1534–43.

——. (2004) 'Weighing the evidence for expanding physician supply', *Annals of Internal Medicine* 141: 705–14.

Cooper, R.A. and Aiken, L.H. (2001) 'Human inputs: the health care workforce and medical markets', *Journal of Health Politics, Policy and Law* 26 (5): 925–38.

Cooper, R.A., Getzen, T.E., McKee, H.J. and Laud, P. (2002) 'Economic and demographic trends affecting physician supply and utilization signal an impending physician shortage', *Health Affairs* 21(1): 140–53.

Cooper, R.A., Getzen, T.E. and Laud, P. (2003) 'Economic expansion is a major determinant of physician supply and utilization', *Health Services Research* (38): 675–96.

Cooper, R.A., Stoflet, S.J. and Wartman, S.A. (2003) 'Perceptions of medical school deans and state medical society executives about physician supply', *Journal of the American Medical Association* 290 (22): 2292–5.

Cornia, G.A. (ed.) (2004) *Inequality, Growth and Poverty in an Era of Liberalisation and Globalisation, Studies in Development Economics*, Oxford: Oxford University Press.

Cornia, G.A., Addison, T. and Kiiski, S. (2004) 'Income distribution changes and their impact in the post-Second World War period', in G.A. Cornia (ed.), *Inequality, Growth and Poverty in an Era of Liberalization and Globalization; UNU – WIDER Studies in Development Economics*, Oxford: Oxford University Press, 26–54.

Council on Graduate Medical Education (1994) *Fourth Report: Recommendations to Improve Access to Health Care through Physician Workforce Reform*, Washington, DC: US Department of Health and Human Services.

—— (2003a) *Statement on the Physician Workforce*, Washington, DC: Council on Graduate Medical Education.

—— (2003b) *Reassessing Physician Workforce Policy Guidelines for the US 2000–2020*, Washington, DC: US Department of Health and Human Services.

Cournot, A. (1929) *Mathematical Principles of the Theory of Wealth*, New York: Macmillan.

Cowing, T.G., Holtman, A.G., and Powers, S. (1983) 'Hospital cost analysis: a survey and evaluation of recent studies', in R.M. Scheffler and L.F. Rossiter (eds), *Advances in Health Economics and Health Services Research* 4, Greenwich, CT: JAI Press, 257–303.

Culyer, A.J. (1973) *The Economics of Social Policy*, London: Martin Robertson.

——. (1985) 'A health economist on medical sociology: reflections by an unreconstructed reductionist', *Social Science and Medicine* 20 (10): 1013–21.

Culyer, A.J. (1989) 'The normative economics of health care finance and provision', *Oxford Review of Economic Policy* 5: 35–8.

——. (1991) 'The normative economics of health care finance and provision', in A. McGuire, P. Fenn and K. Mayhew (eds), *Providing Health Care: The Economics of Alternative Systems of Finance and Provision*, Oxford: Oxford University Press, 65–98.

——. (1992) 'The morality of efficiency in health care – some uncomfortable implications', *Health Economics* 1 (1): 7–18.

——. (1995) 'Chisels or screwdrivers? A critique of the NERA proposals for reform of the NHS', in A. Towse (ed.), *Financing Health Care in the UK. A Discussion of NERA's Prototype Model to Replace the NHS*, London: Office of Health Economics, 23–37.

——. (1998) 'How ought health economists to treat value judgments in their analyses?' in M.L. Barer, T.E. Getzen and G.L. Stoddart (eds), *Health, Health Care and Health Economics*, Chichester: John Wiley and Sons Ltd., 363–71.

——. (2001a) 'Equity – some theory and its policy implications', *Journal of Medical Ethics* 27: 275–83.

——. (2001b) 'Economics and ethics in health care', *Journal of Medical Ethics* 27 (4): 217–22.

——. (2005a) 'Involving stakeholders in health care decisions – the experience of the National Institute for Health and Clinical Excellence (NICE) in England and Wales', *Healthcare Quarterly* 8 (3): 56–60.

——. (2005b) *The Dictionary of Health Economics*, Cheltenham, UK: Edward Elgar Publishing.

Culyer, A.J., van Doorslaer, E. and Wagstaff, A. (1992) 'Utilisation as a measure of equity by Mooney, Hall, Donaldson and Gerard', *Journal of Health Economics* 11 (1): 93–8.

Culyer, A.J. and Wagstaff, A. (1993a) 'Equity and equality in health and health care', *Journal of Health Economics* 12 (4): 431–59.

Culyer, A.J. and Wagstaff, A. (1993b) 'QALYs versus HYEs (healthy year equivalents)', *Journal of Health Economics* 12 (3): 311–23.

Culyer, A.J. and Wagstaff, A. (1995) 'QALYs versus HYEs (healthy year equivalents): a reply to Gafni, Birch and Mehrez', *Journal of Health Economics* 14 (1): 39–45.

Culyer, A.J. and Evans, R.G. (1996) 'Mark Pauly on welfare economics: normative rabbits from positive hats', *Journal of Health Economics,* 15: 243–51.

Culyer, A.J. and Newhouse, J.P. (eds) (2000) *Handbook of Health Economics,* vol.1, North Holland: Elsevier, B.V.

Cutler, A.C., Hauffler, V. and Porter, T. (eds) (1999) *Private Authority and International Affairs*, New York: University of New York Press.

Danzon, P.M. and Furukawa, M.F. (2003) 'Prices and availability of pharmaceuticals: evidence from nine countries', *Health Affairs, Suppl. Web Exclusives* W_3, 521–36.

Dawes, M., Badenoch, D. and Goddard, O. (2000) *Informed Clinical Practice*, NHS R&D Centre for Evidence-Based Medicine, Thames Valley: Royal College of General Practitioners.

De Ferranti, D. (1985) *Paying for Health Services in Developing Countries: an Overview. World Bank Staff Working Papers No. 721*, Washington, DC: World Bank.

Degeling, P., Sorenson, R., Maxwell, S. et al. (2000) *The Organisation of Hospital Care and its Effects*, Sydney: Centre for Hospital Management and Information Systems Research.

Denzin, N. and Lincoln, Y. (eds) (2000) *The Handbook of Qualitative Research*, 4th edn, Thousand Oaks, CA: Sage Publications.

Department of Health (1999) *The Government's Expenditure Plans 1999–2000*, London: Stationery Office.

—— (2000) *A Health Service for All the Talents: Developing the NHS Workforce. Consultation Document on the Review of Workforce Planning*, London: Department of Health.

Department of Health and Social Security (1976) *Sharing Resources for Health in England. Report of the Resource Allocation Working Party*, London: Her Majesty's Stationery Office.

de Pouvoirville, G. and Kimberly, J. (eds) (1993) *The Migration of Managerial Innovation. Diagnosis-Related Groups and Health Care Administration in Western Europe*, San Francisco: Jossey-Bass.

de Pouvoirville, G., Ulmann, P., Nixon, J. et al. (2005) 'The diffusion of health economics knowledge in Europe: the EUROHEED (European Network of Health Economics Evaluation Database) project', *Pharmacoeconomics* 23 (2): 113–20.

Des Harnais, S., Chesney, J. and Fleming, S. (1998) 'The early effects of the prospective payment system on inpatient utilization and the quality of care', *Inquiry* 24: 7–16.

Dickson, M., Hurst, J. and Jacobzone, S. (2003) *Survey of Pharmacoeconomic Assessment Activity in Eleven Countries*, Paris: WHO.

Docteur, E. and Oxley, H. (2003) *Healthcare Systems: Lessons from the Reform Experience, OECD Economics Department Working Papers No.374*, Paris: OECD.

Docteur, E., Suppanz, H. and Woo, J. (2003) *The US Health System: An Assessment and Prospective Directions for Reform. Economics Department Working Papers No.350*, Paris: OECD.

Dolan, P. (2000) 'The measurement of health-related quality of life for use in resource allocation decisions in health care', in A.J. Culyer and

J.P. Newhouse (eds), *Handbook of Health Economics,* vol.1, North Holland: Elsevier, B.V., 1723–60.

Dolan, P., Gudex, C., Kind, P., and Williams, A. (1996) 'Valuing health states: a comparison of methods', *Journal of Health Economics* 15 (2): 209–31.

Dolan, P. and Edlin, R. (2002) 'Is it really possible to build a bridge between cost-benefit analysis and cost-effectiveness analysis?', *Journal of Health Economics* 21 (5): 827–43.

Dolan, P., Olsen, J.A., and Menzel, P. (2003) 'An inquiry into the different perspectives that can be used when eliciting preferences in health', *Health Economics* 12 (7): 545–52.

Dolan, P., Shaw, A., Tsuchiya, N. and Williams, A. (2005) 'QALY maximisation and people's preferences; a methodological review of the literature', *Health Economics* 14(2): 197–208.

Donaldson, C. and Mooney, G. (1991) 'Needs assessment, priority-setting and contracts for health care: an economic view', *British Medical Journal* 303 (6816): 1529–30.

Donaldson, C. and Gerard, K. (1993) *Economics of Health Care Financing, the Visible Hand,* Basingstoke: Macmillan.

Donaldson, C., Birch, S., and Gafni, A., et al. (2002) 'The distribution problem in economic evaluation: income and the valuation of costs and consequences of health care programmes', *Health Economics* 11 (1): 55–70.

Donaldson, C., Gerard, K., Jan, S. et al. (2005) *Economics of Health Care Financing: The Visible Hand,* 2nd edn, Basingstoke: Palgrave Macmillan.

Donaldson, L. (1992) 'Maintaining excellence', *British Medical Journal* 305: 1280–4.

Dowie, J. (2001) 'Analysing health outcomes', *Journal of Medical Ethics* 27: 245–50.

Drucker, P.F. (1981) 'Toward the next economics', in D. Bell and Kristol, I. (eds), *The Crisis in Economic Theory,* New York: Basic Books, 4–18.

Drummond, M. and Torrance, G. (1993) 'Cost-effectiveness league tables: more harm than good?' *Social Science and Medicine* 37 (1): 33–40.

Drummond, M., Jönsson, B. and Rutten, F. (1997) 'The role of economic evaluation in the pricing and reimbursement of medicines', *Health Policy* 40 (3): 199–215.

Drummond, M. and McGuire, A. (2001) *Economic Evaluation in Health Care,* 2nd edn, Oxford: Oxford University Press.

Drummond, M. and Donaldson, C. (2003) 'In the land of blind decision making, is one-eyed economics the king?' *Applied Health Economics and Health Policy* 2 (2): 73–6.

Drummond, M. and Sculpher, M. (2005) 'Common methodological flaws in economic evaluations', *Medical Care* 43 (suppl. 7): 5–14.

Drummond, M.F. (1998) 'A reappraisal of economic evaluation of pharmaceuticals. Science or marketing?' *Pharmacoeconomics* 14 (1): 1–9.

——. (2001) 'Introducing economic and quality of life measurements into clinical studies', *Annals of Medicine* 33 (5): 344–9.

Drummond, M.F. and O'Brien, B. (1997) *Methods for the Economic Evaluation of Health Care Programmes*, 2nd edn, Oxford: Oxford University Press.

Duckett, S.J. (1995) 'Hospital payment arrangements to encourage efficiency: the case of Victoria', *Health Policy* 34: 113–34.

——. (2000a) 'The Australian health workforce: facts and futures', *Australian Health Review* 23 (4): 60–77.

——. (2000b) *The Australian Health Care System*, Melbourne: Oxford University Press.

Duckett, S.J. and Jackson, T.J. (2002) 'The new health insurance rebate: an inefficient way of assisting public hospitals', *Medical Journal of Australia* 172: 439–42.

Duffield, C. and O'Brien-Pallas, L. (2002) 'The nursing workforce in Canada and Australia: two sides of the same coin', *Australian Health Review* 25 (2): 136–44.

——. (2003) 'The consequences of nursing shortages: a helicopter view of the research', *Australian Health Review* 26 (1): 186–93.

Dwyer, J.M. (2004) 'Australian health system restructuring: what problem is being solved', *Australia and New Zealand Health Policy* 1: 1–16.

Easterly, W. (2006) *The White Man's Burden: Why the West's Efforts to Aid the Rest Have Done So Much Ill and So Little Good*, Oxford: Oxford University Press.

Edlin, R. (2004) 'Anti-social welfare functions: a reply to Hansen et al.', *Journal of Health Economics* 23: 899–905.

Eiteman, W.J. and Guthrie, G.E. (1952) 'The shape of the average cost curve', *American Economic Review* 42: 617–24.

Emanuel, E.J. and Fuchs, V.R. (2005) 'Health care vouchers – a proposal for universal coverage', *New England Journal of Medicine* 352 (12): 1255–60.

Enthoven, A.C. (1980) 'How interested groups have responded to a proposal for economic competition in health services', *American Economic Review* 70 (2): 142–8.

——. (1985) *Reflections on the Management of the National Health Service*: London: Nuffield Provincial Hospitals Trust.

——. (1988) *Theory and Practice of Managed Competition in Health Care Finance*, Amsterdam: North Holland Publishing Company.

——. (1993) 'The history and principles of managed competition', *Health Affairs* 10 (Suppl): 24–48.

Evans, R.G. (1971) '"Behavioural" cost functions for hospitals', *Canadian Journal of Economics* 4: 198–215.

——. (1974) 'Supplier-induced demand', in M. Perlman (ed.), *The Economics of Health and Medical Care*, London: Macmillan: 162–73.

——. (1982) 'A retrospective on the new perspective', *Journal of Health Politics, Policy and Law* 7 (summer): 325–44.

——. (1984) *Strained Mercy: The Economics of the Canadian Health Care System*, Toronto: Butterworth.

——. (1986) 'Finding the levers, finding the courage: lessons from cost containment in North America', *Journal of Health Politics, Policy and Law* 11: 585–615.

——. (1990) 'The dog in the night time: medical practice variations and health policy', in T.F. Andersen and G. Mooney, *The Challenge of Medical Practice Variations*, London: Macmillan.

——. (1994) 'Introduction', in R.G. Evans, M.L. Barer, and T.R. Marmor, *Why are some People Healthy and Others not? The Determinants of Health of Populations*, New York: Aldine de Gruyter.

——. (1997) 'Going for gold: the redistributive agenda behind market-based health case reform', *Journal of Health Politics, Policy and Law* 22 (2): 423–66.

——. (1998) 'Towards a healthier economics: reflections on Ken Bassett's problem', in M.L. Barer, T.E. Getzen and Stoddart, G.L. (eds), *Health, Health Care and Health Economics*, Chichester: John Wiley and Sons Ltd.

——. (2000) 'Canada', *Journal of Health Politics, Policy and Law* 25(5): 889–97.

——. (2005) 'Fellow travellers on a contested path: Power, purpose and the evolution of European health care systems', *Journal of Health Politics, Policy and Law* 30 (1–2): 277–94.

Evans, R.G., Lomas, J. and Barer, M. et al. (1989) 'Controlling health expenditures – the Canadian reality', *New England Journal of Medicine* 320: 571–7.

Evans, R.G. and Stoddart, G.L. (1990) 'Producing health and consuming health care', *Social Science and Medicine* 31(12): 1347–63.

Evans, R.G., Barer, M.L. and Marmor, T.R. (1994) *Why are some People Healthy and Others not? The Determinants of Health of Populations*, New York: Aldine de Gruyter.

Evans, R.G. and Roos, N.P. (1999) 'What is right about the Canadian health care system?' *Milbank Quarterly* 77 (3): 393–9.

Evans, R.G. and Vujicic, M. (2005) 'Political wolves and economic sheep: the sustainability of public health insurance in Canada', in Maynard, A. (ed.),

The Public-Private Mix for Health, Oxford: The Nuffield Trust and Radcliffe Publishing, 117–40.

Feldman, R. and Dowd, B. (1991) 'A new estimate of the welfare loss of excess health insurance', *American Economic Review* 81: 297–301.

Feldstein, M.S. (1967) *Economic Analysis for Health Service Efficiency*, Amsterdam: North Holland Publishing Company.

——. (1970) 'The rising price of physicians' services', *Review of Economics and Statistics* 52 (2): 121–33.

——. (1971) 'Hospital cost inflation: a study of non-profit price dynamics', *American Economic Review* 61: 853–72.

——. (1973) 'The welfare loss of excess health insurance', *Journal of Political Economy* 81: 251–80.

Feldstein, M.S. and Gruber, J. (1997) 'A major risk approach to health insurance reform', *National Bureau of Economic Research, Inc., NBER Working Papers No. 4852,* New York: NBER.

Feldstein, P.J. (1999) *Health Care Economics*, 5th edn, Albany, New York: Delmar.

Fenwick, E. and O'Brien, B.J. (2004) 'Cost-effectiveness acceptability curves – facts, fallacies and frequently asked questions', *Health Economics* 13 (5): 405–15.

Ferlie, E., Fitzgerald, L. and Wood, M. (2000) 'Getting evidence into clinical practice: an organisational behaviour perspective', *Journal of Health Services and Research Policy* 5 (2): 96–102.

Ferlie, E., Dopson, S., Locock, L. et al. (2001) 'Evidence based medicine and organisation change: an overview of some recent qualitative research', in L. Ashburner, *Organisational Behaviour and Organisational Studies in Health Care: Reflections on the Future*, Basingstoke: Palgrave Macmillan.

Fetter, R.B. (ed.) (1991) *DRGs: Their Design and Development*, Ann Arbor: Health Administration Press.

Fetter, R.B., Thompson, J.D. and Mills, R.B. (1976) 'A system for cost and reimbursement control in hospitals', *The Yale Journal of Biology and Medicine* 49 (2): 123–36.

Fetter, R.B., Shin, Y. and Freeman, J. et al. (1980) 'Case mix definition by diagnosis-related groups', *Medical Care* (suppl.2) 18: 1–53.

Fetter, R.B., Palmer, G.R. and Freeman, J.L. (1988) 'International comparisons of hospital utilisation based on DRGs', in G. Duru et al. (eds), *System Science in Health Care: Information in Health Care Systems*, Paris: Masson.

Fine, B. (1980) *Economic Theory and Ideology*, London: Edward Arnold.

Finkler, S.A. and Ward, D.M. (1999) *Cost Accounting for Health Care Organisations. Concepts and Applications*, 2nd edn, Gaithersburg: Aspen Publications.

Fisher, E.S., Wennberg, D.E., Stukel, T.A. et al. (2003a) 'The implications of regional variations in Medicare spending. Part 1: The content, quality and accessibility of care', *Annals of Internal Medicine* 138: 273–87.

——. (2003b) 'The implications of regional variations in Medicare spending. Part 2: Health outcomes and satisfaction with care', *Annals of Internal Medicine* 138: 288–99.

Folland, S.T. and Stano, M. (1989) 'Sources of small variations in the use of medical care', *Journal of Health Economics* 8: 85–107.

Folland, S., Goodman, A.C. and Stano, M. (1993) *The Economics of Health and Health Care*, 2nd edn, New Jersey: Prentice Hall.

Foster, J. (2004) *From Simplistic to Complex Systems in Economics, Discussion Paper No. 335*, Brisbane: School of Economics, The University of Queensland.

Foster, J. and Metcalfe, J. (2001) *Frontiers of Evolutionary Economics: Competition, Self-Organisation, and Innovation Policy*, Cheltenham: Edward Elgar Publishing.

Frank, R.G. and McGuire, T.G. (1999) *Economics and Mental Health, Working Paper 7052*, Massachusetts: National Bureau of Economic Research.

——. (2000) 'Economics and mental health', in A.J. Culyer and J.P. Newhouse (eds), *Handbook of Health Economics*, vol.1, North Holland, Elsevier, B.V., 893–954.

Freeman, F. (1994) 'Health promotion for Aboriginal communities', *World Health Forum* 15: 25–28.

Frenk, J. (1995) 'Comprehensive policy analysis for health system reform', *Health Policy* 32 (1): 255–77.

Fuchs, V.R. (1966) 'The output of the health industry', in M.H. Cooper and A.J. Culyer (eds) (1973), *Health Economics*, Middlesex: Penguin Books.

——. (1974a) 'Who shall live?', in V.R. Fuchs, *Health, Economics and Social Choice*, New York: Basic Books.

——. (1974b) 'Some economic aspects of mortality in developed countries', *Journal of Epidemiology and Community Health* 32: 200–5.

——. (1978) 'The supply of surgeons and the demand for operations', *Journal of Human Resources* 13 (Suppl): 35–56.

——. (1986) *The Health Economy*, Cambridge, MA: Harvard University Press.

——. (1996) 'Economics, values and health care reform', Presidential Address to the American Economic Association, *American Economic Review* 86 (1): 1–24.

——. (2000) 'The future of health economics', *Journal of Health Economics* 19 (2): 141–57.

——. (2004a) 'More variation in use of care, more flat-of-the-curve medicine', *Health Affairs Web Exclusive* 10.1377/hltaff.var. 104–7.

——. (2004b) 'Reflections on the socio-economic correlates of health', *Journal of Health Economics* 23: 653–61.

——. (2005) 'Health care expenditures re-examined', *Annals of Internal Medicine* 143 (1), 5 July: 76–8.

Fuchs, V.R. and Hahn, J.S. (1990) 'How does Canada do it? A comparison of expenditures for physicians' services in the United States and Canada', *New England Journal of Medicine* 323: 884–90.

Fuchs, V.R. and Emanuel, E.J. (2005) 'Health Care Reform: Why? What? When? What it might take to effect comprehensive change', *Health Affairs* 25 (6): 1399–414.

Fustukian, S., Sethi, D. and Zwi, A. (2002) 'Workers' health safety in a globalising world', in K. Lee, K. Buse and S. Fustukian (eds), *Health Policy in a Globalising World*, Cambridge: Cambridge University Press.

Garber, A.M. (2000) 'Advances in cost-effectiveness analysis of health interventions', in A.J. Culyer and J.P. Newhouse (eds), *Handbook of Health Economics*, vol.1, North Holland: Elsevier, B.V., 181–221.

Garber, A.M., Sox, H.C. (2004) 'The US physician workforce: serious questions raised, answers needed', *Annals of Internal Medicine* 141: 732–4.

Gavel, P. (2003) 'Physician workforce planning: what have we learned? An Australian perspective', in *Proceedings of the 7th International Medical Workforce Conference*.

——. (2004) 'Medical workforce planning in Australia: process, methodology and technical issues', *Cahiers Sociological Demographic Medicine*, Jan–Mar (44): 7–42.

Gerdtham, U-G. and Jönsson, B. (2000) 'International comparisons of health expenditure: theory, data and econometric analysis', in A.J. Culyer and J.P. Newhouse (eds), *Handbook of Health Economics*, vol.1, North Holland: Elsevier, B.V., 11–53.

Gertler, P., Locay, L. and Sanderson, W. (1987) 'Are user fees regressive? The welfare implications of healthcare financing proposals in Peru', *Journal of Econometrics* 36: 67–88.

Gilson, L. (1988) *Government Health Care Charges: Is Equity Being Abandoned?* London: London School of Hygiene and Tropical Medicine.

Ginsberg, P.B. (1981) 'Altering the tax treatment of employment-based health plans', *Milbank Memorial Fund Quarterly* 59: 224–55.

Goodman, D.C., Fisher, E.S., Bubolz, T.A. et al. (1996) 'Benchmarking the US physician workforce: an alternative to needs-based or demand-based planning', *Journal of the American Medical Association* 276 (22): 1811–17.

Gray, P., Saggers, S., Drandich, M. et al. (1995) 'Evaluating government health and substance abuse for indigenous people: a comparative review,' *Australian Journal of Public Health* 19: 567–72.

Grol, R. and Grimshaw, J. (1999) 'Evidence-based implementation of evidence-based medicine', *Joint Commission Journal on Quality Improvement* 25 (10): 503–13.

Grossman, M. (1972a) 'On the concept of health capital and the demand for health', *Journal of Political Economy* 80: 223–55.

——. (1972b) *The Demand for Health: A Theoretical and Empirical Investigation*, New York: Columbia University Press.

——. (2000) 'The human capital model', in A.J. Culyer and J.P. Newhouse (eds), *Handbook of Health Economics*, vol.1, North Holland: Elsevier, B.V., 347–408.

Grumbach, K. (2002a) 'Fighting hand to hand over physician workforce policy', *Health Affairs* 21 (5): 13–27.

——. (2002b) 'The ramifications of specialty-dominated medicine', *Health Affairs* (21): 155–7.

Guba, E. and Lincoln, Y. (2000) 'Competing paradigms in qualitative research', in N. Denzin and Y. Lincoln (eds), *The Handbook of Qualitative Research*, 4th edn, Thousand Oaks, CA: Sage Publications.

Haines, R. and Jones, R. (1994) 'Implementing findings of research', *British Medical Journal* 308 (6942): 1488–92.

Hakansson, S. (2000) 'Productivity changes after introduction of prospective hospital payments in Sweden', *Casemix* 2: 2.

Hall, J. and Mooney, G. (1990a) 'What every doctor should know about economics, part 1. The benefits of costing', *Medical Journal of Australia* 152 (7): 29–31.

——. (1990b) 'What every doctor should know about health economics, part 2. The benefits of economic appraisal', *Medical Journal of Australia* 152 (2): 80–2.

Hall, J. and Savage, E. (2005) 'The role of the private sector in the Australian healthcare system', in Maynard, A. (ed.), *The Public-Private Mix for Health*, Oxford: The Nuffield Trust and Radcliffe Publishing, 247–78.

Ham, C. and Coulter, A. (2001) 'Explicit and implicit rationing: taking responsibility and avoiding blame for health care choices', *Journal of Health Services Research and Policy* 6 (3): 163–9.

Hardin, G. (1968) 'The tragedy of the commons', *Science* 162: 1243–8.

Harmon, M. and Mayer, R. (1986) *Organizational Theory for Public Administration*, Boston: Little and Brown.

Harris, J.E. (1977) 'The internal organization of hospitals: some economic implications', *Bell Journal of Economics* 8: 467–82.

Harris, J. (1987) 'Qualifying the value of life', *Journal of Medical Ethics* 13: 117–23.

Heilbroner, R.L. and Ford, A.M. (1971) *Is Economics Relevant?* California: Goodyear Publishing Company.

Herzlinger, R.E. and Parsa-Parsi, R. (2004) 'Consumer-driven health care: lessons from Switzerland', *Journal of the American Medical Association* 292 (10): 1213–20.

Hiatt, H.H. (1975) 'Protecting the medical commons: who is responsible?' *New England Journal of Medicine* 293: 235–41.

Himmelstein, D.U., Woolhandler, S. (1986) 'Cost without benefit: administrative waste in US health care', *New England Journal of Medicine* 314: 441–5.

Hodgson, G.M. (1998) *The Foundations of Evolutionary Economics*, Cheltenham: Edward Elgar.

Hopley, C., Salkeld, G., Wang, J.J. et al. (2004) 'Cost utility of screening and treatment for early age related macular degeneration with zinc and antioxidants', *British Journal of Opthalmology* 88 (4): 450–4.

Hornbrook, M.C. and Monheit, A.C. (1985) 'The contribution of case mix severity to the hospital cost-output relation', *Inquiry* 22: 259–71.

Hsiao, W.C. (1987) 'Resource-based relative value scale: an option for physician payment', *Inquiry* 24: 360–1.

Hsiao, W.C. and Stason, W.B. (1979) 'Toward developing a relative value scale for medical and surgical services', *Health Care Financing Review* 1 (Fall): 23–9.

Hsiao, W.C. and Braun, P. (1988) 'Resource based relative values: an overview', *Journal of the American Medical Association* 260: 2347–53.

Hurley, J. (1998) 'Welfarism, extra-welfarism and evaluative economic analysis in the health sector', in M.L. Barer, T.E. Getzen and Stoddart, G.L. (eds), *Health, Health Care and Health Economics*, Chichester: John Wiley and Sons, 374–95.

——. (2000) 'An overview of the normative economics of the health sector', in A.J. Culyer and J.P. Newhouse (eds), *Handbook of Health Economics*, vol.1, North Holland: Elsevier, B.V., 55–118.

——. (2002) 'Medical savings accounts will not advance Canadian health care objectives', *Canadian Medical Association Journal* 167: 151–4.

Hurst, J. (1998) 'The impact of health economics on health policy in England and the impact of health policy on health economics 1972–97', *Health Economics* 7: S47–S62.

Hurst, J. and Jee-Hughes, M. (2001) *Performance Measurement and Performance Management in OECD Health Systems*, Paris: WHO.

Hurst, J. and Siciliani, L. (2003) *Tackling Excessive Waiting Times for Elective Surgery: a comparison of policies in twelve OECD countries*, *OECD Health Working Papers No.6*, Paris: OECD.

Iglehart, J.K. (1998) 'Physicians as agents of social control: the thoughts of Victor Fuchs', *Health Affairs* 17 (1): 90–6.

Irvine, D. and Evans, M. (1995) 'Job satisfaction and turnover amongst nurses: integrating research findings across studies', *Nursing Research* 44: 246–53.

Isaacs, D. and Fitzgerald, D. (2000) 'Seven alternatives to EMB', *British Medical Journal* (319): 1618.

Jacobs, P. (1974) 'A survey of economic models of hospitals', *Inquiry* 11: 83–97.

——. (1997) *The Economics of Health and Medical Care*, 4th edn, Maryland: Aspen Publishers.

Jacobs, P., Ohinmaa, A. and Brady, B. et al. (2005) 'Providing systematic guidance in pharmacoeconomic guidelines for analysing costs', *Pharmacoeconomics* 23 (2): 143–53.

Jan, S. (1998) 'A holistic approach to the economic evaluation of health programs using institutionalist methodology', *Social Science and Medicine* 47 (10): 1565–72

——. (2000) 'Institutional considerations in priority setting: transaction cost perspective on PBMA', *Health Economics* 9: 631–41.

——. (2003a) 'A perspective on the analysis of credible commitment and myopia in health sector decision making', *Health Policy* 63: 269–78.

——. (2003b) 'Why does economic analysis in health care not get implemented any more? Towards a greater understanding of the rules of the game and the costs of decision making', *Applied Health Economics and Health Policy* 2 (1): 17–24.

Jan, S., Dommers, E. and Mooney, G. (2003) 'A politico-economic analysis of decision making in funding health service organisations', *Social Science & Medicine* 57: 427–35.

Jevons, W.S. (1911) *Theory of Political Economy*, 4th edn, London: Macmillan: 164–6.

Jones, J., Wilson, A., Parker, H. et al. (1999) 'Economic evaluation of hospital at home versus hospital care: cost minimalisation analysis of data from randomised control trial', *British Medical Journal* 319: 1547–9.

Joyce, C., McNeil, J. and Stoelwinder, J. (2004) 'Time for a new approach to medical workforce planning', *Medical Journal of Australia* 180 (5 April): 343–6.

Kakwani, N. (1977) 'Measurement of tax progressivity: an international comparison', *Economic Journal* 87: 71–80.

Kaplan, R.S. and Anderson, S.R. (2007) *Time-Driven Activity-Based Costing*, Harvard: Harvard Business School Press.

Karmel, T. and Li, J. (2002) 'The nursing workforce 2010', *National Review of Nursing Education 2002*, Canberra: Commonwealth of Australia.

Kaul, L., Grunberg, L. and Stern, M. (eds) (1999) *Global Public Goods: International Co-operation in the 21st Century*, Oxford: Oxford University Press.

Keen, S. (2001) *Debunking Economics. The Naked Emperor of the Social Sciences*, Annandale, NSW: Pluto Press Australia Ltd.

Keenan, P. and Kennedy, J. (2003) *The Nursing Workforce Shortage: Causes Consequences, Proposed Solutions. Issue Brief, April 2003*, New York: The Commonwealth Fund.

Kerridge, I., Lowe, M. and Henry, D. (1998) 'Ethics and evidence based medicine', *British Medical Journal* 16: 1151–3.

Kerssens, J.J. and Groenewegen, P.P. (2003) 'Consumer choice of socio-health insurance', *Health Expectations* 6 (4): 312–22.

——. (2005) 'Consumer preferences in social health insurance', in *European Journal of Health Economics* 6 (1): 8–15.

Kessel, R. (1958) 'Price discrimination in medicine', *Journal of Law and Economics* 1: 20–58.

Kessler, R.C., Berglund, P., Demler, O. et al. (2003) 'The epidemiology of major depressive disorder: results from the National Co-Morbidity Survey Replication (NCS-R)', *Journal of the American Medical Association* 289: 3095–105.

Ketley, D. and Woods, K.L. (1993) 'Impact of clinical trials on clinical practice: example of thrombolysis for acute myocardial infarction', *Lancet* 342: 891–4.

Keynes, J.M. (1936) *The General Theory of Employment, Interest and Money*, London: Macmillan.

Kimberly, J. (1993) 'DRGs in Western Europe. Lessons and comparisons in managerial innovation', in J. Kimberly and G. de Pouvourville, *The Migration of Managerial Innovation: Diagnosis-related Groups and Health Care Administration in Western Europe*, San Francisco: Jossey Bass, 340–62.

Kimberly, J. and de Pouvoirville, G. (1993) *The Migration of Managerial Innovation: Diagnosis-related groups and Health Care Administration in Western Europe*, San Francisco: Jossey Bass.

Klarman, H.E. (1965) *The Economics of Health*, New York: Columbia University Press.

Klein, R. (1998) 'Why Britain is reorganizing its national health service – yet again', *Health Affairs* 7 (4): 111–25.

——. (2001) *The New Politics of the NHS*, 4th edn, Essex: Prentice Hall.

——. (2005) 'The public-private mix in the UK', in A. Maynard (ed.), *The Public-Private Mix for Health*, Oxford: The Nuffield Trust and Radcliffe Publishing, 43–62.

——. (2006) 'The troubled transformation of Britain's National Health Service', *New England Journal of Medicine* 355(4): 409–15.

Knapp, M. (1999) 'Economic evaluation and mental health: sparse past … fertile future', *The Journal of Mental Health Policy and Economics* 2: 163–7.

Koen, V. (2000) 'Public expenditure reform: the health care sector in the United Kingdom', *Economics Department Working Papers No. 256*, Paris: OECD.

Kumaranayake, L. (1997) 'The role of regulation: influencing private sector activity within health sector reform', *Journal of International Development* 9 (4): 641.

Kumaranayake, L. and Walker, D. (2002) 'Cost-effectiveness analysis and priority-setting: global approach without local meaning?' in K. Lee, K. Buse and S. Fustukian (eds), *Health Policy in a Globalising World*, Cambridge: Cambridge University Press.

Kuntz, K., Tsevar, J., Weinstein, M. et al. (1999) 'Expert panel vs decision-analysis recommendations for post-discharge coronary angiography after myocardial infarction', *Journal of the American Medical Association* 282: 2246–51.

Labelle, R.J., Stoddart, G.L. and Rice, T.H. (1994a) 'A re-examination of the meaning and importance of supplier-induced demand', *Journal of Health Economics* 13 (3): 347–68.

——. (1994b) 'Response to Pauly on a re-examination of the meaning and importance of supplier-induced demand', *Journal of Health Economics* 13 (4): 491–4.

Labonte, R., Schreker, T. and Gupta, A.S. (2005) *Health for Some: Death, Disease and Disparity in a Globalizing Era*, Toronto: Centre for Social Justice.

Lave, J.R. (1989) 'The effect of the Medicare prospective payment system', *Annual Review of Public Health* 10: 141–61.

Lave, J.R. and Lave, L.B. (1984) 'Hospital cost functions', *Annual Review of Public Health* 7: 193–214.

Lave, J.R., Frank, R.G., Schulberg, H.C. et al. (1998) 'Cost-effectiveness of treatments for major depression in primary care practice', *Archives of General Psychiatry* 55 (7): 645–51.

Laverick M.D., Croal, S.A. and Mollan, R.A.B. (1991) 'Orthopaedic surgeons and thromboprophylaxis', *British Medical Journal* 303 (6802): 549–50.

Lee, K. (1998) 'Shaping the future of global health cooperation: where can we go from here?' *Lancet* 351: 899–902.

——. (2001) 'Globalisation – a new agenda for health?' in M. McKee, P. Garner and R. Stott (eds), *International Co-operation and Health*, Oxford: Oxford University Press.

Lee, K., Buse, K. and Fustukian, S. (eds) (2002) *Health Policy in a Globalising World*, Cambridge: Cambridge University Press.

Lee, K. and Goodman, H. (2002) 'Global policy networks: the propagation of health care financing reforms since the 1980s', in K. Lee, K. Buse and S. Fustukian (eds), *Health Policy in a Globalising World*, Cambridge: Cambridge University Press.

Le Grand, J. and Mays, N. (1998) 'The reforms: success, failure, or neither?' in J. Le Grand, V. Mays and J. Mulligan (eds), *Learning from the NHS Internal Market: A Review of the Evidence*, London: King's Fund.

Le Grand, J., Mays, N. and Dixon, J-A. (1998) 'The reforms: success or failure or neither', in Le Grand, J., Mays, N. and Dixon, J-A., *Learning from the NHS Internal Market: a Review of the Evidence*, London: King's Fund, 117–43.

Le Grand, J. and Mays, N. et al. (1998) *Learning from the NHS Internal Market*, London: King's Fund.

Leibenstein, H. (1966) 'Allocative efficiency versus x-efficiency', *American Economic Review* 56: 397–409.

——. (1981) 'Microeconomics and x-efficiency theory', in D. Bell and Kristol, I. (eds), *The Crisis in Economic Theory*, New York: Basic Books.

Liedtka, J. and Whitten, E. (1997) 'Building better patient care services: a collaborative approach', *Health and Management Review* 22 (3): 16–24.

Littlejohns, P., Leng, G., Culyer, T., Drummond, M. (2004) 'NICE clinical guidelines: maybe health economists should participate in guideline development', *British Medical Journal* 329 (7465): 571.

Loewy, E. (1980) 'Cost should not be a factor in medical care', *New England Journal of Medicine* 302: 12.

Lohr, K.N., Brook, R.H., Kamberg, C.I. et al. (1986) 'Use of medical care in the Rand Health Insurance Experiment. Diagnosis and service-specific analyses in a randomised controlled trial', *Medical Care* 24: 81–7.

Lugon, M. and Secker-Walters, J. (eds) (1999), *Clinical Governance: Making It Happen*, London: Royal Society of Medicine Press.

Maarse, H., Paulus, A. and Kuiper, G. (2005) 'Supervision in social health insurance: a four country study', *Health Policy* 71 (3): 333–46.

MacDonald, G. (1993) 'The costs of costing', *Australian and New Zealand Journal of Medicine* 123: 338.

Mach, E.P. and Abel-Smith, B. (1983) *Planning the Finances of the Health Sector. A Manual for Developing Countries*, Geneva: World Health Organization.

Madden L., Hussey R., and Mooney, G. (1995) 'Public health and economics in tandem: programme budgeting, marginal analysis and priority setting in practice', *Health Policy* 33 (2): 16–18.

Makinda, S. (2000) 'Recasting global governance', in R.Thakur and E. Newman (eds), *On the Threshold: the United Nations and Global Governance in the New Millennium*, New York: United Nations.

Malloch, K., Davenport, S., Mitton, D. and Hatter, C. (2003) 'Nursing workforce management: using benchmarking and outcomes monitoring', *Journal of Nursing Administration* 33 (10): 538–43.

Manning, W.G., Newhouse, J.P., Duan, N. et al. (1987) 'Health insurance and the demand for medical care: evidence from a randomised trial', *American Economic Review* 77 (3): 251–77.

March, J.G. and Simon, H.H. (1958) *Organisations*, New York: Wiley.

Mark, A.L. and Dopson, S. (eds), *Organisational Behaviour in Health Care: The Research Agenda*, London: Macmillan.

Marmor, T.R. (ed.) (1983) *Political Analysis and American Medical Care: Essays*, Cambridge: Cambridge University Press.

Marmor, T.R., Wittman, D.A. and Heagy, T.C. (1983) 'The politics of inflation', in T.R. Marmor (ed.), *Political Analysis and American Medical Care: Essays*, Cambridge: Cambridge University Press.

Marmot, M.G. and Theorell, T. (1988) 'Social class and cardiovascular disease: the contribution of work', *International Journal of Health Services* 18: 659–74.

Marmot, M.G. and Mustard, J.F. (1994) 'Coronary heart disease from a population perspective', in R.G. Evans, M.L. Barer and T.R. Marmor (eds), *Why Are Some People Healthy and Others Not? The Determinants of Health of Populations*, New York: Aldine de Gruyter.

Marshall, A. (1961) *Principles of Economics*, 8th edn, London: Macmillan.

Mason, J., Drummond, M. and Torrance, G. (1993) 'Some guidelines on the use of cost effectiveness league tables', *British Medical Journal* 306 (6877): 570–2.

Mathers, C.D. (1996) 'Trends in health expectancies in Australia 1981–1993', *Journal of the Australian Population Association* 13: 1–16.

Maxwell, S. and Ho, M.T. (2004) *Guide to Evidence-Based Clinical Management*, Sydney: UNSW School of Public Health and Community Medicine.

Maynard, A. (ed.) (2005) *The Public-Private Mix for Health*, Oxford: The Nuffield Trust and Radcliffe Publishing.

——. (2005a) 'UK healthcare reform: continuity and change', in A. Maynard (ed.), *The Public-Private Mix for Health*, Oxford: The Nuffield Trust and Radcliffe Publishing, 63–81.

——. (2005b) 'Common challenges in the healthcare markets', in A. Maynard (ed.), *The Public-Private Mix for Health*, Oxford: The Nuffield Trust and Radcliffe Publishing, 279–92.

Maynard, A. and Walker, A. (1997) *The Physician Workforce in the United Kingdom: Issues, Prospects and Policies*, London: Nuffield Trust.

Maynard, A. and Bloor, K. (2001) 'Reforming the contract of UK consultants', *British Medical Journal* 322 (7285): 541–3.

Maynard, A. and Sheldon, T. (2001) 'Limits to demand for health care: rationing is needed in a national health service', *British Medical Journal* 322 (7288): 734.

Maynard, A. and Bloor, K. (2003) 'Trust and performance management in the medical marketplace', *Journal of the Royal Society of Medicine* 96: 532–9.

Maynard, A. and McDaid, D. (2003) 'Evaluating health interventions: exploiting the potential', *Health Policy* 63 (2): 215–26.

McDonald, R. (2002) *Using Health Economics in Health Services: Rationing Rationally?* Buckingham: Open University Press.

McDonald, R., Haycox, A. and Walley, T. (2001) 'The impact of health economics on healthcare delivery. The health economists' perspective', *Pharmacoeconomics* 19 (8): 803–9.

McGuire, A. (1985) 'The theory of the hospital: a review of the models', *Social Science and Medicine* 20 (11): 1177–84.

McGuire, T.G. (2000) 'Physician agency', in A.J. Culyer and J.P. Newhouse (eds), *Handbook of Health Economics*, vol.1, North Holland: Elsevier, B.V., 461–536.

McKee, M., Garner, P. and Stott, R. (eds) (2001) *International Co-operation and Health*, Oxford: Oxford University Press.

McKie, J., Richardson J., Singer, P. et al. (1998) *The Allocation of Health Care Resources: an Ethical Evaluation of the 'QALY' Approach*, Hampshire: Ashgate Publishing.

McKinlay, J.B. and McKinlay, S. (1977) 'The questionable contribution of medical measures to the decline of mortality in the United States in the twentieth century', *Milbank Memorial Fund Quarterly/Health and Society* 55: 405–28.

McPake, B., Kumaranayake, L. and Normand (2002) *Health Economics: An International Perspective*, London: Routledge.

McPherson, K., Wennberg, J.E., Hovind, O. et al. (1982) 'Small area variations in the use of common surgical procedures: an international comparison of New England, England and Norway', *New England Journal of Medicine* 307: 1310–14.

Mechanic, D. (1976) 'Rationing health care', *Hastings Center Report* 6: 34–7.

——. (1997) 'Muddling through elegantly: finding the proper balance in rationing', *Health Affairs* 16 (5): 83–92.

Mills, A. (1995) 'Health policy in less developed countries: past trends and future directions', *Journal of International Developments* 7 (3): 299–328.

——. (1997) 'Leopard or chameleon? The changing character of international health economics', *Tropical Medicine and International Health* 2 (10): 963–77.

——. (1998) 'Health policy reforms and their impact on the practice of tropical medicine', *British Medical Bulletin* 54 (2): 503–13.

Mills, A.C. and Blaesing, S.L. (2000) 'A lesson from the last nursing shortage: the influence of work values on career satisfaction with nursing', *Journal of Nursing Administration* 30 (6): 309–15.

Miners, A.H., Garau, M.F. and Fidan, P. et al. (2005) 'Comparing estimates of cost-effectiveness submitted to the National Institute for Clinical Excellence (NICE) by different organisations: retrospective study', *British Medical Journal* 330 (7482): 65.

Mishan, E.J. (1969) *Welfare Economics: An Assessment*, Amsterdam: North Holland.

Mitton, C. and Donaldson, C. (2003) 'Setting priorities and allocating resources in health regions: lessons from a project evaluating programme budgeting and marginal analysis (PBMA)', *Health Policy* 64 (3): 335–48.

——. (2004) *Priority Setting Tool Kit: A Guide to the Use of Economics in Healthcare Decision Making*, London: BMJ Books.

Mitton, C., Peacock, S., Donaldson, C. et al. (2003) 'Using PBMA in health care priority setting: description, challenges and experience', *Applied Health Economics and Health Policy* 2: 121–34.

Mobbs, R. (1991) 'In sickness and in health: the socio-cultural context of Aboriginal well-being, illness and healing', in J. Reid and P. Trompf, *The Health of Aboriginal Australia*, Sydney: Harcourt, Bruce, Jovanovich.

Mooney, G. (1992) *Economics, Medicine and Health Care*, 2nd edn, Hemel Hempstead: Harvester Wheatsheaf.

——. (1998a) ' "Communitarianism claims" as an ethical basis for allocating health care resources', *Social Science and Medicine* 47 (9): 1171–80.

——. (1998b) 'Economics, communitarianism and health care', in M.L. Barer, T.E. Getzen and G.L. Stoddart (eds), *Health Care and Health Economics*, Chichester: John Wiley and Sons Ltd.

——. (2000) 'Judging goodness must come before judging quality – but what is the good of health care?', *International Journal for Quality in Health Care* 12 (5): 389–94.

——. (2001) 'Communitarianism and health economics', in J. Davis (ed.), *The Social Economics of Health Care*, London: Routledge, 24–42.

——. (2003) *Economics, Medicine and Health Care*, 3rd edn, London: Prentice-Hall.

——. (2005) 'Communitarian claims and community capabilities: furthering priority setting', *Social Science and Medicine* 60 (2): 247–55.

Mooney, G., Gerard, K., Donaldson, C. and Farrar, S. (1992) *Priority Setting in Purchasing: Some Practical Guidelines*, Scotland: National Association of Health Authorities and Trusts.

Mooney, G., Jan, S. and Seymour, J. (1994) 'The NSW health outcomes initiative and economic analysis', *Australian Journal of Public Health* 18 (3): 244–8.

Mooney, G. and Russell, E. (2003) 'Equity in health care: the need for a new economics paradigm?', in A. Scott, A. Maynard and R. Elliott (eds), *Advances in Health Economics*, London: Allen and Unwin, 205–21.

Mooney, G. and Scotton R. (eds) (1998), *Economics and Australian Health Policy*, Sydney: Allen and Unwin.

Morgan, G. (1997) 'Interests, conflict and power', in G. Morgan, *Images of Organisation*, chapter 6, Thousand Oaks, CA: Sage Publications.

Murray, C.J. (1996) 'Rethinking QALYs', in C.J. Murray and A.D. Lopez (eds), *The Global Burden of Disease*, Cambridge, MA: Harvard University Press.

Murray, C.J., Evans, R.B., Acharya, A. et al. (2000) 'Development of WHO guidelines on generalized cost-effectiveness analysis', *Health Economics* 9 (3): 235–51.

Murtagh, M.T. and Cresswell, P. (2003) *Ageing and Inequalities. Tackling Inequalities in Older Peoples' Health in the North East of England*, Stockton: Northern & Yorkshire Public Health Observatory.

Mytelka, L.K. and Delapierre, M. (1999) 'Strategic partnerships, networked oligopolies and the state', in A.C. Cutler, V. Hauffler and T. Porter (eds), *Private Authority and International Affairs*, New York: University of New York Press.

Needleman, J., Buerhaus, P. and Mattke S. (2002) 'Nurse staffing levels and the quality of care in hospitals', *New England Journal of Medicine* 346 (22): 1715–22.

Neuman, W.L. (2000) 'The meanings of methodology', in W.L. Neuman, *Social Research Methods: Qualitative and Quantitative Approaches*, 4th edn, Boston: Allyn and Bacon, chapter 4.

——. (2000) *Social Research Methods: Qualitative and Quantitative Approaches*, 4th edn, Boston: Allyn and Bacon.

Neumann P.J. (2005) *Using Cost-Effectiveness Analysis to Improve Health Care: Opportunities and Barriers*, New York: Oxford University Press.

Neumann, P.J., Greenberg, G., Olchanski, N.V. et al. (2005) 'Growth and quality of the cost-utility literature, 1976–2001', *Value in Health* 8 (1): 3–9.

Newhouse, J.P. (1970) 'Toward a theory of non-profit institutions: an economic model of a hospital', *American Economic Review* 60 (1): 64–74.

——. (1998) 'US and UK health economics: two disciplines separated by a common language?', *Health Economics* 7: S79–S92.

Newhouse, J.P. and Phelps, C.E. (1976) 'New estimates of price and income elasticities for medical care services', in R. Rosett (ed.), *The Impact of Health Insurance on the Health Services Sector*, New York: National Bureau of Economic Research.

Newhouse, J.P., Manning, W.G., Morris, C. et al. (1981) 'Some interim results from a controlled trial of cost sharing in health insurance', *New England Journal of Medicine* 305: 1501–7.

Newhouse, J.P. and the Insurance Experiment Group (1993) *Free for All? Lessons from the RAND Health Insurance Experiment*, Cambridge MA: Harvard University Press.

NHS Medical Workforce Standing Advisory Committee (1997) *Planning the Medical Workforce, Third Report*, London: Department of Health.

Nord, E., Richardson, J., Street, A. et al. (1995a) 'Who cares about cost? Does economic analysis impose or reflect social values?', *Health Policy* 34 (2): 79–94.

——. (1995b) 'Maximizing health benefits vs. egalitarianism: an Australian survey of health issues', *Social Science and Medicine* 41: 1429–37.

Nord, E., Street, A., Richardson, J. (1996) 'The significance of age and duration of effect in social evaluation of health care', *Health Care Analysis* 4: 103–11.

Nusshaum, M.C. and Sen, A.K. (eds) (1993) *The Quality of Life*, Oxford: Oxford University Press.

Nusshaum, M.C., Needleman, J., Buerhaus, P. et al. (2002) 'Nurse staffing levels and the quality of care in hospitals', *New England Journal of Medicine* 346 (22): 1715–22.

Nyman, J.A. (1998) 'Theory of health insurance', *Journal of Health Administration Education* 16 (1): 41–66.

——. (1999a) 'The value of health insurance: the access motive', *Journal of Health Economics* 18 (2): 141–52.

——. (1999b) 'The economics of moral hazard revisited', *Journal of Health Economics* 18 (5) December: 811–24.

——. (2003) *The Theory of Demand for Health Insurance*, Stanford, CA: Stanford University Press.

——. (2004) 'Is "moral hazard" inefficient? The policy implications of a new theory', *Health Affairs* 23 (5): 194–9.

Nyman, J.A., Martinson, M.S., Nelson, D. et al. (2002) 'Cost-effectiveness of gemfibrozil for coronary heart disease patients with low levels of high density lipoprotein cholesterol intervention trial', *Archives of Internal Medicine* 162 (2): 177–82.

O'Brien-Pallas, L., Birch, S. et al. (2001) *Integrating Workforce Planning, Human Resources and Service Planning*, Geneva: WHO.

O'Brien-Pallas, L., Baumann, A. et al. (2001) 'Forecasting models for human resources in health care', *Journal of Advanced Nursing* 33 (1): 120–9.

O'Brien-Pallas, L., Alksnis, C. et al. (2003) *Bringing the Future into Focus. Projecting RN retirement in Canada*, Ontario: Canadian Institute of Health Information.

OECD (1990) *Health Care Systems in Transition: The Search for Efficiency*, Paris: OECD.

—— (1992) *The Reform of Health Care: A Comparison of Seven OECD Countries*, Paris: OECD.

—— (1994) *The Reform of Health Systems: A Review of Seventeen OECD Countries*, Paris: OECD.

—— (2002) *Measuring Up. Improving Health System Performance in OECD Countries*, Paris: OECD.

—— (2004a) *The OECD Health Project: Towards High-Performing Health Systems*, Paris, OECD.

—— (2004b) *The OECD Health Project: Towards High-Performing Health Systems, Policy Studies*, Paris: OECD.

—— (2005a) *Health at a Glance: OECD Indicators 2005*, Paris: OECD.

—— (2005b) *OECD Health Data 2005*, Paris: OECD.

—— (2005c) *The OECD Health Project: Long-term Care for Older People*, Paris: OECD.

Oxman, A.D., Thomson, M.A., Davis, D.A. and Haynes, R.B. (1995) 'No magic bullets: a systematic review of 102 trials of interventions to improve professional practice', *Canadian Medical Association Journal* 153 (10): 1423–31.

Palmer, G.R. (1985) 'Hospital output and the use of Diagnosis-related groups for purposes of economic and financial analysis', in J.R. Butler and D.P. Doessel (eds), *Economics and Health: 1985 Proceedings of the Seventh Australian Conference of Health Economists*, Sydney: School of Health Administration, 159–81.

——. (1986) 'The economics and financing of hospitals in Australia', *The Australian Economic Review*, 3rd quarter: 60–72.

——. (1996) 'Case-mix funding: objectives and objections', *Health Care Analysis* 4: 185–93.

——. (2000a) 'Evidence-based health policy-making, hospital funding and health insurance', *Medical Journal of Australia* 172: 130–3.

——. (2000b) 'Government policy-making, private health insurance and hospital efficiency issues', *Medical Journal of Australia* 172: 413–14.

——. (2001) 'Case-mix in Australia: AR-DRG – A smooth process involving States and a Commonwealth Government', in F.H. Roger France, I. Mertens, M-C Closon and J. Hofdijk (eds), *Casemix: Global Views, Local Actions: Evolution in Twenty Countries*, Amsterdam: IOS Press, 9–23.

Palmer, G.R. and Freeman, J.L. (1987) 'Comparisons of hospital bed utilisation in Australia and the United States using DRGs', *Quality Review Bulletin* 13 (7): 256–61.

——. (1991) 'International comparisons using DRGs', in R.B. Fetter (ed.), *DRGs: Their Design and Development*, Ann Arbor: Health Administration Press.

Palmer, G.R. and Short, S. (2000) *Health Care and Public Policy: An Australian Analysis*, 3rd edn, Melbourne: Macmillan.

Pauly, M.V. (1968) 'The economics of moral hazard', *American Economic Review* 58: 531–7.

——. (1994) Editorial: 'A re-examination of the meaning and importance of supplier-induced demand', *Journal of Health Economics* 13: 369–72.

——. (1996) 'Reply to Anthony J. Culyer and Robert G. Evans', *Journal of Health Economics* 15 (2): 253–4.

——. (1997) 'Who was that straw man anyway? A comment on Evans and Rice', *Journal of Health Politics, Policy and Law* 22 (2): 467–74.

Pauly, M. and Redisch, M. (1973) 'The not-for-profit hospital as a physicians' cooperative', *American Economic Review* 63: 87–100.

Peacock, S. (1998) *An Evaluation of Program Budgeting and Marginal Analysis Applied to South Australian Hospitals*, Melbourne: Centre for Health Program Evaluation, Monash University.

Peacock, S., Ruta, D., Mitton, C. et al. (2006) 'Using economics to set pragmatic and ethical priorities', *British Medical Journal* 332: 482–5.

Permanent Working Group of European Junior Hospital Doctors (1996) *Medical Manpower in Europe by the Year 2000 – from Surplus to Deficit*, Brussels: PWG.

Pew Health Professions' Commission (1995) *Critical Challenges: Revitalizing the Health Professions for the Twenty-first Century*, San Francisco: University of California.

Phelps, C.E. (1975) 'Effects of insurance on demand for medical care', in R. Andersen, O. Anderson and J. Kravits (eds), *Equity in Health Services: Empirical Analyses in Social Policy*, Cambridge, MA: Ballinger Publishing Company, 105–30.

Pleskovic, B. and Stiglitz, C.J. (eds) (2000) *Annual World Bank Conference on Development Economics 1999*, Washington: World Bank.

Preston, B. (2002) *Australian Nurse Supply and Demand to 2006. A Projections Model and its Application. A Report Prepared for the Council of Deans of Nursing*, Melbourne: Australian Council of Deans of Nursing.

——. (2003) *Australian Nurse Supply and Demand to 2006. A Projections Model and its Application*, Melbourne: Council of Deans of Nursing and Midwifery.

Pirraglia, P.A., Rosen, A.B. and Herman, R. et al. (2004) 'Cost-utility analysis, studies of depression management: a systematic review', *American Journal of Psychiatry* 161 (2): 2155–62.

Productivity Commission (2003) *The Health Workforce Issues Paper*, Canberra: Australian Government Productivity Commission.

—— (2005a) *Australia's Health Workforce*, Canberra: Australian Government Productivity Commission.

—— (2005b) *The Health Workforce Issues Paper*, Canberra: Australian Government Productivity Commission.

Punch, K. (2005) 'Qualititative research: overview, design and grounded theory', in K. Punch (ed.), *Introduction to Social Research: Quantitative and Qualitative Approaches*, 2nd edn, London: Sage Publications.

Quadagno, J. (2005) *One Nation, Uninsured: Why the US has no National Health Insurance*, New York: Oxford University Press.

Rae, D. (2005) *Getting Better Value for Money from Sweden's Health Care System*, OECD Economics Department Working Papers No. 443, Paris: OECD.

Ranson, M.K., Beaglehole, R., Correa, C.M. et al. (2002) 'The public health implications of multilateral trade agreements', in K. Lee, K. Buse and

S. Fustukian (eds), *Health Policy in a Globalising World*, Cambridge: Cambridge University Press.

Redelmeier, D.A. and Fuchs, V.R. (1993) 'Hospital expenditures in the United States and Canada', *The New England Journal of Medicine*, 328 (11), 18 Mar: 772–8.

Reinhardt, U. (1972) 'A production function for physicians' services', *Review of Economics and Services* 54: 55–66.

——. (1985) 'The theory of physician-induced demand. Reflections after a decade', *Journal of Health Economics* 4: 187–93.

——. (1992) 'A re-examination on the meaning of efficiency: can efficiency be separated from equity?', *Yale Law and Policy Review* 10 (2): 302–15.

——. (1994) 'Planning the nation's health workforce: let the market in', *Inquiry* 31: 250–63.

——. (1998) 'Abstracting from distributional effects, this policy is efficient', in M.L. Barer, T.E. Getzen and G.L. Stoddart (eds), *Health, Health Care and Health Economics*, Chichester: John Wiley and Sons Ltd, 1–52.

——. (1999) 'The economist's model of physician behaviour', *Journal of the American Medical Association* (281): 462–5.

——. (2002) 'Analysing cause and effect in the US physician workforce', *Health Affairs* 21: 165–6.

——. (2003) 'Does the aging population really drive the demand for health care?', *Health Affairs* 22: 27–39.

——. (2004) 'The Swiss health system: regulated competition without managed care', *Journal of the American Medical Association* 292 (10): 1227–31.

——. (2005) 'The mix of public and private payers in the US health system', in A. Maynard (ed.), *The Public-Private Mix for Health*, Oxford: The Nuffield Trust and Radcliffe Publishing, 83–115.

——. (2006) 'The pricing of US hospital services: chaos behind a veil of secrecy: an economist's insights into what causes the variation in pricing and what to do about it', *Health Affairs* 25 (1): 57–69.

Reinhardt, U., Hussey, P.S. and Andersen, G. et al. (2002) 'Cross-national comparisons of health systems using OECD data, 1999', *Health Affairs* 21 (3): 169–81.

Reinhardt, U., Hussey, P.S. et al. (2004) 'US health care spending in an international context', *Health Affairs* 23: 10–25.

Ricardo, D. (1920) *Principles of Economics*, 8th edn, London: Macmillan.

Rice, T. (1998a) *The Economics of Health Reconsidered*, Chicago: Health Administration Press.

——. (1998b) 'The desirability of market-based health reforms: a reconsideration of economic theory', in M.L. Barer, T.E. Getzen and G.L. Stoddart (eds), *Health, Health Care and Health Economics*, Chichester: John Wiley and Sons Ltd, 415–63.

Rice, T. and Labelle, R.J. (1989) 'Do physicians induce demand for medical service?', *Journal of Health Politics, Policy and Law* 14: 587–600.

Richardson, J. (1987) 'Ownership and regulation in the health care sector', in P. Abelson (ed.), *Privatisation: An Australian Perspective*, Sydney: Australian Professional Publications, 249–74.

Richardson, J. and McKie, J. (2004) 'Empiricism, ethics and orthodox economic theory: what is the appropriate basis for decision-making in the health sector?', *Social Science and Medicine* 60 (2) Jan 2005: 265–75.

Robbins, L. (1932), *An Essay on the Nature and Significance of Economic Science*, London: Macmillan.

Robinson, J. (1962) *Economic Philosophy*, London: C.A. Watts and Co. Ltd.

——. (1969) *The Economics of Imperfect Competition*, 2nd edn, London: Macmillan.

——. (2001) 'Theory and practice in the design of physician payment incentives', *The Milbank Quarterly* 79(2): 149–77.

Roemer, M.I. (1961) 'Bed supply and hospital utilisation: a natural experiment', *Hospitals*, 1 November: 35–42.

Roger France, F.H., Mertens, I., Closon, M-C., and Hofdijk, J. (eds) (2001) *Casemix: Global Views, Local Actions: Evolution in Twenty Countries*, Amsterdam: IOS Press.

Rowson, M. (2000) 'Globalisation and health – some issues', *Medicine, Conflict and Survival* 16: 162–74.

Rubin, R.M. and Chang, C.F. (2003) 'A bibliometric analysis of health economics articles in the economics literature: 1991–2000', *Health Economics* 12 (5): 403–14.

Runde, J. (1997) 'Abstraction, idealisation and economic theory', in P. Arestis, G. Palma and M. Sawyer (eds), *Markets, Unemployment and Economic Policy: Essays in Honour of Geoff Harcourt*, London: Routledge.

Russell, L. (1989) *Medicare's New Hospital Payment System*, Washington, DC: Brookings Institute.

Russell, L.B., Gold, M.R. and Siegel, J. (1996) 'The role of cost-effectiveness analysis in health and medicine', *Journal of the American Medical Association* 276 (14): 1172–7.

Ruta, D., Mitton, C., Bate, A. et al. (2005) 'Program budgeting and marginal analysis: bridging the divide between doctors and managers', *British Medical Journal* 330: 1501–3.

Saltman, R.B. and Bergman, S-E. (2005) 'Renovating the commons: Swedish health care reforms in perspective', *Journal of Health Politics, Policy and Law* 30 (1–2): 253–76.

Samuelson, P.A. and Nordhaus, W.D. (2005) *Economics*, 18th edn, London: McGraw Hill.

Santerre, R.F. and Neun, S.P. (2000) *Health Economics: Theories, Insights and Industry Studies*, rev. edn, Orlando, FL: Harcourt Brace.

Scherer, F.M. (2000) 'The pharmaceutical industry', in A.J. Culyer and J.P. Newhouse (eds), *Handbook of Health Economics*, vol.1, North Holland: Elsevier B.V., 1297–336.

Schieber, G.J. and Poullier, J-P. (1990) 'Overview of international comparisons of health care expenditures', in OECD, *Health Care Systems in Transition. The Search for Efficiency*, Paris: OECD, 9–15.

Schroeder, S.A. (1996) 'How can we tell whether there are too many or too few physicians? The case for benchmarking', *Journal of the American Medical Association* 276: 1841–3.

Schultz, T.P. (2004) 'Health economics and applications in developing countries', *Journal of Health Economics* 23: 637–41.

Scott, A., Maynard, A. and Elliott, R. (eds) (2003) *Advances in Health Economics*, London: Allen and Unwin, 205–21.

Scotton, R.B. (1974) *Medical Care in Australia: An Economic Diagnosis*, Melbourne: Sun Books.

——. (1998) 'The doctor business', in G. Mooney and R.B. Scotton (eds), *Economics and Australian Health Policy*, Sydney: Allen and Unwin.

Scotton, R.B. and Macdonald, C.R. (1993) *The Making of Medibank, Australian Studies in Health Services Administration, no. 26*, Sydney: University of New South Wales.

Sculpher, M., Drummond, M. and Buxton, M. (1997) 'The iterative use of economic evaluation as part of the process of health technology assessment', *Journal of Health Services and Research Policy* 2 (1): 26–30.

Secretary of State for Health (2000) *The NHS Plan: A Plan for Investment, a Plan for Reform*, London: Stationery Office.

Sen, A.K. (1977) 'Rational fools: a critique of the behavioural foundations of economic theory', *Philosophy and Public Affairs* 6: 317–44.

——. (1979) 'Personal utilities and public judgments: or, what's wrong with welfare economics?', *Economic Journal* 87: 537–58.

——. (1980) 'Equity of what?', *The Tanner Lectures on Human Values*, Cambridge: Cambridge University Press.

——. (1986) *Commodities and Capabilities*, Amsterdam: North Holland.

——. (1987) *On Ethics and Economics*, Oxford: Blackwell.

——. (1993) 'Capability and well-being', in M.C. Nusshaum and A.K. Sen (eds), *The Quality of Life*, Oxford: Oxford University Press.

——. (2006) 'The man without a plan', *Foreign Affairs*, March/April, 85 (2). Accessed at www.foreignaffairs.org

Shah, C. and Burke, G. (2001) 'Job growth and replacement needs in nursing occupations', *National Review of Nursing Education 2002: The Nursing Workforce*, Canberra: Commonwealth of Australia.

Siegel, J.E., Weinstein, M.C., Russell, L.B. et al. (1996) 'Recommendations for reporting cost-effectiveness analyses', *Journal of the American Medical Association* 276: 1339–41.

Simoens, S., Villeneuve, M. and Hurst, J. (2005) *Tackling Nurse Shortages in OECD Countries, OECD Health Working Papers No.19*, Paris: OECD.

Simon, H.H. (1947) *Administrative Behaviour*, New York: Macmillan.

Sloan, F.A. (2000) 'Nor-for-profit ownership and hospital behaviour', in A.J. Culyer and J.P. Newhouse (eds), *Handbook of Health Economics*, vol.1, North Holland: Elsevier B.V., 1141–74.

Smith, A. and Brown, G.C. (2000) 'Understanding cost-effectiveness: a detailed review', *British Journal of Opthalmology* 54: 794–8.

Solow, R.M. (1997) 'How did economics get that way and what way did it get', *Daedalus. Journal of the American Culture in Transformation: Fifty years, Four Disciplines* 126 (1): 39–58.

Sox, H.C. (2005) 'Understanding rising health care costs: introducing a series of articles', *Annals of Internal Medicine* 142 (10): 865.

Sraffa, P. (1926) 'The law of returns under competitive conditions', *Economic Journal* 40: 538–50.

——. (1960) *Production of Commodities by Means of Commodities: Prelude to a Critique of Political Economy*, Cambridge: Cambridge University Press.

Stanley, J. (1989) 'The Appleton Consensus Conference: suggested international guidelines for decisions to forego medical treatment', *Journal of Medical Ethics* 15: 129–36.

Starr, P. (1982) *The Social Transformation of American Medicine*, New York: Basic Books.

Stigler, G.J. (1965) *Essays in the History of Economics*, Chicago: University of Chicago Press.

Stiglitz, J.E. (1988) *Economics of the Public Sector*, 2nd edn, New York: Norton.

——. (1999) 'The underpinnings of a stable and equitable global financial system: from old debates to new paradigm', in B. Pleskovic and J. Stiglitz (eds) (2000), *Annual World Bank Conference on Development Economics 1999*, Washington World Bank, 91–130.

Stockman, A. (1996) *Introduction to Microeconomics*, New York: Dryden Press.

Stoddart, G.L. and Barer, M.L. (1999) 'Will increasing medical school enrolment solve Canada's physician supply problems?', *Canadian Medical Association* 161 (8): 983–5.

Stolk, E.A. and Poley, M.J. (2005) 'Criteria for determining a basic health services package. Recent developments in The Netherlands', *European Journal of Health Economics* 6 (1): 2–7.

Stone, P.W., Chapman, R.H., Sandberg, E.A. et al. (2000) 'Measuring costs in cost-utility analyses. Variations in the literature', *International Journal of Technology Assessment in Health Care* 16 (1): 111–24.

Strauss, S. and McAlister, F. (2000) 'Evidence-based medicine: a commentary on common criticisms', *Canadian Medical Association Journal* 15, 163 (7): 837–41.

Street, A. and Duckett, S. (1996) 'Are waiting lists inevitable?', *Health Policy* 36 (1): 1–15.

Tarabusi, C. and Vickery, G. (1998) 'Globalisation in the pharmaceutical industry: part 1', *International Journal of Health Sciences* 28 (1): 67–105.

Thurow, L.C. (1983) *Dangerous Currents: The State of Economics*, New York: Random House.

Tisdell, C. (1995) 'Evolutionary economics and research and development', in S. Dowrick (ed.), *Economic Approaches to Innovation*, Aldershot: Edward Elgar.

Tomblin Murphy, G. and O'Brien-Pallas, L. (2002) *How do Health, Human Resources Policies and Practices Inhibit Change? A Plan for the Future. Discussion Paper No. 30*, Toronto: Commission on the future of health care in Canada.

Torgerson, P.J., Maynard, A.K. and Gosden, T. (1998) 'International comparisons of health care expenditure: a dismal science?', *Quarterly Journal of Medicine* 91(2): 69–70.

Torrance, G.W. (1986) 'Measurement of health state utilities for economic appraisal', *Journal of Health Economics* 5: 1–30.

Tsuchiya, A. (2000) 'QALYs and ageism: philosophical theories and age weighting', *Health Economics* 9: 57–68.

Tsuchiya, A. and Williams, A. (2004) 'Welfare economics and economic evaluation', in M. Drummond and A. McGuire (eds), *Economic Evaluation in Health Care. Merging Theory with Practice*, Oxford: Oxford University Press, 22–45.

United Nations (2000) *Security Council Press Release 6890, Pre-deployment Testing, Counselling for Peace Keeping Personnel*, New York: United Nations.

United Nations Development Programme (2005) *Human Development Report 2005. International Co-operation at a Crossroads: Aid, Trade and Security in an Unequal World*, New York: UNDP.

van Doorslaer, E., Wagstaff, A. and van der Burg, H. et al. (1999) 'The redistributive effect of health care finance in twelve OECD countries', *Journal of Health Economics* 18: 291.

van Doorslaer, E., Wagstaff, A. (2000) 'Equity in the delivery of health care in Europe and the US', *Journal of Health Economics* 19 (5): 553–83.

van Doorslaer, E., and Schut, F.T. (2000) 'Belgium and the Netherlands revisited', *Journal of Health Politics, Policy and Law* 25 (5): 875–87.

van Doorslaer, E., and Masserid, C. (2004) *Income-Related Inequality in the use of Medical Care in 21 OECD Countries*, Paris: OECD.

Von Neumann, J. and Morgenstern, O. (1944) *Theory of Games and Economic Behaviour*, Princeton, NJ: Princeton University Press.

Waddington, C.J. and Enyimayew, K.A. (1989) 'A price to pay: the impact of user charges on Ashanti – Akim district of Ghana', *International Journal of Health Planning and Management* 4: 17–47.

Wagstaff, A. (1986) 'The demand for health: some new empirical evidence', *Journal of Health Economics* 5 (3): 195–233.

——. (1991) 'QALYs and the equity-efficiency trade-off', *Journal of Health Economics* 10: 21–41.

Wagstaff, A., and van Doorslaer, E. (1992) 'Equity in the finance of health care', *Journal of Health Economics* 11: 361–87.

——. (1993) 'Equity in the finance and delivery of health care: concepts and definitions', in E. van Doorslaer, A. Wagstaff and F. Rutten (eds), *Equity in the Finance and Delivery of Health Care: An International Perspective*, Oxford: Oxford University Press.

——. (1997) 'Progressivity, horizontal equity and reranking in health care finance: a decomposition analysis for The Netherlands', *Journal of Health Economics* 16 (5): 499–516.

——. (1999) 'Equity in the finance of health care: some further international comparisons', *Journal of Health Economics* 18: 263–90.

——. (2000) 'Equity in health care finance and delivery', in A.J. Culyer and J.P. Newhouse (eds), *Handbook of Health Economics*, vol.1, North Holland: Elsevier, B.V., 1803–62.

Walker, A. and Maynard, A. (2003) 'Managing medical workforces: from relative stability to disequilibrium in the UK NHS', *Applied Health Economics and Health Policy* 2 (1): 25–36.

Walt, G. (1994) *Health Policy: An Introduction to Process and Power*, London: Zed Books.

Weinstein, M.C. (1981) 'Economic assessments of medical practices and technologies', *Medical Decision Making* 1: 309–30.

Weinstein, M.C. and Stason, W.B. (1977) 'Foundations of cost-effectiveness analysis for health and medical practices', *New England Journal of Medicine* 296: 716–21.

——. (1982) 'Cost-effectiveness of coronary artery bypass surgery', *Circulation* 66 (Suppl.) 111: 56–66.

Weinstein, M.C. (2001) 'Should physicians be gatekeepers of medical resources?', *Journal of Medical Ethics* 27: 268–74.

Weinstein, M.C., Siegal, J.E., Gold, M.R. et al. (1996) 'Recommendations of the panel on cost-effectiveness in health and medicine', *Journal of the American Medical Association* 276 (14): 1253–8.

Weisman, V. and Mooney, G. (1998) 'Burden of illness estimates for priority setting: a debate revisited', *Health Policy* 43 (3): 243–51.

Wennberg, J.E. (1984) 'Dealing with medical practice variations: a proposal for action', *Health Affairs* 3: 6–32.

Wennberg, J.E. and Gittelsohn, A. (1973) 'Small area variations in health care delivery: a population-based health information system can guide planning and regulatory decision making', *Science* 182: 1102–7.

——. (1982a) 'Professional uncertainty and the problem of supplier-induced demands', *Social Science and Medicine* 16 (7): 811–24.

——. (1982b) 'Variations in medical care among small areas', *Scientific American* 246: 100–11.

Wennberg, J.E., Freeman, J.L. and Culp, W.J. (1987) 'Are hospital services rationed in New Haven or over-utilized in Boston?', *The Lancet* 1: 1185–9.

Wennberg, J.E., Freeman, J.L. and Culp, W.J. (1989) 'Hospital use and mortality among Medicare beneficiaries in Boston and New Haven', *New England Journal of Medicine* 321: 1168–73.

Westert, G.P., Schellevia, F.G., de Bakker, D.H. et al. (2005) 'Monitoring health inequalities through general practice: the Second Dutch National Survey of General Practice', *European Journal of Public Health* 15 (1): 59–65.

White House (1999) *A National Security Strategy for a New Century*, Washington, D.C.: The White House.

Williams, A. (1985) 'Economics of coronary artery bypass grafting', *British Medical Journal* 291: 326–9.

——. (1988) 'Health economics: the end of clinical freedom?', *British Medical Journal* 297: 1183–91.

——. (1992) 'Cost-effectiveness analysis: is it ethical?', *Journal of Medical Ethics* 18: 7–11.

——. (1997) 'Intergenerational equity: an exploration of the fair innings argument', *Health Economics* 6 (2): 117–32.

——. (1998a) 'If we are going to get a fair innings, someone will need to keep the score!', in M.L. Barer, T.E. Getzen and G.L. Stoddart (eds), *Health, Health Care and Health Economics: Perspectives on Distribution*, London: John Wiley and Sons.

——. (1998b) 'Primeval health economics in Britain: a personal retrospective of the pre-HESG period', *Health Economics* 7: S3–S8.

——. (2005) 'The pervasive role of ideology in the optimisation of the public-private mix in public healthcare systems', in A. Maynard (ed.), *The Public-Private Mix for Health*, Oxford: The Nuffield Trust and Radcliffe Publishing, 7–20.

Williams, A. and Cookson, R. (2000) 'Equity in health', in A.J. Culyer and J.P. Newhouse (eds), *Handbook of Health Economics*, vol.1, North Holland: Elsevier, B.V., 1863–910.

Williamson, O. (1999) 'Public and private bureaucracies: a transaction cost economics perspective?', *The Journal of Law, Economics and Organisation* 15(1): 306–42.

Wiseman, V., Mooney, G., Berry, G. et al. (2003) 'Involving the general public in priority setting: experiences from Australia', *Social Science and Medicine* 56: 1001–12.

Wood, M., Ferlie, E. and Fitzgerald, L. (1998) 'Achieving clinical behaviour change: a case of becoming indeterminate', *Social Science and Medicine* 47 (11): 1729–38.

Woods, K.L. et al. (1998) 'Beta-blockers and antithrombotic treatment for secondary prevention after acute myocardial infarction: towards an understanding of factors influencing clinical practice: The European Secondary Prevention Study Group', *European Heart Journal* 19: 74–9.

Woolhandler, S. and Himmelstein, D.U. (1991) 'The deteriorating administrative efficiency of the US health care system', *New England Journal of Medicine* 324 (8): 1253–8.

Woolhandler, S., Campbell, T. and Himmelstein, D.U. (2003) 'Costs of health care administration in the United States and Canada', *New England Journal of Medicine* 349 (8): 768–75.

World Bank (1987) *Financing Health Services in Developing Countries: an Agenda for Reform. A World Bank Policy Study*, Washington, DC: World Bank.

—— (1993) *World Development Report 1993: Investing In Health*, Washington, DC: World Bank.

—— (1997) *World Development Report 1997: The State in a Changing World*, Washington, DC: World Bank.

—— (2000) *Assessing Globalisation. Briefing Paper*, Washington, DC: World Bank, April.

—— (2005) *World Development Report 2006. Equity and Development*, Washington, DC: World Bank.

World Health Organisation (2000) *The World Health Report 2000, Health Systems: Improving Performance*, Geneva: WHO.

—— (2001) *The World Health Report 2001: Mental Health: New Understanding, New Hope*, Geneva: WHO.

—— (2003) *Guide to Producing National Health Accounts with Special Applications for Low-income and Middle-income Countries*, Geneva: WHO.

—— (2006) *The World Health Report: National Health Accounts*, Geneva: WHO.

Yett, D.E. (1970) 'The nursing shortage', in M.H. Cooper and A.J. Culyer (eds) (1973), *Health Economics*, Middlesex: Penguin Books.

——. (1975) *An Economic Analysis of the Nurse Shortage*, Lexington, MA: Lexington Books.

Zuckermann, S., Hadley, J. and Iezzoni, L. (1994) 'Measuring hospital efficiency and frontier cost functions', *Journal of Health Economics* 13: 255–80.

Zweifel, P. and Frech, H.E. III (eds) (1990) *Health Economics Worldwide*, Boston: Kluwer Academic Publishers.

Zweifel, P. and Breyer, F. (1997) *Health Economics, New York*, Oxford: Oxford University Press.

Zweifel, P. and Manning, W.G. (2000) 'Moral hazard and consumer incentives in health care', in A.J. Culyer and J.P. Newhouse (eds), *Handbook of Health Economics*, vol.1, North Holland: Elsevier B.V., 409–59.

Zweifel, P., Felder, S. and Werblow, A. (2004) 'Population ageing and health care expenditure: new evidence on the "red herring"', *Geneva Papers on Risk and Insurance: Issues and Practice* 29 (4): 652–66.

Zwi, A.B., Ho, M.T. and Grove, N.J. (2005) 'Health and Australia's program of overseas development assistance: keeping track of ODA and keeping ODA on track', *Medical Journal of Australia* 183 (3): 119–20.

Index

Printed and bound by CPI Group (UK) Ltd, Croydon, CR0 4YY